Living Language™
ADVANCED
CONVERSATIONAL
FRENCH

THE LIVING LANGUAGE™ SERIES
BASIC COURSES ON CASSETTE

*Spanish
*French
*German
*Italian
*Japanese
*Portuguese (Continental)
Portuguese (South American)
Advanced Spanish
Advanced French
Children's Spanish
Children's French
Russian
Hebrew
English for Native Spanish Speakers
English for Native French Speakers
English for Native Italian Speakers
English for Native German Speakers
English for Native Chinese Speakers

*Also available on Compact Disc

LIVING LANGUAGE PLUS®

Spanish
French
German
Italian

LIVING LANGUAGE TRAVELTALK™

Spanish
French
German
Italian
Russian

Living Language™

ADVANCED CONVERSATIONAL

FRENCH

By Mary Finocchiaro,

PROFESSOR OF EDUCATION, HUNTER COLLEGE;
SPECIALIST, LANGUAGE AND LINGUISTICS, U.S.
STATE DEPARTMENT

Remunda Cadoux,

DIRECTOR, INSTITUTE FOR TEACHERS OF
FOREIGN LANGUAGE, HUNTER COLLEGE;
SUPERVISOR, FOREIGN LANGUAGE
BROADCASTING, BUREAU OF RADIO AND
TELEVISION

BASED ON THE METHOD DEVISED BY
RALPH R. WEIMAN, FORMER CHIEF OF
LANGUAGE SECTION, U.S. WAR DEPARTMENT

SPECIALLY PREPARED FOR USE WITH THE
LIVING LANGUAGE COURSE® IN ADVANCED
FRENCH

Crown Publishers, Inc., New York

Copyright © 1968, 1986 by Crown Publishers, Inc.
All rights reserved.

THE LIVING LANGUAGE COURSE is a registered trademark, and
CROWN, and LIVING LANGUAGE and colophon are trademarks of
Crown Publishers, Inc., 201 East 50th Street, New York, New York 10022

Library of Congress Catalog Card Number: R68-3056

Manufactured in the United States of America

This work was previously published under the title
Living Language Conversation Manual, French Advanced Course.

ISBN 0-517-55888-2

1986 Updated Edition

10   9   8   7   6   5

CONTENTS

INTRODUCTION   xiv
INSTRUCTIONS   xvi

LESSON 41   1

RENDEZ-VOUS AU CAFÉ   1

A. *ON FIXE LE RENDEZ-VOUS*   1
B. *ON SE RENCONTRE AU CAFÉ*   2

NOTES   5
GRAMMATICAL ITEMS   9
  I. *VENIR DE*   9
  II. *TENIR À*   9
  III. *VOICI: VOILÀ*   10
  IV. *AVOIR ENVIE DE*   10
  V. PREPOSITIONS BEFORE INFINITIVES   11
      A. *DE*   11
      B. *A*   12
      C. NO PREPOSITION AFTER CERTAIN VERBS   12

LESSON 42   16

AU KIOSQUE   16

NOTES   21
GRAMMATICAL ITEMS   23
  I. *CE QUI*   23
  II. *CE QUE*   24
  III. DEMONSTRATIVE ADJECTIVES   24
      A. *CE, CET, CETTE; CES*   24
      B. *-CI, -LÀ*   24
  IV. ADJECTIVES OF NATIONALITY   25
  V. *EN* + PRESENT PARTICIPLE   25

LESSON 43   30

AU *TÉLÉPHONE*   30

A. *UN APPEL INTERURBAIN*   30
B. *UNE COMMUNICATION LOCALE*   32

NOTES   34
GRAMMATICAL ITEMS   35
  I. A. *QUEL* (AS INTERROGATIVE)   35
    B. *QUEL* (AS EXCLAMATION)   36
  II. *NE...RIEN*   36
  III. OBJECT PRONOUNS BEFORE   38
     COMPLEMENTARY INFINITIVE
  IV. FUTURE TENSE   38
  V. IMPLIED FUTURITY (WITH *QUAND, AUSSITOT QUE,*
    ETC.)   40
  VI. *IL FAUT* WITH INDIRECT OBJECT PRONOUNS   41

LESSON 44   46

LES TRANSPORTS EN VILLE   46

A. *LE MÉTRO*   46
B. *L'AUTOBUS*   48
C. *LE TAXI*   50

NOTES   51
GRAMMATICAL ITEMS   53
  I. COMPARISON OF ADJECTIVES   53
  II. IMPERATIVE   54
  III. FUNCTIONS OF *ON*   55
  IV. FUNCTIONS OF *DEVOIR*   55
  V. THE SUBJUNCTIVE   56

LESSON 45   61

FAISONS UNE PROMENADE À PIED   61

A. *AVANT LA PROMENADE*   61
B. *À LA RÉCEPTION*   62
C. *QUINZE MINUTES PLUS TARD*   64
D. *DE RETOUR À L'HOTEL*   65

NOTES   66
GRAMMATICAL ITEMS   68
  I. "DISJUNCTIVE" (EMPHATIC) PRONOUNS   68
  II. REFLEXIVE VERBS   70

LESSON 46   75

DANS UN GRAND MAGASIN   75

A. *AU RAYON DES GANTS*   75
B. *AU RAYON DES ROBES*   77
C. *AU COMPTOIR DES MOUCHOIRS*   79

NOTES   80
GRAMMATICAL ITEMS   81
  I. CONDITIONAL   81
 II. POSSESSIVES WITHOUT NOUNS (*LE MIEN, LE TIEN,*
     ETC.)   83
III. DEMONSTRATIVES WITHOUT NOUNS (*CELUI-CI,*
     CELLE-LÀ, ETC.)   84
IV. DOUBLE OBJECT PRONOUNS   85

LESSON 47   91

ON SE FAIT COIFFER   91

A. *CHEZ LE COIFFEUR*   91
B. *DANS LA RUE*   93

NOTES   94
GRAMMATICAL ITEMS   96
  I. *QUE JAMAIS* (IN COMPARISONS)   96
 II. *POUVOIR* + INFINITIVE   97
III. *SE FAIRE* + INFINITIVE   97
IV. DEFINITE ARTICLE WITH PARTS OF THE BODY   98
 V. CONTRACTIONS   99
VI. *CHEZ*   99

LESSON 48   104

AU THÉÂTRE   104

A. *AU BUREAU DE LOCATION*   104
B. *AU THÉÂTRE FRANÇAIS*   105
C. *À L'ENTR'ACTE, AU FOYER*   107

NOTES   109
GRAMMATICAL ITEMS   111
  I. *NE... QUE* (ONLY)   111
 II. PARTITIVE ARTICLE   111
III. IMPERATIVE FORMS WITH PRONOUNS   115
IV. VERBS CONJUGATED WITH *ÊTRE*   116

LESSON 49   121

AU MUSÉE DU LOUVRE   121

NOTES   126
GRAMMATICAL ITEMS   127
  I. *FAIRE* + INFINITIVE   127
 II. *IL Y A*   128
III. *ALLER* + *Y*   128
IV. *DONT*   129

LESSON 50   135

LES PRODUITS DE L'ARTISANAT: LA PEINTURE   135

A. *ON DÉCIDE D'ALLER AU MARCHÉ AUX PUCES*   135
B. *ON ARRIVE AU MARCHÉ AUX PUCES*   136
C. *DANS UNE GALERIE D'ART*   138

NOTES   140
GRAMMATICAL ITEMS   142
  I. RELATIVE PRONOUN *QUI*   142
 II. RELATIVE PRONOUN *QUE*   143
III. RELATIVE PRONOUN *OÙ*   144
IV. SUPERLATIVES   144
 V. COLORS MODIFIED BY OTHER ADJECTIVES OR
    NOUNS   146

LESSON 51   150

ON FAIT DES PHOTOGRAPHIES   150

A. *ON SE PRÉPARE*   150
B. *DANS LE MAGASIN DE PHOTOGRAPHIE*   152
C. *À L'ARC DE TRIOMPHE*   153
D. *À LA PLACE DE LA CONCORDE*   154
E. *À LA PLACE DU TERTRE*   154

NOTES   156
GRAMMATICAL ITEMS   158
  I. *EN* (SOME OF IT, SOME OF THEM, ETC.)   158
 II. *ASSEZ DE*   160
III. *QU'EST-CE QUI*   160
IV. *POUR* + INFINITIVE   161

LESSON 52   164

AGENCE DE VOYAGES   164

A. *ON DEMANDE DES RENSEIGNEMENTS*   164
B. *LE LENDEMAIN*   167

NOTES   170
GRAMMATICAL ITEMS   172
  I. PREPOSITIONS *EN, À, DANS* WITH PLACE NAMES   172
  II. PREPOSITION *DE* WITH PLACE NAMES   174
  III. PREPOSITIONS WITH MEANS OF
     TRANSPORTATION   176
  IV. SUBJUNCTIVE AFTER THE INTERROGATIVE OR
     NEGATIVE OF *CROIRE* AND *PENSER*   176

LESSON 53   180

VOITURES—LOCATION OU ACHAT   180

A. *LOCATION D'UNE VOITURE*   180
B. *ACHAT D'UNE VOITURE*   183

NOTES   184
GRAMMATICAL ITEMS   185
  I. INTERROGATIVE PRONOUN *QUEL*   185
  II. INTERROGATIVE ADJECTIVE *QUEL*   186
  III. *PAR* IN EXPRESSIONS OF TIME   187
  IV. *FALLOIR* WITH INDIRECT OBJECT PRONOUNS   187
  V. *PENSER* + INFINITIVE   188

LESSON 54   192

À LA STATION-SERVICE   192

NOTES   196
GRAMMATICAL ITEMS   197
  I. *Y* (THERE, ETC.)   197
  II. *ALLER* + INFINITIVE   198
  III. IRREGULAR ADJECTIVES   199

LESSON 55   203

LA DOUANE   203

A. *ON APPROCHE DE LA FRONTIÈRE ESPAGNOLE*   203
B. *À LA FRONTIÈRE*   204
C. *PLUS TARD*   206

NOTES   207
GRAMMATICAL ITEMS   209
  I. *ENTENDRE, VOIR* + INFINITIVE   209
  II. *VOULOIR* + SUBJUNCTIVE   209
  III. FORMS OF THE PAST PARTICIPLE   210
  IV. VERBS ENDING IN *-CER*   212
  V. VERBS ENDING IN *-GER*   212

LESSON 56   216

À LA BANQUE   216

A. *AU GUICHET DE CHANGE*   216
B. *AU BUREAU DU DIRECTEUR*   217

NOTES   221
GRAMMATICAL ITEMS   222
  I. *AVANT DE* + INFINITIVE   222
  II. *APRÈS* + *AVOIR* OR *ÊTRE* + PAST PARTICIPLE 223
  III. CONDITIONAL PERFECT   224
  IV. SENTENCES WITH "IF"   225
  V. FORMS OF ADVERBS   226

LESSON 57   231

À LA POSTE   231

A. *AU GUICHET "AFFRANCHISSEMENTS"*   231
B. *AU GUICHET "POSTE RESTANTE"*   232
C. *AU GUICHET "TÉLÉGRAMMES"*   233
D. *AU GUICHET "COLIS"*   234
E. *AU BUREAU DE LA S.N.C.F.*   235

NOTES   235
GRAMMATICAL ITEMS   236
  I. *EN* AND *DANS* IN TIME EXPRESSIONS   236
  II. *AVOIR À*   237
  III. POSITION OF PRONOUNS BEFORE
    COMPLEMENTARY INFINITIVES   238

LESSON 58   241

LES VÊTEMENTS   241

A. *BLANCHISSAGE ET DÉGRAISSAGE*   241
B. *NETTOYAGE*   243
C. *CHEZ LE TAILLEUR*   244
D. *CHEZ LA COUTURIÈRE*   245

NOTES   245
GRAMMATICAL ITEMS   247
  I. PREPOSITIONS BEFORE INFINITIVES   247
  II. PRESENT TENSE OF VERBS *MENER, PRÉFÉRER*   248
  III. PAST PARTICIPLES USED AS ADJECTIVES   249

LESSON 59   252

LE DENTISTE, LE MÉDECIN, ET LE PHARMACIEN   252

A. *CHEZ LE DENTISTE*   252
B. *LA VISITE DU MÉDECIN*   254
C. *A LA PHARMACIE*   256

NOTES   256
GRAMMATICAL ITEMS   258
  I. PRESENT TENSE WITH *DEPUIS*   258
  II. WAYS TO EXPRESS "AGO"   258
  III. *IL SE PEUT* + SUBJUNCTIVE   260
  IV. DEFINITE ARTICLE WITH PARTS OF THE BODY   261

LESSON 60   265

LES CULTES   265

A. *LES OFFICES DIVINS*   265
B. *UN MARIAGE FRANÇAIS*   268
C. *CHARLES PARLE AU TÉLÉPHONE AVEC MICHEL*   269

NOTES   270
GRAMMATICAL ITEMS   272
  I. *FALLOIR* + SUBJUNCTIVE   272
  II. TIME EXPRESSIONS WITH DAYS OF THE WEEK   273
  III. SOME USES OF *IL EST* AND *C'EST*   273

SUMMARY OF FRENCH GRAMMAR   279

ABOUT THE SOUNDS   279

1. THE ALPHABET   281
2. THE CONSONANTS   281
3. SIMPLE VOWELS   283
4. THE NASALIZED VOWELS   285
5. THE APOSTROPHE   286
6. THE DEFINITE ARTICLE   287
7. THE INDEFINITE ARTICLE   288
8. THE POSSESSIVE   289
9. CONTRACTIONS   289
10. GENDER   289
11. PLURAL OF NOUNS   292
12. FEMININE OF ADJECTIVES   293
13. PLURAL OF ADJECTIVES   294
14. AGREEMENT OF ADJECTIVES   295
15. POSITION OF ADJECTIVES   295
16. COMPARISON OF ADJECTIVES   297
17. POSSESSIVE ADJECTIVES   297
18. POSSESSIVE PRONOUNS   299
19. DEMONSTRATIVE ADJECTIVES   300
20. DEMONSTRATIVE PRONOUNS   301
21. PERSONAL PRONOUNS   301
22. POSITION OF PRONOUNS   303
23. RELATIVE PRONOUNS   305
24. INDEFINITE PRONOUNS   305
25. NOUN USED AS INDIRECT OBJECT   305
26. REPETITION OF PREPOSITIONS   306
27. THE PARTITIVE   306
28. NEGATION   307
29. WORD ORDER IN QUESTIONS   307
30. ADVERBS   308
31. THE INFINITIVE   311
32. THE PAST PARTICIPLE   311
33. THE INDICATIVE   312
34. THE IMPERATIVE   316
35. VERBS FOLLOWED BY THE INFINITIVE   316
36. THE SUBJUNCTIVE   317

REGULAR VERB CHARTS 322

A. CLASSES I, II, III 322
B. VERBS ENDING IN -*CER* AND -*GER* 324
C. VERBS ENDING IN -*ER* WITH CHANGES IN THE STEM 326
D. VERBS ENDING IN -*OIR* 328
E. VERBS ENDING IN -*NDRE* 330
F. COMPOUND TENSES OF VERBS CONJUGATED WITH *ÊTRE* 332
G. COMPOUND TENSES OF REFLEXIVE VERBS 332
H. INFREQUENTLY USED AND "LITERARY" TENSES 333

IRREGULAR VERB CHARTS 334

ANSWERS 347

INTRODUCTION

Living Language ™ *Advanced Conversational French*
is designed for students who have completed the 40
lessons of the basic *Living French* course or for
anyone with a sufficient grasp of the language who is
ready for more sophisticated French conversation and
grammar. Although this book is intended for use with
the *Advanced Living French* cassette or record, it may
be used alone as a textbook.

The material in the *Advanced French* course is
substantially more complex than that in the first 40
lessons of the basic *Living French* course. These 20
units incorporate more advanced speech patterns and
more intricate grammatical detail. Each unit is orga-
nized as follows:

Text. The recorded text (in boldface type) consists of
dialogues between an American couple visiting
France and their friends and business acquaintances
in various situations that travelers are likely to
encounter in France. Those words and phrases in
the text printed in boldface italics within the recorded matter refer to material treated in Grammatical Items for Special Study. The English translation
appears directly beneath each line of French.

Notes. The small circles in the body of the text refer
to the notes which immediately follow the text. The
notes contain grammatical details, and comments
on matters of general interest.

Grammatical items. This section treats carefully se-
lected grammatical constructions in thorough detail
and supplements and enlarges upon the material
already presented in the earlier lessons. All students
should read over this material several times, and

those who care to go more thoroughly into the language would do well to study the grammar intensively.

Drills and exercises. The exercises furnish an overall review of the material in the unit. The answer key is in the back of the book. You will find it very useful to work through the complete advanced course, and then do the translation sentences once again; this translation review will serve as a culmination of all your studies.

You will, of course, work through the course as fast or as slowly as is convenient, but we urge that you do a little work every day, if only for ten minutes.

Students will find it helpful to make up little dialogues, to keep a notebook of vocabulary words and phrases for frequent review, and to listen to, speak, and read French as often as they can. Through this constant repetition and practice, the French language—with all the pleasure and utility it affords—will become yours.

Course Material

The material of the *ADVANCED LIVING FRENCH* course consists of the following:

1. *One hour-long cassette or 2 long-playing records.* The label on each face indicates clearly which lessons are contained on that side.

2. *Advanced Conversational French* book. This book is designed for use with the recorded lesson or it may be used alone. It contains the following sections:

Advanced French Vocabulary and Grammar
Summary of French Grammar
Answers to the Drills and Exercises and Quizzes

3. *French-English/English-French Common Usage Dictionary.* A special kind of dictionary that gives literal translations of more than 20,000 French words,

plus idiomatic phrases and sentences to illustrate the everyday use of the more important vocabulary. One thousand essential words are highlighted for quick reference. The *Common Usage Dictionary* doubles as a phrasebook.

How to Use Advanced Conversational French with the Living Language™ Cassette

The lessons, continuing from the basic *Living French* course, are numbered from 41 through 60.

1. Look at page 1. Note the words in boldface type. These are the words you will hear on the cassette.

2. Now read Lesson 41. (The ▣▣ ▣▣ symbols indicate the beginning of the recorded material. In some advanced lessons, information and instructions precede the recording.) Note the points to look for when you play the cassette. Look at the first sentence, **Allô! Qui est à l'appareil?**, and be prepared to follow the voice on the cassette.

3. Play the cassette, listen carefully, and watch for the points mentioned in Lesson 41. Then rewind, play the dialogue again, and this time say the words aloud. Keep repeating until you are sure you know the lesson. The more times you listen and repeat, the longer you will remember the material.

4. Now go on to the next lesson. It's always good to quickly review the previous lesson before starting a new one.

5. At the end of each section there are Drills and Exercises, and a Quiz. Do these exercises faithfully, checking your answers at the back of the book, and if you make any mistakes, study the section again.

Living Language™

ADVANCED
CONVERSATIONAL
FRENCH

LESSON 41

RENDEZ-VOUS AU CAFÉ
APPOINTMENT AT A CAFÉ

A. *On fixe le rendez-vous*° Making the appointment

1. Michel: **Allô!**° **Qui est à l'appareil?**
   Hello! Who's on the wire?

2. Charles: **Ici**° **Charles Lewis, de New York.**
   This is Charles Lewis from New York.

3. Michel: **Quel** *plaisir*° **de vous entendre! Où vous trouvez-vous**° **en ce moment?**
   What a pleasure to hear from you! Where are you right now [lit.: at this moment]?

4. Charles: **A**° **l'Hôtel Merceau.** *Nous venon d'arriver,* **ma femme et moi.**
   At the Hotel Merceau. My wife and I have just arrived.

5. Michel: *Je tiens à vous voir* **le plus tôt possible! Vous êtes libre cet après-midi? A deux heures?**
   I'm eager to see you as soon as possible. Are you free this afternoon? At two o'clock?

6. Charles: **C'est parfait. Où nous retrouverons-nous?**
   Excellent. Where shall we meet?

7. Michel: **Au Café des Deux Magots,**° **Place Saint-Germain. Prenez un taxi.**
   At the Café des Deux Magots, Place Saint-Germain. Take a taxi.

8. Charles: **D'accord.**° **Trouvera-t-on une table libre à cette heure-là?**
   Fine. Will we get a table at that time?

9. Michel: **Sans doute. A tout à l'heure,° alors.**
   No doubt. See you in a little while, then.

10. Charles: **Entendu. A plus tard. Au revoir.**
    Right. See you later. So long.

B. *On se rencontre au café* They meet at the café

11. Michel: **Eh bien, Charles, *vous voici enfin arrivé,*° Soyez° le bienvenu à Paris!°**
    Well, Charles, here you are at last. Welcome to Paris!

12. Charles: **Merci, Michel. Nous sommes tellement°*contents*, Jeanne at moi, *d'être* à Paris.**
    Thank you, Michael. Jane and I are so happy to be in Paris.

13. Michel: **Voulez-vous vous asseoir à l'intérieur ou sur la terrasse?**
    Do you want to sit indoors or out on the terrace?

14. Charles: **a la terrasse, bien entendu!**
    Outdoors, of course!

15. Michel: **Ah! *Voilà une table libre* au deuxième rang. Mais . . . où est Jeanne?**
    Ah! There's an empty table in the second row, But . . . where's Jane?

16. Charles: **Elle est restée° à l'hôtel pour défaire les bagages. D'ailleurs, le voyage a été long et fatigant.**
    She stayed at the hotel to unpack. Moreover, the trip was long and tiring.

17. Garçon: **Qu'est-ce que vous prendrez,° messieurs?°**
    Waiter: What will you have, gentlemen?

18. Michel: **Un citron pressé,°** s'il vous plaît. Il
    fait si chaud!°
    A lemonade, please. It's so warm!

19. Charles: **Et pour moi°** un demi° blonde.°
    And for me a large glass of light beer.

20. Garçon: **Tout de suite,°** messieurs.
    Right away, gentlemen.

21. Charles: **Quelle° agréable initiation à la vie°**
    française! Tiens!° *Voici déjà°* **le garçon** qui
    nous apporte° les boissons!° A votre santé!
    What a pleasant introduction to French life!
    Look! Here's the waiter bringing our drinks
    already! To your health!

22. Michel: **A la vôtre!°** Et bon séjour°à Paris!
    To yours! And an enjoyable stay in Paris!

23. Charles: **On est° vraiment bien ici.** *J'ai envie*
    de° rester° **ici toute la journée.°**
    It's really nice here. I feel like staying here the
    whole day.

24. Michel: **Vous avez le** *droit de passer°* **toute**
    l'après-midi au café.
    You have the right to spend all afernoon at the
    café.

25. Charles: *On ne demande* **jamais°** *aux clients*
    de partir?
    They never ask the customers to leave?

26. Michel: **Pas du tout! Et, si vous voulez, vous**
    pouvez lire le journal, écrire des lettres,
    bavarder avec des amis, ou, tout simple-
    ment, regarder passer les gens.
    Not at all! And, if you wish, you can read the
    newspaper, write letters, chat with friends, or
    simply look at the people passing by.

27. Charles: **Quand on demeure à New-York,°
    on oublie bien vite° *l'art de se détendre.***
    When you live in New York, you quickly
    forget the art of relaxing.

28. Michel: **J'espère° que vous avez fait bon
    voyage.° C'est° par le *France* que° vous êtes
    venus,° n'est-ce pas?**
    I hope you've had a good trip. You came on the
    France, didn't you?

29. Charles: **Oui, et la traversée° a été excel-
    lente. Nous avons trouvé nos compagnons de
    voyage° très sympathiques,° et la vie à
    bord° était toujours très gaie.**
    Yes, and the trip was excellent. We found our
    traveling companions very congenial, and life
    on board was always very gay.

30. Michel: **Dites donc,° si vous n'avez pas de
    projets° pour demain, on pourra peut-être
    faire un petit tour° à pied.°**
    Say, if you don't have any plans for tomorrow,
    maybe we can take a little walk.

31. Charles: **Quelle bonne idée!° Je suis sûr que
    Jeanne aura envie de nous accompagner.
    Merci, mon vieux.**
    What a good idea! I'm sure Jane will want to
    come with us. Thank you, my friend.

32. Michel: **Garçon, l'addition,° s'il vous plaît.
    Je vais régler l'addition, donner un pour-
    boire,° et nous partons...Mais non,
    Charles. C'est moi qui vous invite pour fêter
    votre arrivée à Paris.**
    Waiter! The check, please. I'm going to pay
    the bill, leave a tip, and we'll go...No, no,
    Charles, I'm treating you to celebrate your
    arrival in Paris.

NOTES

A. *On fixe le rendez-vous: On* is a catch-all pronoun meaning "we," "they," indefinite "you," "people," etc. See Lesson 44 for full explanation. See also Note 23 *below.*

1. *Allô!:* What to say when answering the telephone. *J'écoute* is also used.

2. *Ici:* Used on the telephone to indicate the speaker. Ex.: *Ici Marianne.* This is Marianne.

3. *Quel plaisir:* Note the use of *quel* to express "What a . . . !" This is discussed fully in Lesson 45.
   vous trouvez-vous: Forms of *se trouver* (lit.: to find oneself) are often used in place of *être* (to be). *Se trouver* is a reflexive verb. Other reflexive verbs in this lesson are *se rencontrer, s'asseoir, se détendre.* Reflexive verbs are discussed in detail in Lesson 45.

4. *A l'hôtel:* Note that A has no accent. Capital letters generally do not take accents.

7. *(le) Café des Deux Magots:* A landmark on the Left Bank in Paris, and a celebrated meeting-place for intellectuals and artists.

8. *D'accord:* Agreed, O.K. *Entendu,* in sentence 10 of the text, means the same thing.

9. *A tout à l'heure:* See you in a little while. A frequently used expression.

11. *Vous voici enfin arrivé:* lit.: Here you are finally arrived.
    Soyez: imperative form of the verb *être.*
    Soyez le bienvenu: lit.: Be welcome. A common courtesy formula
    à Paris: See Lesson 52.

12. *tellement* = *si* (so).

16. *Elle est restée:* Note the use of *être* as a helping verb instead of *avoir*. See Lesson 48 for full discussion.

17. *prendrez:* form of *prendre*, literally "to take." *Prendre* is used when offering or asking for food.
    messieurs: plural of *monsieur* (similarly: *mesdames, mesdemoiselles*).

18. *un citron pressé:* lemonade (lit.: a squeezed lemon). There is another drink called *limonade*, which is carbonated.
    il fait si chaud: The verb *faire* is generally used in weather expressions. Examples: *il fait froid* ("it's cold"); *il fait beau* ("the weather is fine"); *Qu'il faisait doux!* ("How nice it was!").

19. *pour moi:* Note disjunctive pronoun after preposition *pour*. See Lesson 45 for explanation of disjunctive pronoun forms and uses.
    un demi: short for *un demi-litre* (a half-liter). A liter is approximately equal to a quart. In France, and throughout most of Continental Europe, the metric system is generally used for all measures.
    blonde: a light beer. The word *bière* (beer) is understood. A dark beer is *une brune*.

20. *Tout de suite:* immediately, right away.

21. *Quelle agréable initiation:* See Note 3 above. Notice that *quelle* is feminine, to agree with the feminine noun *initiation*.
    la vie française: The definite article is used with nouns to express a general concept or idea. Examples: *La vie est belle.* Life is beautiful; *La santé est importante.* Health is important.

Tiens!: Look! What do you know! A familiar exclamation.

déjà: Notice its position in the sentence immediately after *voici.*

le garçon qui nous apporte: lit.: "the waiter who is bringing us..."

boissons: from the verb *boire,* to drink.

22. *A la vôtre = à votre santé:* a familiar toast.
    bon séjour: lit.: good sojourn, stay.

23. *on est:* equivalent to *nous sommes.* See A. above.
    j'ai envie de: equivalent to *je voudrais, j'aimerais* (I'd like to, I feel like). For fuller explanation, see Grammatical Item IV in this lesson.
    rester: to stay, to remain. Do not confuse with *se reposer,* to rest.
    la journée: This feminine form of "day" is used to indicate duration or extension of time. Note also *toute la matinée* ("all morning," "the entire morning"), *toute la soirée* ("all evening," "the entire evening"). Contrast with the masculine *tous les jours* ("every day"), *tous les matins* ("every morning"), *tous les soirs* ("every evening").

24. *passer:* to spend (time); *dépenser,* to spend (money).

25. *ne... jamais:* never.

27. *on demeure à New-York = on habite New-York* or *on vit à New-York:* One lives in New York.
    bien vite = très vite (very quickly). *Bien* is used to intensify the word it precedes. Examples: *Il est bien gentil.* ("He's quite nice."); *Elle danse ici bien souvent.* ("She dances here quite often.")

28. *j'espère:* from verb *espérer.* In verbs which have *é* as the last vowel of the stem, the *é* changes to *è* before the silent endings *-e, -es* and *-ent.* However, the *é* remains throughout the future and conditional tenses. Other verbs similarly conjugated: *préférer* (to prefer), *répéter* (to repeat), *céder* (to yield), *s'inquiéter* (to worry), *posséder* (to possess), *protéger* (to protect).

avait fait bon voyage: had a good trip. Note idiomatic omission of indefinite article *un.*

C'est par le France *que . . . :* It's by the *France* that . . .

le France: masculine to agree with *paquebot* (liner) or *navire* (ship), understood. The country is *la* France.

venus: plural, because both husband and wife are referred to. See Lesson 48 for discussion of participle agreement.

29. *la traversée:* the crossing (*traverser:* to cross).

compagnons de voyage: traveling companions. (Note word order.)

sympathiques: nice, pleasant, congenial. Do not confuse with *sympathetic.*

la vie à bord: shipboard life.

30. *Dites donc:* Say; Listen; By the way.

pas de projets: de and not *des* because of the negative partitive construction. See Lesson 48 for detailed explanation of the partitive.

projets: plan, projects.

faire un petit tour: faire une petite promenade (take a little walk).

à pied: on foot.

31. *Quelle bonne idée!:* What a good idea!

32. *l'addition:* a bill in a restaurant or café.

un pourboire: It is customary to leave a tip for

the waiter. Notice "pour boire" (lit., "for drinking") but used to indicate a tip for any service.

GRAMMATICAL ITEMS FOR SPECIAL STUDY

I. *venir de:* to have just (lit., "to come from")
   Study:

Subject	venir	de	Pronoun	Infinitive	Complement
1. Je	viens	de	lui	parler.	
2. Il	venait	de	l'	acheter.	
3. Il	venait	de		lire	le journal.

1. *I have just spoken to him. (I come from speaking to him.)*

2. *He had just bought it. (He came from buying it.)*

3. *He had just read the newspaper. (He came from reading the newspaper.)*

Note: See *Summary of French Grammar* for review of object pronouns and the *Irregular Verb Charts* for forms of *venir*.

II. *tenir à:* to be eager to, to want to very much
    Study:

Subject	tenir	à	Pronoun	Infinitive	Complement
1. Il	tient	à	vous	parler.	
2. Nous	tenions	à		voir	Michel.

1. *He wants very much to talk to you.*

2. *We were eager to see Michel.*

Note: See the *Irregular Verb Charts* for forms of *tenir*.

III. *voici; voilà*

A. Notice:

Direct object pronoun	voici or voilà
1. Me	voici.
2. Les	voilà.

1. *Here I am.*
2. *There they are.*

Note: In modern usage, *voilà* is often used instead of *voici.*

B. Study

Me	voici.	Nous	voici.
Te	voici.	Vous	voici.
Le	voici.	Les	voici.
La	voici.		

IV. *avoir envie de:* to feel like. to want to (used primarily in the *present, imperfect past,* and *future*)

Study:

Subject	avoir	envie	de	Object Pron.	Infin.	Comp.
1. J'	ai	envie	de		dormir.	
2. Il	avait	envie	de	le	voir.	
3. Elle	aura	envie	d'		acheter	le livre.

1. *I feel like sleeping.*

2. *He wanted to see him.*

3. *She will want to buy the book.*

Note: Review forms of *avoir* in the *Irregular Verb Charts.*

V. **Prepositions before infinitives.**

Note: Nouns generally take the preposition *de* before a following infinitive. See examples below.

A. *de*

1. After nouns:

	Noun	Prep.	Infinitive	Complement
1. J'ai	envie	de	partir.	
2. Quel	plaisir	de	voir	Paris!
3. C'est	le moment	de	parler.	
4. Il a	le droit	de	rester.	

1. *I feel like leaving.*

2. *What a pleasure to see Paris!*

3. *It's the time to speak.*

4. *He has the right to stay.*

Certain adjectives and certain verbs take either the preposition *de* or the preposition *à* before the following infinitive. These must be memorized, because there is no set rule to determine their use in all cases. See examples below, and also Lesson 58.

2. After certain adjectives:

	Adjective	Prep.	Infinitive	Complement
a. Nous sommes	contents	de	partir.	
b. Je suis	enchanté(e)	de	faire	votre connaissance.

a. *We are happy to leave.*
b. *I am pleased to make your acquaintance.*

3. After certain verbs:

a. Il refuse	de venir.
b. Il essaie	de parler.
c. Il demande aux clients	de partir.

    a. *He refuses to come.*
    b. *He tries to speak.*
    c. *He asks the clients to leave.*

B. *à*

1. After certain adjectives:

a. Nous sommes prêts	à	partir.
b. C'est facile	à	faire.

    a. *We are ready to go.*
    b. *It's easy to do.*

2. After certain verbs.

Verb	Prep.	Infinitive	Complement
a. Je commence	à	parler	français.
b. Il tient	à	régler	l'addition.

    a. *I am beginning to speak French,*
    b. *He wants very much to settle the bill.*

C. No preposition after certain verbs (following are the most common):

	Verb	Infinitive	Complement
1. *aller;*	Je vais	téléphoner.	
2. *vouloir:*	Je voudrais	laisser	un pourboire.
3. *falloir:*	Il faut	fixer	le rendez-vous.
4. *pouvoir:*	Vous pouvez	lire	le journal.
5. *savoir:*	Nous savons	nager.	

1. *I'm going to phone.*

2. *I'd like to leave a tip.*

3. *One must make the appointment.*

4. *You can read the paper.*

5. *We know how to swim.*

Note: Forms of the above irregular verbs are given in the *Irregular Verb Charts*.

DRILLS AND EXERCISES

I. Substitute each of the words in parentheses for the italicized word in the pattern sentence. Write the complete sentence and say aloud.

   A. Example: Il fait *beau.*/Il fait *chaud.*
      (chaud, froid, frais, doux, bon, mauvais, du soleil, du vent)
   B. C'est *moi* qui l'invite.
      (son ami, lui, elle, son père, Michel, sa soeur)
   C. Quel plaisir de vous *voir!*
      (connaître, entendre, parler, revoir, écouter)

II. Replace the subject pronoun *je* by the other subject pronouns *(tu, il, elle, nous, vous, ils, elles)*. Make the appropriate changes in the verb. (Study verb forms in the *Irregular Verb Charts*.)

   A. *Je* viens de l'acheter.

   B. *Je* tiens à le voir.

   C. *J'ai* envie de lui parler.

III. Replace the italicized object pronoun by the other appropriate pronouns *(me, te, le, la, nous, vous, les)*, and translate.

   A. *Me* voici.

   B. *Te* voilà.

IV. Translate the following sentences into French;
    then say them aloud.

1. I'm going to meet Charles.

2. He's not going to see Jane.

3. Are we going to find a free table?

4. I want to telephone.

5. Do you want to speak French?

6. She wants to make an appointment.

7. It's necessary to sit indoors (à l'intérieur).

8. It is necessary to pay the bill.

9. She can take a little walk.

10. We can celebrate your arrival.

11. I know how to read a French newspaper.

12. Do you know how to write a letter in (en)
    French?

13. I'm beginning to unpack.

14. Are you beginning to understand?

15. She wants very much to see him.

16. I refuse to stay here.

17. He has asked Robert to stay.

18. I'm happy to be in Paris.

19. It's time to meet Michael.

20. I have the right to accompany Michael.

21. Have we the right to enter (entrer)?

Answers at back of book.

QUIZ

From among the three choices given, choose the one
which correctly renders the English given at the

beginning of each sentence, write the complete sentence, and translate.

1. *(have just)* Je_____arriver.
   - (a) tiens à
   - (b) ai envie d'
   - (c) viens d'

2. *(right away)*_____, messieurs.
   - (a) A la vôtre
   - (b) Heureusement
   - (c) Tout de suite.

3. *(drinks)* Tiens, voici déjà le garçon qui nous apporte les_____.
   - (a) verres
   - (b) boissons
   - (c) pourboires.

4. *(never)* Et on ne demande_____aux clients de partir?
   - (a) jamais
   - (b) plus
   - (c) rien

5. *(of course)* A la terrasse,_____.
   - (a) pas du tout
   - (b) bien entendu
   - (c) tout à fait

6. *(It's)*_____chaud.
   - (a) Il est
   - (b) C'est
   - (c) Il fait

7. *(I feel like)*_____ marcher.
   - (a) Je me sens
   - (b) Je demande
   - (c) J'ai envie de

8. *(pay)* Je vais_____l'addition et laisser un
   pourboire.
   (a) rejoindre
   (b) retrouver
   (c) régler

9. *(crossing)* Oui, et c'était une
   excellente_____.
   (a) bienvenu
   (b) traversée
   (c) journée

10. *(Here he is)*_____.
    (a) La voici
    (b) Le voici
    (c) Les voici

Answers at back of book.

LESSON 42

AU KIOSQUE°
AT THE NEWSSTAND

1. Charles: *au marchand de journaux* **Nous
   venons d'arriver à Paris, monsieur, et je ne
   connais° pas les journaux français. Pour-
   riez-° vous nous aider?**
   (to the news vendor) We've just arrived in Paris,
   sir, and I'm not familiar with French newspapers. Could you help us?

2. Marchand: **Volontiers, monsieur. Pour la politique et l'information générale, nous avons
   bon nombre de quotidiens° à Paris. Puis,
   nous avons aussi des journaux littéraires...**

Gladly, sir. For politics and general information, we have a good many dailies in Paris. Then too, we also have literary newspapers . . .

3. Jeanne: **"Quotidiens," vous avez dit? Je ne connais pas *ce mot-là*.**
"Quotidiens," did you say? I don't know that word.

4. Marchand: **Cela veut dire qu'il y a un numéro tous les jours,° madame. Il y a aussi des hebdomadaires,° qui ne° paraissent qu'une fois par semaine.**
That means that there's an edition every day, madam. There are also weeklies, which come out only once a week.

5. Charles: **Si je ne me trompe pas, je vois là une quinzaine° de quotidiens!**
If I'm not mistaken, I see there about fifteen dailies!

6. Jeanne: **Mais quel journal a le plus grand tirage, monsieur? Si on veut connaître un pays . . .**
But which paper has the largest circulation, sir? If one wants to get to know a country . . .

7. Marchand: **Alors là, madame, il n'y a pas à dire: c'est *France-Soir*. *En choisissant ceci*, vous ne vous tromperez pas. Tenez, vous voulez regarder?°**
As for that, madam, there's no doubt: it's *France-Soir*. You won't make a mistake choosing this one. Here, would you like to look at it?°

8. Charles: **Tant d'images! Mais je ne vois, en première page, que des histoires de crimes et de scandales! Je ne vois ni politique ni information générale.**

So many pictures! But on the front page I see only stories about crimes and scandals! I see neither politics nor general information.

9. Marchand: **Mais non, monsieur, vous avez là tout *ce qu'*il vous faut° dans un journal: actualités,° spectacles, radio et télévision, mondanités, la rubrique sportive, même les courses.**
Why no, sir, you have there everything you need in a newspaper: news, shows, radio and television, society news, the sports section, even the races.

10. Charles: **Quand même, n'auriez-vous pas quelque chose d°'un peu plus sobre?**
Still, wouldn't you have something a bit more serious?

11. Marchand: **Prenez alors *Le Figaro,* monsieur, ou bien *Le Monde.***
Then take *Le Figaro,* sir, or *Le Monde.*

12. Charles: **Eh bien, je commence par *Le Monde.***
All right, I'll begin with *Le Monde.*

13. Jeanne: **Je vois que vous avez là des revues de tous les pays—revues *françaises, italiennes, allemandes, anglaises, américaines,* et même *russes!***
I see you have magazines there from every country—French, Italian, German, English, American, and even Russian magazines!

14. Marchand: **Oui, madame, et de tous les genres. Il y a des revues hebdomadaires et mensuelles, et d'autres qui paraissent toutes les deux semaines.**

Yes, madam, and all kinds. There are weekly
and monthly magazines, and others which
come out every other week.

15. Jeanne: **Celles-là sont d'intérêt général,
n'est-ce pas—*Paris-Match* et *Jours de
France*?**
Those over there are of general interest, aren't
they—*Paris-Match* and *Jours de France?*

16. Marchand: **C'est ça, madame, et de *côté-ci*
nous avons tout *ce qui* peut intéresser une
femme—revues de mode, albums de tricot,
et puis *Marie France, Elle*...**
That's right, madam, and on this side we have
everything that could interest a woman—
fashion magazines, knitting magazines, and
then *Marie France, Elle*...

17. Jeanne: **Puis-je regarder un moment ce
numéro de *Marie France*?**
May I look at this issue of *Marie France* for a
moment?

18. Marchand: **Mais oui, madame. Vous voyez
ici dans le sommaiore, il y a le courrier des
livres, des disques, de la télévision...et
aussi des rubriques maison, jardin, cuisine,
enfants, beauté, santé...**
Of course, madam. You see here in the table of
contents, there are reports on books, records,
television...and also columns on the house,
garden, cooking, children, beauty, health...

19. Charles: **Que c'est ennuyeux!**
What a bore!

20. Jeanne: **Tais-toi, chéri, puisque tu n'en° sais
rien! Quand j'aurai fini de la lire, je te
passerai les mots croisés.**

Be quiet, dear, since you know nothing about it! When I finish reading it, I'll give you the crossword puzzle.

21. Marchand: **Est-ce que je peux vous suggérer aussi** *cette petite revue-ci, Une Semaine de Paris?*° **Elle vous donne le programme de tous les spectacles.**
May I also suggest to you this little magazine, *Une Semaine de Paris?* It gives you the programs of all the shows.

22. Charles: **C'est exactement** *ce qu'*il **nous faut, monsieur.**
That's exactly what we need, sir.

23. Charles: **Auriez-vous aussi un plan de la ville avec tous les monuments importants?**
Would you also have a map of the city with all the important monuments?

24. Marchand: **Bien sûr. En voilà un qui se vend**° **beaucoup.**
Certainly. Here's one [of them] that is widely sold.

25. Jeanne: **Nous avons naturellement notre** *Michelin,*° **mais il nous faut un guide illustré format de poche.**
We have our *Michelin*, of course, but we need a pocket-sized illustrated guide.

26. Marchand: **Voici quelque chose qui fera votre affaire.**
Here is something that will meet your needs.

27. Charles: **Jeanne, regarde ces cartes routières. Elles montrent**° **toutes les nouvelles routes et se vendent trois francs cinquante chacune.**

Jane, look at these road maps. They show all
the new roads and are sold for three francs
fifty each.

28. Charles: **Vous avez été si aimable, monsieur.
Pourriez-vous nous indiquer un magasin
tout près d'ici où l'on vend des disques° et
des bandes magnétiques?**
You have been so kind, sir. Could you direct us
to a store near here where they sell records and
tapes?

29. Marchand: **Il y en a un à deux pas d'ici, au
coin de la rue. Au revoir, monsieur, madame.**
There is one (of them) very close by, at the
corner of this street. Good-bye, sir, madam.

NOTES

Title. *kiosque:* a newsstand. There are kiosques on
almost every street corner in Paris, where one
can buy newspapers, magazines, street maps,
guides, and sometimes road maps. Most kiosques are very colorful because they display
posters announcing theatre programs, con-
certs, art exhibitions, and other attractions.

1. *connais:* from *connaître,* "to know," in the
sense of "to be acquainted with," "to be
familiar with." See also 3 and 6 of text.
Pourriez-vous: The conditional is used in expressions of courtesy; see also 10, 23, and 28.
See *Irregular Verb Charts* for conditional
forms of *pouvoir* and *avoir,* and Lesson 46 for
discussion of the conditional of courtesy.

2. *quotidien:* daily.

4. *tous les jours:* every day. See Lesson 41, note
23 for a discussion of this use of *tout.*

hebdomadaire: weekly. (Other words in this family are *mensuel:* monthly, and *annuel:* yearly.)

ne . . . [verb] . . . que: only. See also 8 of the text.

5. *quinzaine:* "aine" at the end of a number indicates an approximate amount. Note, however, *douzaine,* which means *a dozen.*

7. Notice the omission of "it" in the French.

9. *il vous faut:* you need (lit.: It is necessary to you.) This is derived from the verb *falloir,* "to be necessary to." It is used only in the third person singular. Note also, in 22 and 25 of the text: *il nous faut:* we need (lit.: It is necessary to us.) See Lesson 43 for full discussion.

   actualités: from *actuel* (contemporary, at the present time, at this moment). Do not confuse it with the English "actual," which is equivalent to the French *réel* or *véritable.*

10. *quelque chose de:* something. As in *quelque chose d'intéressant* (something interesting); *quelque chose de nécessaire* (something necessary). Also notice *Donnez-moi quelque chose.* (Give me something.)

20. *en:* a catch-all pronoun meaning "some of it, some of them, any of it, any of them, about it, etc." This pronoun is always expressed in French, though it may be merely implied in English. Note also the use of *en* in 24 of the text. *En* is discussed in Lesson 51.

21. *Une Semaine de Paris:* a pocket-sized weekly guide to events of cultural and general interest; names of restaurants, hotels, movies, plays, etc.

24. *se vend:* Notice that the reflexive form of the verb *vendre* is used to express the passive "is sold." Contrast with the active use of *vend* in 28 of the text.

25. *Michelin:* comprehensive detailed guides to the various regions of France and other European and African countries.

27. *Elles montrent:* An alternative way to express the same idea would be: *Elles indiquent toutes les nouvelles routes...*

28. *disques:* Notice that the word "discothèque" comes from the word "disque."

And from the same root, the following useful vocabulary:

disque microsillon: microgroove.
disque de 45, 33, 78 tours: records of 45, 33 and 78 r.p.m.
disque stéréo(phonique): stereo.

Other related terms are:

un électrophone: a phonograph.
un magnétophone: a tape recorder.
une bande (un ruban) magnétique: a tape.
haute fidélité: hi-fi.

GRAMMATICAL ITEMS FOR SPECIAL STUDY

I. *ce qui:* that which, what (used as **subject**)

Study:

Verb	ce qui	Verb	
1.	Ce qui	n'est pas	clair n'est pas français.
2. Je vois	ce qui	est	sur la table.

1. *That which is not clear is not French.*

2. *I see what is on the table.*

II. *ce que:* that, which, what (used as *object*)

Study:

Verb	ce que	Subject	Verb	
1.	Ce que	vous	dites	est intéressant.
2. Je comprends	ce que	Michel	a dit.	

1. *What you're saying is interesting.*

2. *I understand what Michael said.*

III. *Demonstrative adjectives*

A. *ce, cet, cette:* this or that; *ces:* these or those

Study:

MASCULINE		FEMININE	
Sing.	*Plu.*	*Sing.*	*Plu.*
ce garçon	ces garçons	cette femme	ces femmes
cet ami	ces amis	cette amie	ces amies
cet hôtel	ces hôtels	cette histoire	ces histoires

B. *-ci* (derived from *ici*—here) designates something close to the speaker, and *-là* (there) indicates something at a distance.

Study:
1. Je n'aime pas   cette revue-ci.
2. Je préfère   ce journal-là.
3. Je ne veux pas   ces disques-là.
4. Je veux   ces bandes-ci.

1. *I don't like this magazine.*

2. *I prefer that newspaper.*

3. *I don't want those records.*

4. *I want these tapes.*

IV. **Adjectives of nationality** (always written with a small letter)

Study:

Feminine	Masculine	
belge	belge	*Belgian*
suisse	suisse	*Swiss*
espagnole	espagnol	*Spanish*
française	français	*French*
anglaise	anglais	*English*
chinoise	chinois	*Chinese*
danoise	danois	*Danish*
américaine	américain	*American*
africaine	africain	*African*
italienne	italien	*Italian*
canadienne	canadien	*Canadian*
allemande	allemand	*German*

1) Note that the above adjectives, like all adjectives, agree in gender and number with the nouns they modify or describe.

2) When adjectives of nationality are used as nouns, they are capitalized. Contrast:

C'est un livre français.   Il est Français.
It's a French book.   *He is a Frenchman.*

V. *en* + present participle

A. Study:
1. **(parler)**   En parl*ant*, il a fait des erreurs.
2. **(choisir)**   En choisiss*ant* ceci, vous ne vous trompez pas.
3. **(apprendre)** Elle a pleuré en appren*ant* la vérité.
4. **(lire)**   En lis*ant,* on apprend beaucoup.

1. *While speaking, he made some mistakes.*

2. *You're not making a mistake in choosing this one.*

3. *She cried upon learning the truth.*

4. *One learns a great deal through reading.*

B. Notes:

1. *En* may be translated by *while, by, upon, through, in.*

2. *En* + present participle may come at the beginning, in the middle, or at the end of a sentence.

3. See the *Irregular Verb Charts* for present participles of irregular verbs.

4. Note that this is not the same use of *en* mentioned in Note 20 of this lesson.

DRILLS AND EXERCISES

I. Substitute the word(s) or expressions in the list for the italicized word(s) or expressions in the pattern sentence. Write the complete sentence and say aloud.

A. Je ne comprends pas ce que vous *dites*. (voulez, écrivez, faites, expliquez, voulez dire)

B. Je vois ce qui *est sur la table*. (arrive, se passe, ne va pas, vous inquiète)

C. J'aime ce *manteau*-ci. (livre, disque, complet, journal, garçon)

II. Make each of the following masculine. Write complete sentences.

Example: Elle est *Française:*/Il est *Français*.

Anglaise
Chinoise
Américaine
Italienne
Espagnole

III. Expand the following sentences by placing *En choisissant cela* in front of each; then say aloud and translate.

_____, il s'est trompé.

_____, elle a bien fait.

_____, elle ne s'est pas trompée.

_____, elle avait raison.

_____, nous avons payé trop cher

IV. Translate the following sentences into French; then say them aloud.

1. Could you tell us . . . ?

2. Could you show *(montrer)* us . . . ?

3. Could you direct us *(nous indiquer)* to a store?

4. Would you have a daily (paper)?

5. If I'm not mistaken, here's a literary newspaper.

6. Here is something interesting *(intéressant)*.

7. Here is something boring *(ennuyeux)*.

8. There is something important.

9. We need some records and some tapes.

10. May I see Jane?

11. May I speak to Charles?

12. Let's choose between this edition *(numéro)* and that edition.

13. Look at this article (masc.). Don't look at that article.

14. I don't like these newspapers. I prefer those newspapers.

15. I don't like these magazines. I prefer those magazines.

16. Show me that tape recorder.

17. Take those tapes.

18. Take these records.

19. Here's what you're looking for.

20. Here's what I mean. *(vouloir dire)*

21. What I want? A road map!

22. What he's looking for? A tape!

23. What she's reading? Our *Michelin!*

24. I have everything you're looking for.

25. I understand everything she's saying.

26. He likes what's important.

27. We read what's necessary *(nécessaire)*.

28. Do you see what's happening *(se passer)*?

29. By reading one learns to read.

30. By writing one learns to write.

Answers at back of book.

QUIZ

From among the three choices given, choose the one which correctly renders the English given at the beginning of each sentence, write the complete sentence, and translate.

1. *(I don't know)* _____ les journaux.
   (a) Je ne sais pas
   (b) Je ne vois pas
   (c) Je ne connais pas

2. *(Could you)* _____ nous aider?
   (a) Pourriez-vous
   (b) Auriez-vous
   (c) Seriez-vous

3. *(a week)* Ces journaux paraissent une fois _____.
   (a) la semaine
   (b) par semaine
   (c) une semaine

4. *(So many)* _____ images!
   (a) Trop d'
   (b) Beaucoup d'
   (c) Tant d'

5. *(with)* Je commence _____ Le Monde.
   (a) par
   (b) sans
   (c) comme

6. *(all)* Nous avons des revues de _____ les genres.
   (a) toutes
   (b) tous
   (c) tout

7. *(That's right)* _____, madame.
   (a) C'est raison
   (b) C'est droite
   (c) C'est ça

8. *(a map)* Avez-vous _____ de la ville?
   - (a) un plan
   - (b) une route
   - (c) une mappe

         Answers at back of book.

LESSON 43

AU TÉLÉPHONE°
ON THE TELEPHONE

A. *Un appel interurbain*   A long-distance call

> *Charles parle à l'employée près des cabines téléphoniques au Bureau des P et T.*
> Charles speaks to the employee near the telephone booths at the Post Office.

1. Charles: **Puis-je faire ici un appel interurbain°, mademoiselle?**
   May I make a long-distance call here, Miss?

2. Employée: *C'est pour quelle ville, monsieur?*
   To what city, sir?

3. Charles: **Pour Bordeaux, mais je ne connais pas le numéro.**
   To Bordeaux, but I don't know the number.

4. Employée: **Cela *ne* fait *rien,* monsieur. *Je peux le demander* au service des renseignements.**
   That doesn't matter, sir. I can ask information for it.

5. Charles: **Ne vous en donnez pas la peine. *Je vais le chercher* moi-même° dans l'annuaire.**
   Don't trouble. I'll look for it myself in the telephone book.

6. Employée: **Très bien, monsieur.** *Vous trouverez* **le Bottin°** **là-bas, à droite.**
   Very well, sir. You'll find the directory over there, to the right.

7. Charles: **Merci, mademoiselle. Voyons...** **Ah! Duclos, Philippe... 48.62.57°** **(quarante-huit, soixante-deux, cinquante-sept).**
   Thank you, Miss. Let's see... Ah! Duclos, Philippe... 48.62.57.

8. Employée: **Vous l'avez trouvé, je vois.** *Ce sera* **huit francs pour trois minutes.°**
   You found it, I see. That will be eight francs for three minutes.

9. Charles: **Et si c'est plus de trois minutes, je paie un supplément, n'est-ce pas?**
   And if it's more than three minutes, I pay extra, don't I?

10. Employée: **C'est ça, monsieur. Veuillez°** **entrer dans la cabine huit, et** *je vous ferai signe dès que j'aurai* **la communication.** *(Elle appelle la téléphoniste.)*
    That's right sir. Please go into booth number eight, and I'll let you know (lit.: I'll signal you) as soon as I have your party. *(She calls the operator.)*

11. Téléphoniste: **J'écoute.°**
    Number, please.

12. Employée: **Mademoiselle, passez-moi le 48.62.57 à Bordeaux, s'il vous plaît.**
    Operator, connect me with 48.62.57 at Bordeaux, please.

13. Téléphoniste: **Ne quittez pas... Vous avez la communication.**
    Just a moment... Here's your party.

14. Employée: **Merci, mademoiselle.** *(Elle fait signe à Charles.)*
    Thank you, operator. *(She motions to Charles.)*

15. Charles: *(dans la cabine 8)* **Allô. Je voudrais parler à M. Duclos, s'il vous plaît.**
    (in booth number 8) Hello. I'd like to speak to Mr. Duclos, please.

16. Une bonne: **C'est de la part de qui, s'il vous plaît?**
    Who's calling, please?

17. Charles: **Ici Charles Lewis, à Paris.**
    This is Charles Lewis, in Paris.

18. Une bonne: **Je vais voir s'il est là ... Non, monsieur, il vient de sortir. Voudriez-vous laisser un mot?°**
    I'll see if he's here ... No, sir, he's just left. Do you wish to leave a message?

19. Charles: **Quel dommage! Dites-lui que *je le rappellerai* ce soir. Je dois lui parler.**
    What a pity! Tell him that I'll call him back this evening. I must speak to him.

20. Une bonne: **Très bien, monsieur. *Je ferai* votre commission.**
    Very well, sir. I'll deliver your message.

21. Charles: **Merci beaucoup, mademoiselle. Au revoir.**
    Thank you very much. Good-bye.

B. *Une communication locale*   A local call

22. Charles: *(au guichet°)* **Je regrette de vous déranger encore, mademoiselle, mais ...**
    (at the desk) I'm sorry to bother you again, Miss, but ...

23. Employée: **Je vous en prie, monsieur.**
That's quite all right, sir.

24. Charles: **Je n'ai pas encore l'habitude de vos téléphones automatiques, vous savez.**
I'm not yet used to your dial telephones, you know.

25. Employée: **Ce n'est pas très compliqué, monsieur. Vous connaissez le numéro?**
It's not very complicated, sir. Do you know the number?

26. Charles: **Oui, cette fois-ci je veux donner un coup de fil dans Paris même, ANJou 75-69.°**
Yes, this time I want to make a call within Paris itself, ANJou 75-69.

27. Employée: *Il vous faudra* **un jeton,° monsieur. Décrochez° le récepteur, mettez le jeton dans la fente, attendez le bourdonnement,° et composez votre numéro.**
You'll need a token, sir. Pick up the receiver, insert the token in the slot, wait for the dial tone, and dial your number.

28. Charles: **J'y suis, jusqu'ici.** *Mais quels sont ces boutons?*
I get it (I understand), so far. But what are these buttons?

29. Employée: **Eh bien, vous entendez la sonnerie, et** *quand votre correspondant répondra,* **vous enfoncerez le bouton A.°**
Well, you hear the ringing, and when your party answers, you push button A.

30. Charles: **Mais si on ne répond pas? Ou si la ligne est occupée? Ou si j'ai un faux numéro?**
But if no one answers? Or if the line is busy? Or if I get a wrong number?

31. Employée: **Alors là, vous raccrochez, voilà
    tout. Vous attendez un peu et vous commen-
    cez de nouveau.**
    Well then, you hang up, that's all. You wait a
    little and then you begin again.

32. Charles: **Vous êtes bien aimable, mademoi-
    selle. Grâce à vous je suis sûr que *je saurai*
    me dèbrouiller.**
    You're very kind, Miss. Thanks to you I'm
    sure that I'll know how to manage.

                        NOTES

Title. *téléphone:* One can make telephone calls from
       a café, a post office, and many other public
       places. Post offices include telephone service,
       as part of the government agency known as the
       P et T—*Postes et Télécommunications.*

  1. *interurbain:* between two cities.

  5. *moi-même:* myself. Study the following:

     toi-même   yourself
     lui-même   himself
     elle-même   herself
     nous-mêmes   ourselves
     vous-mêmes   yourself or yourselves
     eux-mêmes   themselves (masc.)
     elles-mêmes   themselves (fem.)
     soi-même   oneself

  6. *Bottin:* the name of the company which issues
     the telephone directory. In Paris the different
     directories are compiled according to family
     name, to streets, and to occupations.

  7. *48.62.57:* Phone numbers containing four or
     more numbers are said in groups of two.

8. Long-distance telephone calls are usually paid for in advance.

10. *veuillez:* a more formal way to say *s'il vous plaît.* It is always followed by the infinitive.

11. *j'écoute:* a formula used in answering the telephone, or by the operator asking for a number.

18. *un mot:* lit., a word. In this context, it means a message.

22. *guichet:* a desk, window, counter, etc., as in a bank, post office, theater. Behind the *guichet* sits *un employé.*

26. *ANJou 75-69:* The French recently dropped their traditional telephone exchanges and changed to all-digit numbers. Thus, the Paris number ANJou 75-69 has become 553-75-69. However, throughout this course we have continued to use the exchanges.

27. *jeton:* a metal token used in place of money in a telephone slot. These tokens must be purchased ahead of time.
    décrochez: the imperative form, explained in Lesson 44.
    bourdonnement: The dial tone may also be referred to as *le signal.*

29. *le bouton A:* The caller has to press a button *after* he hears a voice at the other end, in order for his voice to be heard.

GRAMMATICAL ITEMS FOR SPECIAL STUDY

I. *quel*—what
   A. *quel* (as an *interrogative*)

Study:

1. Quel livre voulez-vous?	*What book do you want?*
2. Quelle robe voulez-vous?	*What dress do you want?*
3. Quels livres désirez-vous?	*What books do you want?*
4. Quelles robes désirez-vous?	*What dresses do you want?*

B. *quel* (in *exclamations*). Notice the English equivalents, particularly. The forms are like those of the interrogative.

1. Quel garçon!	*What a boy!*
2. Quelle belle robe!	*What a beautiful dress!*
3. Quels beaux yeux!	*What beautiful eyes!*
4. Quelles belles maisons!	*What beautiful homes!*

II. *ne . . . rien*—nothing

Study:

A. Subject	ne	Ind. Obj.	Main Verb	rien
1. Je	ne		vois	rien.
2. Il	ne	me	disait	rien.

1. *I see nothing. (I don't see anything.)*

2. *He said nothing to me. (He wasn't saying anything to me.)*

B. Subject	ne	Indirect Object	Auxiliary	rien	Past Participle
1. Je	n'		ai	rien	vu.
2. Nous	n'		avons	rien	trouvé.
3. Il	ne	s'	est	rien	acheté.
4. Je	ne	lui	ai	rien	donné.

1. *I saw nothing. (I didn't see anything.)*

2. *We found nothing. (We didn't find anything.)*

3. *He bought nothing for himself. (He didn't buy anything for himself.)*

4. *I gave him nothing. (I didn't give him anything.)*

	Rien	ne	Verb
C. 1.	Rien	n'	est si beau.
2.	Rien	ne	s'est passé.

1. *Nothing is so beautiful.*

2. *Nothing happened.*

D. *rien*—used alone:

Study:

1. Qu'est-ce qui se passe? Rien.	1. *What is happening? Nothing.*
2. Que vois-tu? Rien.	2. *What do you see? Nothing.*

Note: When *rien* is used as a one-word utterance, *ne* is ommitted.

III. *Object pronouns before complementary infinitives.* Note that they immediately precede the infinitive.

Study:

Subject	Main verb	Object pronouns	Infinitive
1. Je	peux	le lui	demander.
2. Je	dois	le	chercher.
3. Je	sais	le	faire.
4. Je	vais	l'	acheter.

1. *I can ask him for it.* (*demander* means "to ask [for].")

2. *I must look for it.* (*chercher* means "to look for.")

3. *I know how to do it.* (*savoir* before an infinitive means "to know how.")

4. *I'm going to buy it.*

IV. *The future tense*
   A. The future tense is formed by adding the endings *-ai, -as, -a, -ons, -ez, -ont* either (1) to the infinitive, or (2) to an irregular stem. The irregular stem is a modification of the infinitive and always ends in *r*.
   B. Study the formation of the future tense of these regular verbs.

1st conjugation	2nd conjugation	3rd conjugation
arriver, to arrive	*choisir,* to choose	*attendre,* to wait (for)
infin. + endings	infin. + endings	Drop final -e of infinitive + endings.
j' arriver*ai*	choisir*ai*	attendr*ai*
(I'll arrive, etc.)	(I'll choose, etc.)	(I'll wait, etc.)
tu arriver*as*	choisir*as*	attendr*as*
il arriver*a*	choisir*a*	attendr*a*
elle arriver*a*	choisir*a*	attendr*a*
nous arriver*ons*	choisir*ons*	attendr*ons*
vous arriver*ez*	choisir*ez*	attendr*ez*
ils arriver*ont*	choisir*ont*	attendr*ont*
elles arriver*ont*	choisir*ont*	attendr*ont*

C. Future tense of the three most common irregular verbs.

avoir, to have	**être,** to be	**aller,** to go
stem + endings	stem + endings	stem + endings
j'aurai	*serai*	*irai*
(I'll have, etc.)	(I'll be, etc.)	(I'll go, etc.)
tu *auras*	*seras*	*iras*
il *aura*	*sera*	*ira*
elle *aura*	*sera*	*ira*
nous *aurons*	*serons*	*irons*
vous *aurez*	*serez*	*irez*
ils *auront*	*seront*	*iront*
elles *auront*	*seront*	*iront*

D. For additional examples of the formation of the future tense of regular verbs, see the *Regular Verb Charts.*

E. For the formation of the future tense of verbs with irregular future stems, see the *Irregular Verb Charts.*

F. The future tense in French is generally used in the same way as the future tense in English.

Example: Nous parlerons français en France. *We'll speak French in France,* French also uses the future tense as discussed in Section V below.

V. *Future after* quand, lorsque, dès que, ausitôt que *when futurity is implied*

Study:

Word	Subject	Object Pronoun	Future Verb	Future or Imperative Verb Phrase
1. Quand	il		viendra	je lui parlerai.
2. Lorsque	tu		rentreras	téléphone-moi.
3. Dès qu'	il	me	verra	il dira, "Bonjour."
4. Aussitôt que	vous		arriverez	venez me voir.

1. *When he comes (will come), I shall speak to him.*

2. *When you return (will return), phone me.*

3. *As soon as he sees me (will see me), he will say, "Good day."*

4. *As soon as you arrive (will arrive), come to see me.*

VI. **The indirect objects are used with** *il faut* (third person singular of *falloir*). Study the following sentences. See also Lesson 53.

Il	Ind. Obj.	faut	Direct Obj.	Meanings
1. Il	me	faut	un franc.	*I need a franc.*
2. Il	te	faut	un jeton.	*You [fam.] need a token.*
3. Il	lui	faut	le numéro.	*He [She] needs the number.*
4. Il	nous	faut	le Bottin.	*We need the directory.*
5. Il	vous	faut	une cabine.	*You need a booth.*
6. Il	leur	faut	de l'espoir.	*They need (some) hope.*

Note: See also Lesson 42, note 9.

DRILLS AND EXERCISES

I. Substitute each of the words in parentheses for the italicized word in the model sentence. Write the complete sentence and say aloud.

A. Je peux le *demander*. (choisir, comprendre, voir. lire, faire, acheter [don't forget *l'* before the vowel])

B. Je *peux* le demander. (dois, vais, veux, sais)

C. Je ne *sais* rien. (vois, comprends, lis, dis, mange, veux)

D. Il n'a rien *vu*. (compris, acheté, choisi, lu, fini, appris)

II. Transform the following sentences into exclamations by using the proper form of *quel,* Say and translate them.

Example: C'est une belle maison./Quelle belle maison!

1. C'est un livre intéressant.

2. C'est un bon garçon.

3. C'est une robe exquise.

4. Ce sont de jolies images.

5. Ce sont de beaux arbres.

III. Replace *dès que, lorsque,* and *aussitôt que* by *quand* in each of the following sentences. Say, write, and translate each sentence.

1. *Dès que* je le verrai, je le saluerai.

2. *Aussitôt qu'*il viendra, dites-lui de manger.

3. *Lorsqu'*il sortira, fermez la porte.

4. *Dès que* vous quitterez la salle, on commencera la discussion.

5. *Aussitôt qu'*il achètera la voiture, il fera un voyage.

IV. Translate the following sentences into French; then say them aloud.

1. I'd like to look for a number.

2. Would you like to speak to Charles?

3. *(téléphoniste,* fem.) What a telephone operator!

4. I see nothing.

5. He finds nothing.

6. You want nothing?

7. She saw nothing.

8. We found nothing.

9. They didn't want anything.

10. What did you find? Nothing.

11. What do you want? Nothing.

12. What do you say? Nothing.

13. Please speak more loudly.

V. Match the English phrases in the first column with their correct French equivalents in the second column. Say and write the French sentences.

1. *Buy a token.*	Décrochez le récepteur.
2. *Look up the number in the directory.*	Raccrochez si vous avez un faux numéro.
3. *Pick up the receiver.*	Achetez un jeton.
4. *Put the token in the slot.*	Composez votre numéro.
5. *Wait for the dial tone.*	Attendez le signal.
6. *Ask Information for the number.*	Mettez le jeton dans la fente.
7. *Dial your number.*	Commencez de nouveau.
8. *Push button A.*	Demandez le numéro au service des renseignements.
9. *Speak with your party.*	Cherchez le numéro dans le Bottin.

10. *Hang up if you   Parlez avec votre
    have a wrong   correspondant.
    number.*
11. *Begin again.*   Enfoncez le bouton A.

VI. Translate the dialogue into French.

Mme: Hello! Is this PASsy 58-17?

M.: Yes, madam.

Mme: I'd like to speak to Monsieur Dupont, please.

M.: Who's calling?

Mme: This is Madame Lenclos.

M.: Hold the wire, please . . . I'm sorry, Ma'am, but his line is busy. Do you wish to wait? It may be long.

Mme: No, thank you. I prefer to leave a message.

M.: As you wish, madam.

Mme: Please tell him that I'll call back tomorrow.

M.: I'll deliver your message.

Mme: Thank you very much. Good-bye, miss.

M.: Good-bye, madam.

Answers at back of book.

QUIZ

From among the three choices given, select the one which correctly renders the English word or phrase given at the beginning of each sentence, write the complete sentence, and translate.

1. (*which*) C'est pour _____ ville?
   (a) quelle
   (b) cette
   (c) quoi

2. (*That's nothing*) _____, monsieur.
   - (a) Cela ne dit pas
   - (b) Cela n'est pas
   - (c) Cela ne fait rien

3. (*on the right*) Le Bottin est à _____.
   - (a) gauche
   - (b) droite
   - (c) bas

4. (*I have*) Dès que _____ la communication, je vous ferai signe.
   - (a) j'ai
   - (b) j'avais
   - (c) j'aurai

5. (*Please*) _____ entrer.
   - (a) Voulez
   - (b) Veuillez
   - (c) Voudriez

6. (*once again*) Je vous dérange _____.
   - (a) encore une fois
   - (b) toujours
   - (c) autrefois

7. (*itself*) C'est dans Paris _____.
   - (a) soi-même
   - (b) même
   - (c) lui-même

8. (*You will need*) _____ un jeton.
   - (a) Vous faudrez
   - (b) Vous faudra
   - (c) Il vous faudra

9. (*I understand*) _____, jusqu'ici.
   - (a) J'y sais
   - (b) J'y suis
   - (c) J'y comprends

10. (*I'll know how*) _____ me débrouiller.
   (a) Je sais
   (b) Je saurai
   (c) Je savais

Answers at back of book.

LESSON 44

LES TRANSPORTS EN VILLE
CITY TRANSPORTATION

A. *Le Métro*°   The subway

1. Charles: **Ecoute, chérie, j'ai une merveilleuse idée! Pour rentrer,° puisque nous avons un si long trajet à faire, *divisions-le* en trois. Nous prendrons le métro, puis l'autobus, et finalement un taxi. Tu veux?°**
   Listen, dear, I have a marvelous idea! To get back home, since we have such a long way to go, let's divide it into three parts. We'll take the subway, then a bus, and finally a taxi. How about it? (Would you like to?)

2. Jeanne: **Tu es fou? *Le taxi nous coûterait* les yeux de la tête!°**
   Are you crazy? The taxi would cost us a fortune!

3. Charles: **Mais ce serait plus amusant, et puis *nous connaîtrions* ainsi tous les moyens de transport.**
   But it would be so much more fun, and then that way we'd get to know all the means of transportation.

4. Jeanne: **Eh bien, je m'en remets à toi. *Allons prendre nos billets.*°**

Well, I'll leave it up to you. Let's go get our
tickets.

5. Employé: **Premières ou secondes,° monsieur?**
   First or second class, sir?

6. Jeanne: **Est-ce plus cher en première?**
   Is it more expensive in first class?

7. Employé: **Oui, madame.** *Mais vous auriez
   avantage* **à prendre un carnet de dix billets.**
   Yes, madam. But it would be to your advan-
   tage to buy a book of ten tickets.

8. Charles: **Alors, un carnet de secondes. Comment** *fait-on* **pour aller à l' "Etoile," s'il
   vous plaît?**
   Well then, a book of second-class tickets. How
   do we get to the "Etoile" station, please?

9. Employé: **Eh bien,** *prenez* **la direction° de
   Neuilly.** *Descendez* **sur le quai par l'escalier
   qui se trouve au bout du couloir.** *Passez* **par
   le portillon automatique° et présentez vos
   billets à l'employé. D'ici à l'Etoile il n'y a
   que sept arrêts, sans correspondance.°**
   Well, take the train that goes to Neuilly. Go
   down to the platform by the staircase at the end
   of the corridor. Go through the automatic gate,
   and give your tickets to the employee. From
   here to the Etoile there are only seven stops,
   without changing trains.

10. Charles: **Merci, monsieur.** *Viens,* **chérie.**
    Thank you, sir. Come, dear.

11. Jeanne: *(dans la voiture)* **Je vois sur le plan
    qu'**on aurait pu **prendre la correspondance
    à "Champs-Elysées-Clemenceau" pour la
    ligne 9, qui va directement chez nous.**

(in the subway car) I see on the map that we could have changed at ''Champs-Elysées-Clemenceau'' for line 9, which goes directly to our place.

12. Charles: **C'est vrai, mais notre projet nous permettra de mieux connaître le métro.**
That's true, but our plan will permit us to become better acquainted with the subway.

B. *L'autobus*   The bus

13. Jeanne: *(à l'arrêt d'autobus)* **Que de monde!**
(at the bus stop) What a crowd!

14. Charles: **Oui, malheureusement c'est l'heure d'affluence;** *nous devrons faire la queue.* **Voyons, je crois que c'est la ligne 22° qu'***il nous faut.*
Yes, unfortunately it's rush hour; we'll have to stand in line. Let's see, I think we need line 22.

15. Jeanne: **Quelle est cette petite machine?**
What's that little machine?

16. Une dame: **Elle distribue des tickets numérotés, madame, qui indiquent votre tour dans la queue.**
It distributes numbered tickets, madam, which indicate your place in the line.

17. Jeanne: **Merci, madame. Tiens, voici l'autobus qui arrive.**
Thank you, madam. Look, here comes the bus.

18. Le receveur:° **Les numéros, s'il vous plaît!**
Ticket collector: Numbers, please!

19. Jeanne: **Pourvu que nous puissions monter!
    Il est bien bondé.°**
    I only hope we can get on. It's quite crowded.

20. Charles: **Mais il y a encore de la place,
    heureusement.** *(Au receveur)* **Quel est le
    tarif, s'il vous plaît?**
    But there's still room, fortunately. *(To the
    ticket collector)* What's the fare, please?

21. Receveur: **Quelle est votre destination, mon-
    sieur? Vous payez selon la longueur du par-
    cours.**
    What is your destination, sir? You pay accord-
    ing to the length of the trip.

22. Charles: **Nous allons à la Place du Troca-
    déro.**
    We're going to the Place du Trocadéro.

23. Receveur: **Alors c'est deux sections, c'est-à-
    dire deux tickets. Mais** *prenez* **plutôt un
    carnet° de vingt tickets. Ça revient moins
    cher.**
    Then that's two sections, or two tickets. But
    take a book of twenty tickets instead. It's
    cheaper.

24. Jeanne: **Oui,** *ça vaudrait mieux.* **Mais nous
    ne trouverons jamais de places assises à
    l'intérieur.**
    Yes, that would be better. But we'll never find
    seats inside.

25. Charles: **Tant mieux, alors. Nous resterons
    ici sur la plateforme.° C'est bien plus agré-
    able.**
    Well, so much the better. We'll stay here on
    the platform. It's much more pleasant.

26. Jeanne: *Regarde* donc la Tour Eiffel là-bas,
de l'autre côté de la Seine. Elle est *plus
grande que* je ne croyais.°
Look at the Eiffel Tower over there, on the
other side of the Seine. It's bigger than I
thought.

27. Charles: **Et plus impressionnante, aussi.
Mais voilà notre arrêt.** *Descendons,* et *cher-
chons* un taxi.
And more impressive, too. But here's our stop.
Let's get off and look for a taxi.

C. *Le taxi* The taxi

28. Charles: **Taxi! Taxi!**
Taxi! Taxi!

29. Jeanne: *Celui-là doit être occupé.* Tu vois, le
petit drapeau est baissé. *Allons* là-bas à la
tête de station.
That one must be taken. You see, the little flag
is down. Let's go over there to the taxi stand.

30. Charles: *(dans le taxi)* **Combien est-ce pour
aller à la rue Molitor?**
(in the taxi) How much is it to go to the rue
Molitor?

31. Chauffeur: **Vous payerez le prix inscrit au
compteur, monsieur. C'est quelle adresse,
s'il vous plaît?**
You pay the price shown on the meter, sir.
What's the address, please?

32. Charles: **Le numéro 33. Et** *ne conduisez pas
trop vite, je vous prie!*
Number 33. And don't drive too fast, please!

33. Jeanne: *Je voudrais voyager* toujours en taxi!
C'est de loin le moyen de transport le plus
confortable.
I'd like to travel by taxi all the time! It's by far
the most comfortable means of transportation.

34. Charles: **Le plus cher aussi, malheureuse-
ment. Ah! voilà enfin notre hôtel.**
The most expensive too, unfortunately. Ah!
There's our hotel at last.

35. Jeanne: **Tu avais raison,° Charles. Avec le
taxi et les deux carnets nous avons dépensé
beaucoup d'argent, mais *on a revu* toutes
sortes de choses intéressantes.**
You were right, Charles. With the taxi and the
two books of tickets, we've spent a good deal
of money, but we saw all sorts of interesting
things again.

NOTES

Title. *Métro:* short for "Métropolitain," the under-
ground or subway system of Paris.

1. *pour rentrer: pour* + infinitive means "in
order to."
tu veux?: The use of the *tu* (familiar) form is
generally limited to members of one's immedi-
ate family, to one's most intimate friends, and
to children below the age of approximately
fourteen years. it is also used in speaking to
animals.
Children and adolescents generally use *tu*
with their peers. The use of *tu* among adults
outside the family is generally agreed upon by
both parties concerned as an indication of mu-
tual affection and regard. The use of *tu* among
adults under other circumstances is improper.
When uncertain, use the *vous* (polite) form.

2. Jane's preoccupation with the taxi fare was unwarranted. Taxis in Paris are not more expensive than in other large cities.

4. Tickets are *billets* on the subway and *tickets* on the bus.

5. *premières ou secondes:* The Paris métro has two classes. Each train has one first-class car—red—in the middle, which is more comfortable, more roomy, and also more expensive.

9. *direction:* Subway lines are identified both by a number and by the names of the last stops at either end.
   portillon automatique: an iron gate which closes automatically when the train enters the station.
   correspondance: literally, a transfer to another subway line. Outside of each subway station and on each platform there is a large map showing the entire subway system, and the possible transfers from one line to another. In the larger stations, a passenger can press a button indicating his station destination, and the most convenient route will immediately light up on the map.

14. Bus lines are identified in the same two ways as subway lines.

18. *Le receveur:* There is a ticket collector on each bus in addition to the driver.

19. Often when buses are full, a sign reading COMPLET is displayed, and no more passengers are allowed to enter.

23. *carnet:* a book of tickets, bought in advance and used as needed.

25. *la plate-forme:* French buses have an outdoor platform where passengers are permitted to stand.

26. *plus grande que je ne croyais:* After the comparative of an adjective, *ne* generally precedes the verbs *croire* (to believe) and *penser* (to think). Example: *Elle est moins belle qu'il ne pensait.* She is less beautiful than he thought.

35. *Tu avais raison: avoir raison*—to be right.

GRAMMATICAL ITEMS FOR SPECIAL STUDY

I. *Comparison of adjectives*
Study:

	aussi/ plus/ moins	Adjective	que	Complement
1. Cette robe est	plus	belle	que	l'autre
2. Ce livre-ci est	plus	intéressant	que	celui-là
3. Mon complet est	moins	beau	que	le vôtre
4. Ces hommes-ci sont	moins	riches	que	ceux-là
5. Cet hôtel est	aussi	bon	que	l'autre
6. Ses repas sont	aussi	délicieux	que	ceux de sa soeur

1. *This dress is more beautiful than the other one.*

2. *This book is more interesting than that one.*

3. *My suit is less handsome than (not as handsome as) yours.*

4. *These men are less rich than (not as rich as) those.*

5. *This hotel is as good as the other one.*

6. *Her meals are as delicious as her sister's.*

II. *Imperative*
Study:

Infinitive	Fam. Sing.	Fam. Plu. and Polite Form	Suggestion (Let's)
1. parler	Parle!	Parlez!	Parlons!
2. finir	Finis!	Finissez	Finissons!
3. apprendre	Apprends!	Apprenez!	Apprenons!
1. *(to) speak*	*Speak!*	*Speak!*	*Let's speak!*
2. *(to) finish*	*Finish!*	*Finish!*	*Let's finish!*
3. *(to) learn*	*Learn!*	*Learn!*	*Let's learn!*

Notes:

1. To form the imperative, take the *tu, vous,* and *nous* forms of the present indicative, and omit the subject pronoun.

2. In general, drop the final "s" of the familiar singular form for verbs conjugated like *parler* and *aller.*

Examples:

Parle français.	*Speak French.*
Va à l'école.	*Go to school.*
Ouvre la porte.	*Open the door.*

Note, however, that for easier pronunciation, the "s" *is* included before the pronouns *en* and *y*.

Examples:

Parles-en.	*Speak of it.*
Vas-y.	*Go there.*

3. The imperative forms of *avoir*, *être*, and *savoir* are irregular, and can be found in the *Irregular Verb Charts*.

III. *on*

Study the function of *on* in the following sentences:

On perd toujours la tête dans ces cas-là.
One always loses one's head in these cases.

On parle français ici.
French is spoken here. or *We speak French here.*

On dit que c'est un voleur.
People say he's a thief. or *They say he's a thief.*

Note: *On* is a kind of "catch-all" subject pronoun. Its literal meaning is "one," as in the first example above, but it is frequently used as well for *you, they, we,* or for *people* in the vague, generalized sense. *On* can also express the passive voice, as in:

On vend les billets ici.   Tickets are sold here.

IV. *devoir*

A. Study the forms of *devoir* in the *Irregular Verb Charts*.

B. Notice some of the functions and equivalents of
devoir in the following sentences:

Subject	Auxiliary Verb	devoir	Infinitive
1. Je		dois	partir.
2. Je		devais	partir.
3. Je		devrai	partir.
4. Je		devrais	partir.
5. J'	ai	dû	partir.
6. J'	aurais	dû	partir.

1. *I must leave.*

2. *I was supposed to leave.*

3. *I'll have to leave.*

4. *I should leave.*

5. *I had to leave*

6. *I should have left.*

C. With nouns, *devoir* means "to owe." Examples:

Il me **doit** six francs.   *He owes me six francs.*
Je lui **dois** la vie.   *I owe my life to him.*

V. *The subjunctive:* This mood expresses doubt,
emotion, volition, possibility, necessity. It is generally used in subordinate clauses after verbs
which define the mood, after *il faut que* (see
Lesson 60), and after certain conjunctions.

A. Study the regular forms of the subjunctive in the
Regular Verb Charts. You will also find the
subjunctives of the most common irregular
verbs in the *Irregular Verb Charts.*

Notice the following examples:

	Main clause	Subordinate clause
Volition	1. Il veut	que **j'aille.**
Doubt	2. Nous doutons	qu'**elles viennent** ici.
Emotion	3. Je regrette	qu'**il soit** mort.

1. *He wants me to go (that I go).*

2. *We doubt that they are coming here.*

3. *I am sorry (that) he is dead.*

B. Study the following examples of the subjunctive with certain conjunctions:

Present/Future/Imperative	Conjunction	Present Subjunctive
1. Je viendrai	pourvu que	vous m'invitiez.
2. Il n'est pas heureux	quoiqu'	il soit riche.
3. Je sortirai	à moins qu'	il ne pleuve.
4. Je le répète	afin que	vous puissiez l'apprendre.
5. Venez	pour que	je puisse vous parler.

1. *I'll come <u>provided</u> you invite me.*

2. *He is not happy <u>although</u> he is rich.*

3. *I shall go out <u>unless</u> it rains.*

4. *I repeat it <u>in order that</u> you may learn it.*

5. *Come <u>so that</u> I can speak to you.*

Note: In example 3, notice that, with the conjunction *à moins que*, *ne* is placed before the subjunctive. This is also done with a few other expressions, such as *de peur que* (for fear that).

DRILLS AND EXERCISES

I. Substitute each of the words or expressions in parentheses for the italicized word or expression in the model sentence. Write the complete sentence and say aloud.

A. Charles est plus *beau* que Jacques. (riche, intelligent, charmant, aimable, pauvre)

B. On parle *français* ici. (anglais, italien, chinois, espagnol, turque)

C. Je dois *partir*. (sortir, étudier, manger, lire, travailler)

D. *Je dois* partir (je devrais, j'ai dû, je devrai, j'aurais dû). [Translate these sentences.]

E. Il me doit *dix francs*. (vingt francs, cent cinquante francs, deux livres, du respect)

II. Transform these familiar singular forms of the imperative to (1) the *vous* form, and (2) to the *nous* (Let's . . .) form.

Example: Parle! / Parlez! / Parlons!
          Finis!
          Sois!
          Apprends!
          Mange!
          Choisis!
          Mets!

III. Translate the following sentences into French; then say them aloud.

1. What's the address?

2. We have to take a bus

3. She must take the subway.

4. That must be the bus stop.

5. I had to get (*prendre*) a ticket.

6. They had to get (*prendre*) a book of second-class tickets.

7. She'll have to stand in line.

8. They'll have to pay.

9. He should pay, but he doesn't want to pay.

10. He should have left.

11. They (fem.) should have come.

12. Let's go look at the Eiffel Tower.

13. Let's go spend (*passer*) the afternoon with Marie.

14. How does one get to (go about arriving at) the Opera?

15. How does one find (go about finding) a taxi?

16. There is only one automatic gate.

17. There are only two changes (*correspondances*) to make.

18. He said that she would take a taxi.

19. He said that they would have the money.

20. They are richer than the others.

21. The tickets are more expensive in first class.

22. English is spoken here.

23. The Eiffel Tower can be seen from here (*d'ici*).

24. People stand in line here.

25. She wants you to go.

26. I am glad that she is happy.

27. We doubt that he can do that.

28. I will go unless it rains.

Answers at back of book.

QUIZ

From among the three choices given, select the one
which correctly renders the English word or phrase
given. Write the complete sentence, and translate.

1. (*To get back*) _____, prenons un taxi.
   (a) A rentrer
   (b) A la rentrée
   (c) Pour rentrer

2. (*Let's go*) _____ prendre nos billets.
   (a) Va
   (b) Allons
   (c) Allez

3. (*at the end*) L'escalier se trouve _____ du
   couloir.
   (a) à la fin
   (b) enfin
   (c) au bout

4. (*stand in line*) Nous devrons _____.
   (a) faire la queue
   (b) faire la ligne
   (c) rester en ligne

5. (*room*) Il y a encore de la _____.
   (a) chambre
   (b) place
   (c) pièce

6. (*according to*) Vous payez _____ la
   longueur du parcours.
   (a) d'accord
   (b) pour
   (c) selon

7. (*better*) Oui, ça vaudrait _____
   (a) bon
   (b) bien
   (c) mieux

8. (*That one*) _____ doit être occupé.
   (a) Cela
   (b) Ceci
   (c) Celui-là

9. (*what*) C'est _____ adresse, s'il vous
   plaît?
   (a) quelle
   (b) quel
   (c) quoi

10. (*You were right*) _____.
    (a) Tu avais droit.
    (b) Tu avais raison.
    (c) Tu étais droite.

Answers at back of book.

LESSON 45

FAISONS UNE PROMENADE À PIED
LET'S TAKE A WALK

A. *Avant la promenade* Before the walk

1. Jeanne: **Si on faisait° une promenade à pied,
   tous les deux? Si on allait voir un quartier
   intéressant, le Quartier Latin,° par exemple?**
   How about taking a walk, both of us? How
   about going to visit an interesting neighborhood
   —the Latin Quarter, for instance?

2. Charles: *Toi et moi?* Seuls? J'ai fait des tours
   à Paris il y a longtemps, mais je ne saurais
   pas te piloter à présent.
   You and I? Alone? I took strolls around Paris a
   long time ago, but I wouldn't know how to show
   you the way now.

3. Jeanne: **C'est facile! Il faudra tout simplement demander le chemin au concierge.°**
   It's easy! You only have to ask the concierge
   the way.

B. *Á la réception*   At the reception desk

4. Charles: **Monsieur, comment fait-on pour al-
   ler à pied au Quartier Latin?**
   Sir, how does one go about walking to the Latin
   Quarter?

5. Concierge: **Dé quel côté voulez-vous aller?**
   Toward what area do you want to go?

6. Charles: **Du côté de la Sorbonne°...**
   Toward the Sorbonne...

7. Concierge: **Eh bien, le Quartier Latin est à
   deux pas° d'ici, puisque nous sommes sur la
   Rive Gauche.° Regardez ce plan de Paris.
   Nous sommes ici.**
   Well, the Latin Quarter is close by here, since
   we are on the Left Bank. Look at this map of
   Paris. We are here.

8. Charles: **Ah! Je vois bien. Nous ne sommes
   pas très loin du Quartier Latin.**
   Ah! I see. We're not very far from the Latin
   Quarter.

9. Concierge: **Vous devez *vous diriger* vers le
   boulevard Saint-Michel° et la rue des
   Ecoles...**

You must head toward the boulevard Saint-Michel and the rue des Ecoles . . .

10. Charles: **Je comprends. On doit** *se diriger* **dans cette direction-ci . . .**
    I understand. One must head in *this* direction . . .

11. Concierge: **C'est ça! Il faut continuer tout droit sur la rue de Seine. Une fois arrivé au boulevard Saint-Germain, vous devez tourner à gauche devant l'église qui fait le coin du boulevard et de la rue Napoléon . . .**
    Right! One must continue straight ahead on the rue de Seine. Once you arrive at the boulevard Saint-Germain, you must turn left in front of the church that is located at the corner of the boulevard and the rue Napoléon.

12. Charles: **Puis, on traverse le boulevard, on marche encore deux rues, et on tourne à droite!**
    Then, you cross the boulevard, you walk two more blocks, and you turn to the right!

13. Concierge: **C'est ça. Et si** *vous vous égarez,* **vous n'avez qu'à demander le chemin à un passant. A propos, ne traversez pas avant de voir l'enseigne au néon "Passez piétons." Et quand on traverse la rue, il faut marcher entre les clous° dans le passage clouté!**
    That's it. And if you get lost, you have only to ask a passerby the way. Incidentally, don't cross before you see the neon traffic sign "Pedestrians Walk." And when you do cross, you have to walk between the nail heads, in the pedestrian crossing.

14. Charles: *Ne vous inquiétez pas!*
    Don't worry!

15. Charles: **Jeanne, chérie, j'ai tout arrangé.
    Nous devrons tout simplement faire dix
    minutes de marche.**
    Jane, dear, I've arranged everything. We'll
    just have to walk for ten minutes.

16. Jeanne: **C'est parfait. Je n'ai pas envie de
    marcher longtemps. Allons!**
    That's fine! I don't feel like walking a long
    time. Let's go!

C. *Quinze minutes plus tard*   Fifteen minutes later

17. Jeanne: **Charles, voilà la Seine! Mais je vois
    Notre-Dame.° *Nous nous sommes égarés!***
    Charles, there's the Seine. But I see Notre
    Dame. We've lost our way!

18. Charles: **Un instant. Je vais demander le
    chemin à ce monsieur.°**
    Just a minute. I'm going to ask this man the
    way.
    **Monsieur, s'il vous plaît ... pour aller au
    Quartier Latin ... à la Sorbonne ... quelle
    rue faut-il prendre? Je n'ai aucune idée ...**
    Please, sir, to go to the Latin Quarter ... to the
    Sorbonne ... which street must you take? I
    have no idea ...

19. Monsieur: **Mais vous marchez° dans le
    mauvais sens, monsieur.**
    But you're walking in the wrong direction, sir.

20. Charles: **Comment? Je ne marche° pas dans
    le bon sens?**
    What? I'm not walking in the right direction?

21. Monsieur: **Je le regrette, monsieur, mais
    vous devez rebrousser chemin et remonter
    cette rue.**

I'm sorry sir, but you must retrace your steps and go back up this street.

22. Charles: **Tu entends, Jeanne? Nous devons refaire le chemin.**
Did you hear, Jane? We have to start all over again.

23. Jeanne: **Je te parie qu'en quittant l'hôtel nous aurions dû tourner à gauche quand nous avons tourné à droite!**
I'll bet you that on leaving the hotel we should have turned left when we turned right!

D. *De retour à l'hôtel*   Back at the hotel

24. Concierge: **Bonsoir, monsieur, 'dame. Avez-vous fait une bonne promenade cet après-midi?**
Good evening, sir, madam. Did you have a nice walk this afternoon?

25. Charles: **Ah oui. Une fois que nous avons trouvé le bon chemin.**
Oh, yes, Once we found the right way.

26. Concierge: **Mais comment! Mes indications n'étaient pas justes?**
What? My directions weren't correct?

27. Jeanne: **Si, mais c'est *nous* qui *nous sommes trompés*. Nous avons tourné à droite au lieu de tourner à gauche.**
Yes, but it was we who made a mistake. We turned right instead of turning left.

28. Concierge: **Quel dommage! Mais à quelque chose malheur est bon. Vous avez dû voir des endroits intéressants.**
What a pity! But an ill wind always blows

some good. You must have seen some interesting places.

29. Charles: **Ah, vous avez raison. Nous avons revu Notre-Dame, les bouquinistes de la Seine, et la Sainte-Chapelle.°**
Oh, you are right. We again saw Notre Dame, the second-hand book vendors along the Seine, and the Sainte Chapelle.

30. Jeanne: **N'oublie pas que nous avons vu aussi le musée de Cluny° et le Panthéon.°**
Don't forget that we also saw the Cluny Museum and the Panthéon.

NOTES

1. *Si on faisait:* The imperfect is used after *si* to mean "How about?" Example: *Si on parlait au concierge?* (How about speaking to the concierge?)
le Quartier Latin: the section of Paris on the Left Bank (of the Seine River) where the University of Paris is located. It is called the Latin Quarter because, during the Middle Ages, all students spoke Latin.

3. *concierge:* Both in hotels and in apartment houses, the concierge is the recipient and dispenser of all information about tenants, directions, prices, and everything else.

6. *Sorbonne:* the Faculties of Arts and Sciences of the University of Paris.

7. *à deux pas:* lit., "two steps away," but this is often merely wishful thinking.
Rive Gauche: The Seine River divides Paris into the Rive Gauche (Left Bank) and the Rive Droite (Right Bank). In general, the student/

Bohemian/artistic/intellectual quarters of the city are on the Rive Gauche, and the commercial and fashionable quarters on the Rive Droite.

9. *Boulevard Saint-Michel:* Often referred to as the "Boul' Mich,' " it is the main thoroughfare of the Latin Quarter. It is lined with cafés and bookstores.

13. *entre les clous:* The main streets in Paris have large crosswalks delimited by metal discs like large nailheads (*clous:* nails). Pedestrians may be fined if they cross outside of this "passage clouté."

17. The cathedral of Notre Dame is usually referred to simply as "Notre-Dame."

18. *ce monsieur:* Note the use of *ce monsieur* for "that man." In this sort of social context, it is good form to refer to a man as a "gentleman," e.g., *un monsieur.* Similarly, refer to a woman as *cette dame,* a girl as *cette demoiselle.*

19. 20. *marchez... marche:* It would be equally correct to use forms of *aller.* That is, ... "*Vous allez dans le mauvais sens.... *" "*Comment? Je ne vais pas... *"

29. *la Sainte-Chapelle:* a church which is a jewel of Gothic architecture on the Ile de la Cité (a small island in the middle of the Seine). Notre Dame is also on the Ile de la Cité.

30. *le musée de Cluny:* a small museum in the Latin Quarter.
le Panthéon: a building containing the tombs of many of the famous men of France.

GRAMMATICAL ITEMS FOR SPECIAL STUDY

I. *"Disjunctive"* or **emphatic pronouns** (See the *Summary of French Grammar* for all the forms and No. 6 below.)

Study the forms and functions of this class of pronouns:

1. **With prepositions:**

	Preposition	Pronoun
a. Je travaille	pour	lui.
b. Viens	avec	moi.
c. Partons	sans	eux.

    a. *I work for him.*
    b. *Come with me.*
    c. *Let's leave without them.*

2. **After *que* in comparisons:**

	plus/ moins/ aussi	Adjective	que	Pronoun
a. Il est	plus	riche	que	toi.
b. Nous sommes	moins	pressés	que	vous.
c. Vous êtes	aussi	intelligent	qu'	elle.

    a. *He is richer than you* (fam.).
    b. *We are less hurried than you* (polite sing. or plu.).
    c. *You are as intelligent as she.*

3. **After imperatives:**

a. Donne-**moi** le livre.	a. *Give me the book.*
b. Couche-**toi** maintenant.	b. *Go to bed now.*

4. In compound subjects and objects:

a. Charles et **moi** nous allons au cinéma.	a. *Charles and I go to the movies.*
b. **Lui** et **elle** viendront demain.	b. *He and she will come tomorrow.*
c. Je vous aime[1] beaucoup, **toi** et Jeanne.	c. *I like you and Jane very much.*

Notes:

1. In a compound subject, when the two pronouns are of the third person, the subject pronoun is omitted and the verb follows directly (see b. above).
2. In all other cases, the normal subject or object pronoun is included (see a. and c. above).

5. In emphatic statements:

a. **Moi,** je ne le veux pas.	a. *I don't want it.*
b. Je ne sais pas, **moi.**	b. *I don't know.*

6. After *c'est:*

C'est **moi.**	*It's I.*
C'est **toi.**	*It's you.*
C'est **lui.**	*It's he.*
C'est **elle.**	*It's she.*
C'est **nous.**	*It's we.*
C'est **vous.**	*It's you.*
C'est (*or* Ce sont) **eux.** } C'est (*or* Ce sont) **elles.**}	*It's they.*

---

[1]The verb *aimer*, used alone, means "to love." Ex.: *Je t'aime.* I love you. However, when it is qualified, as in *Je vous aime bien* or *Je vous aime beaucoup*, it means "I like you very much."

7. **Alone, as a complete utterance:**
a. Qui a fait cela? **Moi.** *Who did that? I (did).*
b. Qui est entré? **Lui.** *Who entered? He (did).*

II. *Reflexive verbs*—verbs whose object pronouns refer to (reflect back on) the same person or persons as their subjects.

Study the forms and equivalents (See also the *Regular Verb Charts*):

A. *Present tense*

1. Je me lave.	1. *I wash myself.*
2. Tu te laves.	2. *You wash yourself.*
3. Il se lave.	3. *He washes himself.*
4. Elle se lave.	4. *She washes herself.*
5. Nous nous lavons.	5. *We wash ourselves.*
6. Vous vous lavez.	6. *You wash yourself (yourselves).*
7. Ils se lavent.	7. *They wash themselves.*
8. Elles se lavent.	8. *They wash themselves.*

Examples:

Infinitive	Subject	Direct Obj.	Verb	Complement
1. (se lever)	Je	me	lève	à huit heures.
2. (se tromper)	Vous	vous	trompez.	
3. (se dépêcher)	Nous	nous	dépêchons	quand nous sommes en retard.

1. *I get up at eight o'clock.* (lit.: *I raise myself at eight o'clock.*)

2. *You're making a mistake.* (lit.: *You deceive yourself.*)

3. *We hurry (ourselves) when we are late.*

Infinitive		Subj.	Indir. Obj.	Verb	Dir. Obj.	Complement
1. (se brosser)	Est-ce que	tu	te	brosses	les dents	tous les matins?
2. (se laver)		Elle	se	lave	les mains.	

1. *Do you brush your teeth every morning?* (lit.: *Do you brush the teeth for yourself every morning?*)

2. *She is washing her hands.* (lit.: *She is washing the hands for herself.*)

Note: Many verbs which are not reflexive in English are reflexive in French. As you come across reflexive verbs, memorize them. Examples: *se coucher* (to go to bed); *s'arrêter* (to stop [oneself]); *se couper* (to cut [oneself]).

B. *Present Perfect*

1. Je me suis égaré(e).

1. *I lost my way. (lit.: I lost myself.)*

2. Tu t'es égaré(e).
2. *You lost your way.*

3. Il s'est égaré.
3. *He lost his way.*

4. Elle s'est égarée.
4. *She lost her way.*

5. Nous nous sommes égaré(e)s.
5. *We lost our way.*

6. Vous vous êtes égaré(e)(s).
6. *You lost your way.*

7. Ils se sont égarés.
7. *They lost their way.*

8. Elles se sont égarées.
8. *They lost their way.*

Notes:

1. Compound tenses of reflexive verbs, such as the present perfect above, are always formed with *être*.

2. The past participle of reflexive verbs agrees with the preceding *direct* object pronoun *only*. Contrast:

Nous nous sommes lavé(e)s.	*We washed ourselves [got washed]*.
Nous nous sommes lavé les mains.	*We washed our hands*.
Elle s'est coupée.	*She cut herself*.
Elle s'est coupé le doigt.	*She cut her finger*.

DRILLS AND EXERCISES

I. Substitute each of the words in parentheses for the italicized word in the pattern sentence. Write the complete sentence and say aloud.

A. Il travaille pour *moi*. (toi, lui, elle, nous, vous, eux, elles)

B. Il est plus riche que *moi*. (toi, lui, elle, nous, vous, eux, elles)

C. Qui est à la porte? C'est *moi*. (toi, lui, elle, nous, vous, eux, elles)

D. Elle s'est *lavée*. (couchée, arrêtée, dépêchée, levée, égarée, trompée)

II. Replace *Je* by the other subject pronouns. Make all necessary verb changes. Write the sentences, say and translate them.

A. *Je* me couche à neuf heures.

B. *Je* me suis trompé(e).

III. Change the *present* to the *present perfect* or *perfect*. Say, and translate each.

Example: Nous nous couchons./Nous nous sommes couché(e)s.

A. Nous nous lavons.   D. Nous nous dépêchons.

B. Nous nous levons.   E. Nous nous arrêtons.

C. Nous nous trompons.

IV. Translate the following into French; then say them aloud.

1. Ask the concierge the way.

2. Don't ask this gentleman the way.

3. I wouldn't know how to go on foot.

4. Toward what area do you wish to go? Toward Paris.

5. Toward the Louvre.

6. How about going to see the Sainte Chapelle (fem.)?

7. How about taking a walk?

8. We've lost our way.

9. We went toward (*se diriger vers*) the Latin Quarter.

10. Are we walking in the right direction?

11. You're walking in the wrong direction.

12. Turn to the right.

13. I must turn to the left.

14. You should have continued straight ahead.

15. She must retrace her steps.

16. The Sorbonne is right near (*à deux pas d'*) here? Yes, it's very near (*tout près d'*) here.

Answers at back of book.

QUIZ

From among the three choices, select the one which correctly renders the English word or phrase given. Write the complete sentence, and translate.

1. (*How about taking*) _____ une promenade à pied?
   - (a) Comment faire
   - (b) Si on faisait
   - (c) Si on prendrait

2. (*easy*) C'est _____.
   - (a) aisé
   - (b) facile
   - (c) agréable

3. (*Look at*) _____ ce plan de Paris.
   - (a) Cherchez
   - (b) Voyez
   - (c) Regardez

4. (*straight ahead*) Il faut continuer _____.
   - (a) droit devant
   - (b) à droite
   - (c) tout droit

5. (*direction*) Vous allez dans le mauvais _____.
   - (a) sens
   - (b) côté
   - (c) coin

6. (*left*) Nous avons tourné _____.
   - (a) laissé
   - (b) à gauche
   - (c) à droite

7. (*once*) Ah oui, _____ nous avons trouvé le bon chemin.
   - (a) premier
   - (b) une fois que
   - (c) maintenant que

8. (*mistaken*) C'est nous qui nous sommes

   _____.

   (a) égaré
   (b) trompé
   (c) trompés

9. (*What a pity*) _____!
   (a) Quelle pitié!
   (b) Quelle sympathie!
   (c) Quel dommage!

10. (*Don't forget*) _____ que nous avons vu
    Notre-Dame.
    (a) N'oublie pas
    (b) Ne revois pas
    (c) Ne dis pas

Answers at back of book.

LESSON 46

DANS UN GRAND MAGASIN°
IN A DEPARMENT STORE

A. *Au rayon des gants* In the glove department

1. Vendeuse: **Qu'y a-t-il pour votre service, madame?**
   Saleslady: What can I do for you, madam?

2. Jeanne: *Je voudrais* **une paire de gants pour tous les jours, s'il vous plaît; comme** *les miens,* **mais en cuir.**°
   I'd like a pair of gloves for every day, please; like mine, but in leather.

3. Vendeuse: **Nous en avons de tous les genres et de toutes les couleurs. En voici une paire en peau de chevreau ...**

We have all kinds and all colors. Here is a pair
in kid . . .

4. Jeanne: **Oui, *ceux-là* sont assez jolis.
   Voudriez-vous me les montrer en beige, s'il
   vous plaît?**
   Yes, those are quite pretty. Would you show
   them to me in beige, please?

5. Vendeuse: **Quelle est votre pointure,° madame? Les pointures sont les mêmes qu'aux
   Etats-Unis.**
   What size do you take, madam? The sizes are
   the same as in the United States.

6. Jeanne: **Ah oui? Alors six et demi.**
   Ah, yes? Six and a half, then.

7. Vendeuse: **Un instant, je vais vous les chercher. Les voici. Voulez-vous les essayer, madame?**
   One moment, I'll get them for you. Here they
   are. Would you like to try them on, madam?

8. Jeanne: **Ils me vont° parfaitement. Quel en
   est le prix, s'il vous plaît?**
   They fit me perfectly. What's the price,
   please?

9. Vendeuse: **Trente francs.°**
   Thirty francs.

10. Jeanne: **C'est très bien. Voulez-vous *me les
    envelopper,* s'il vous plaît?**
    That's fine. Will you wrap them for me,
    please?

11. Vendeuse: **Voilà, madame. Merci beaucoup.**
    There you are, madam. Thank you very much.

12. Jeanne: ***Pourriez-vous* m'indiquer où se
    trouve le W.C.?°**

Could you tell me [lit.: indicate, point out to
me] where I will find the ladies' room?

13. Vendeuse: **Avec plaisir, Madame. Tournez à
gauche et continuez tout droit.**
Gladly, madam. Turn to the left, and continue
straight ahead.

14. Jeanne: **Je vous en remercie.°**
Thank you.

B. *Au rayon des robes*   In the dress department.

15. Vendeuse: **Madame désire?**
What would you like, madam?

16. Jeanne: **Je cherche une robe de soie en vert
clair—à manches courtes, et pas trop dé-
colletée.**
I'm looking for a light-green silk dress—with
short sleeves and not cut too low.

17. Vendeuse: **Ce modéle-ci, madame, c'est la
nouvelle mode, et une véritable occasion à
150 (cent cinquante) francs.**
This model is the latest style, madam, and a
real bargain at 150 francs.

18. Jeanne: **Oh, c'est vraiment trop cher!
N'auriez-vous rien d'autre, à meilleur
marché?°**
Oh, that's really too expensive! Don't you
have anything else, less expensive?

19. Vendeuse: **Il y a *celle-ci* à 120 (cent vingt)
francs. Voyez comme la coupe est élégante.
Mais quelle est votre taille, madame?**
There's this one at 120 francs. See how elegant
the cut is. But what's your size, madam?

20. Jeanne: **Eh bien, aux Etats-Unis c'est le
dix . . .**
Well, in the United States it's ten . . .

21. Vendeuse: **Cette robe-ci est pour vous alors.
    Passons dans le salon d'essayage . . .**
    This dress is for you, then. Let's go into the
    fitting room . . .

22. Jeanne: **Je la° trouve un peu large aux
    épaules, et trop longue aussi.**
    I find it a little wide in the shoulders, and also
    too long.

23. Vendeuse: **Essayons la taille en dessous,
    alors. Ah, madame, vous êtes ravissante!
    Cette robe vous va à merveille!**
    Let's try the next smaller size, then. Ah,
    madam, you look lovely! This dress suits you
    wonderfully!

24. Jeanne: **En effet, elle est très chic . . . Bon, je
    la prends!**
    Yes, it's really very smart . . . Good, I'll take
    it!

25. Vendeuse: **C'est un excellent choix, ma-
    dame. Veuillez me suivre à la caisse.**
    It's an excellent choice, madam. Will you
    come with me to the cashier's desk, please?

26. Jeanne: (*à la caisse*) **Est-ce que vous acceptez
    les chèques de voyage?°**
    (*at the cashier's desk*) Do you accept traveler's
    checks?

27. Caissière: **Certainement, madame. Désirez-
    vous emporter votre achat?** *Nous pourrons
    vous l'envoyer,°* **si vous préférez.**
    Cashier: Certainly, madam. Do you wish to
    take your purchase with you? We can send it to
    you, if you prefer.

28. Jeanne: **Oui, cela vaudrait mieux. Merci beaucoup.**
Yes, that would be better. Thank you very much.

C. *Au comptoir des mouchoirs*   At the handkerchief counter

29. Vendeur: **Qu'est-ce que vous désirez, madame?**
Salesman: What do you wish, madam?

30. Jeanne: **Je cherche des mouchoirs pour mon mari.**
I'm looking for some handkerchiefs for my husband.

31. Vendeur: **Il aimera beaucoup *ceux-ci*, j'en suis sûr. Ils sont en coton, à 30 (trente) francs la douzaine.**
He'll like these very much, I'm sure. They're cotton, at 30 francs a dozen.

32. Jeanne: *Auriez-vous* **quelque chose de meilleure qualité?**
Would you have something in a better quality?

33. Vendeur: *Ceux-ci* **sont en lin, madame. Ils se vendent à 8 (huit) francs chacun.**
These are linen, madam. They sell for 8 francs each.

34. Jeanne: **Oui, je les aime mieux. *Donnez-m'en* une demidouzaine,° s'il vous plaît.**
Yes, I like these better. Give me a half-dozen of them, please.

35. Vendeur: **Très bien, madame . . . Et voici votre monnaie.° Je vais *vous les envelopper*.**
Very good, madam . . . And here's your change. I'll wrap them up for you.

36. Jeanne: **Merci beaucoup, monsieur.**
    Thank you very much, sir.

37. Vendeur: **A votre service, madame.**
    At your service, madam.

NOTES

Title: *grand magasin:* has two equivalents: a big store
(of any kind) and, more commonly, a department
store. In Paris, most of them are on the Right Bank.

2. *en cuir: en* generally precedes the noun for a
   fabric or material. Examples: *en coton* (in
   cotton); *en laine* (in wool).

5. *pointure:* the term used to indicate sizes for
   socks, shoes, stockings, hats, and gloves. To
   indicate sizes of dresses, suits, coats, and
   shirts, the term *taille* is used. Some sizes are
   the same as in the United States. Other sizes
   are measured in centimeters, and are therefore
   different.

8. *Ils me vont:* They fit me. From *aller* (to fit, to
   suit), used in connection with clothes, etc. See
   also 20 in the text.

9. The unit of currency in France is the franc.
   There are approximately nine francs to a dollar. The rate of exchange fluctuates slightly
   from day to day.

12. *le W.C.:* The toilet is *le W.C.* (water closet) or
    la toilette; the washroom or washbowl is *le
    lavabo; la salle de bains* (bathroom) is where
    you take a bath; and the shower is *la douche.*
    In general, in France and throughout Europe,
    you must ask for the precise facility you want.
    There is no real equivalent to our "rest room,"
    "ladies' room," etc.

14. *Je vous en remercie:* lit.: I thank you for it. This expression is a little more formal than *merci*, but is frequently used.

18. *bon marché:* inexpensive.
    meilleur marché: less expensive.

22. *la:* refers to the dress (*la robe*).

26. Traveler's checks are accepted almost everywhere in France.

27. Purchases are delivered—and graciously—if the customer so desires.

34. *une demi-douzaine:* In compound words, *demi* is invariable.

35. *monnaie:* (small) change or currency. *Argent* is the word for money in general.

GRAMMATICAL ITEMS FOR SPECIAL STUDY
I. The *Conditional*

A. The conditional is formed by adding the endings *-ais, -ais, -ait, -ions, -iez, -aient* to the future stem.

B. Study the following examples of regular verbs:

1st conjugation (future stem = infin.)	2nd conjugation (future stem = infin.)	3rd conjugation (future stem = infin. less final e)
arriver	*choisir*	*attendre*
j'arriver*ais* (I'd come, I would come)	je choisir*ais* (I'd choose, I would choose)	j'attendr*ais* (I'd wait, I would wait)

tu arriver*ais*	tu choisir*ais*	tu attend*rais*
il ⎱ arriver*ait* elle ⎰	il ⎱ choisir*ait* elle ⎰	il ⎱ attend*rait* elle ⎰
nous arriver*ions*	nous choisir*ions*	nous attend*rions*
vous arriver*iez*	vous choisir*iez*	vous attend*riez*
ils ⎱ arriver*aient* elles ⎰	ils ⎱ choisir*aient* elles ⎰	ils ⎱ attend*raient* elles ⎰

C. Study the formation of the conditional of these verbs which have irregular future stems:

avoir	*être*	*aller*

future stem =
  aur-
  j'aur*ais* (I'd have, I would have)
	future stem =
	  ser-
	  je ser*ais* (I'd be, I would be)
		future stem =
		  ir-
		  j'ir*ais* (I'd go, I would go)

tu aur*ais*	tu ser*ais*	tu ir*ais*
il ⎱ aur*ait* elle ⎰	il ⎱ ser*ait* elle ⎰	il ⎱ ir*ait* elle ⎰
nous aur*ions*	nous ser*ions*	nous ir*ions*
vous aur*iez*	vous ser*iez*	vous ir*iez*
ils ⎱ aur*aient* elles ⎰	ils ⎱ ser*aient* elles ⎰	ils ⎱ ir*aient* elles ⎰

D. For additional examples of the conditional, both regular and irregular verbs, see both the *Regular* and *Irregular Verb Charts*.

E. Uses of the conditional.

1. The conditional in French is generally used in much the same way as it is in English. Study these sentences:

   a. Il a dit qu'il *arriverait* demain. *He said he would arrive tomorrow.*

   b. Si j'avais l'argent, j'*irais* au théâtre. *If I had the money, I would go to the theatre.*

   See Lesson 56 for additional examples in which the conditional is used in "if" sentences.

2. Notice this special use of the conditional of *devoir:*

    a. Il *devrait* payer. *He ought to pay.* (*He should pay.*)

3. The conditional is commonly used in expressions of courtesy. Notice the following examples:

    a. Que voudriez-vous? *What would you like?*
    b. Pourriez-vous nous aider? *Could you help us?* (lit.: *Would you be able to help us?*)
    c. Auriez-vous le temps? *Would you have the time?*

II. *Possessives* (without nouns)

A. Notice these examples:

    1. Mon père est plus jeune que *le tien.*
       My father is younger than yours.
    2. J'ai perdu mon dictionnaire. Donnez-moi *le vôtre.*
       I lost my dictionary. Give me yours.
    3. Ces gants sont jolis. Je n'aime plus *les miens.*
       These gloves are pretty. I no longer like mine.
    4. Tu t'occupes de ton travail. Je m'occupe *du¹ mien.*
       You take care of your work. I take care of mine.

B. Study these forms:

	Singular		Plural	
	Masc.	Fem.	Masc.	Fem.
mine	le mien	la mienne	les miens	les miennes
yours	le tien	la tienne	les tiens	les tiennes

¹*de + le = du.* See Lesson 47 for contracted forms.

his,	le sien	la sienne	les siens	les siennes
hers				
ours	le nôtre	la nôtre	les nôtres	les nôtres
yours	le vôtre	la vôtre	les vôtres	les vôtres
theirs	le leur	la leur	les leurs	les leurs

Note: In French, all possessives agree with the thing possessed and not the possessor. Example: *Son père est venu* could mean either "His father has come." or "Her father has come." Since *père* is masculine, it takes the masculine possessive in either case.

III. *Demonstratives* (without nouns)

  A. Notice these examples:

    1. Je n'aime pas cette robe-ci. Donnez-moi **celle-là.**
       I don't like this dress. Give me that one.

    2. Je ne veux pas ce complet-ci. Je prendrai **celui-là.**
       I don't want this suit. I'll take that one.

    3. Cette robe? Je ne l'aime pas. Je préfère **celle** de ma sœur.
       That dress? I don't like it. I prefer my sister's.

    4. Cette robe? Je ne l'aime pas. Je préfère **celle** que vous portez.
       That dress? I don't like it. I prefer the one you are wearing.

  B. Study these forms.

Singular		*Plural*	
Masc.	*Fem.*	*Masc.*	*Fem.*
celui	celle	ceux	celles

Note: The demonstratives must be followed by *-ci* or *-là* except (1) when they are followed by the preposition *de*, or (2) when they introduce a relative clause.

Examples:

La
peinture?
*The
painting?*

1. Celle *de* mon ami est épatante.
   My friend's (the one of my friend) is terrific.

2. Celle *qui* est à gauche est plus jolie. *The one which is at the left is prettier.*

3. Celle *que* je veux est trop chère. *The one that I want is too expensive.*

4. Celle *dont* vous parlez ne me plaît pas.
   The one of which you are speaking doesn't please me.
   (See Lesson 49 for explanation of *dont*.)

IV. *Double object pronouns*

A. Notice these examples:

Il me le donne.	*He gives it to me.*
Il nous les montre.	*He shows them to us.*
Il le lui a prêté.	*He loaned it to him.*
Il les leur a prêtés.	*He loaned them to them.*
Donnez-le-moi.	*Give it to me.*
Ne me le donnez pas.	*Don't give it to me.*
Il m'en donne.	*He gives some to me.*
Donnez-m'en.	*Give me some.*
Ne m'en donnez pas.	*Don't give me any.*
Je l'y mets.	*I'm putting it there.*

B. Study the forms of direct and indirect objects in the *Summary of French Grammar.*

NOTES:

1. Use the following possible combinations of word order in all sentences *except* affirmative imperative.

Indirect	Direct	Indirect	y	en
me				
te $\left.\right\}$ *pre-cedes*	le la $\left.\right\}$ *pre-cedes*	lui leur $\left.\right\}$ *pre-cedes*	y *pre-cedes*	en
nous	les			
vous				

2. The order of double object pronouns in affirmative imperative is as follows:

Direct	Indirect	y	en
	moi		
	toi		
le $\left.\right\}$	lui		
la $\left.\right\}$ *precedes*	nous $\left.\right\}$ *precedes* y *precedes*		en
les	vous		
	leur		

Note: *Me* and *te* become *moi* and *toi* after *le, la, les.*

DRILLS AND EXERCISES

I. Substitue each of the words or expressions in parentheses for the italicized word or expression in the model sentence. Write the complete sentence and say aloud.

A. Pourriez-vous le *faire?* (lire, demander, choisir, contrôler, payer)

B. J'aime *le mien.* (le tien, le sien, le nôtre, le vôtre, le leur)

C. Je m'occuperai *des miens.* (des tiens, des siens, des nôtres, des vôtres, des leurs)

II. Replace the adjective-noun combination with the pronoun.

Example: Je ne veux pas *cette robe-ci.*/Je ne veux pas *celle-ci.*

1. Donnez-moi *ce crayon-ci.*
2. Je préfère *ces livres-là.*
3. Regardez *ces tables-ci.*
4. Prenez *ces numéros-ci.*

III. Expand the following by placing *Celui dont je vous ai parlé* in front of each. Writ the entire sentence, say it, and give the English equivalent.

1. _____ a été vendu.
2. _____ coûte trop cher.
3. _____ ne me plaît pas.
4. _____ est excellent.
5. _____ est le frère de Michel.
6. _____ est venu me voir.

IV. Replace the italicized nouns by object pronouns, and translate them.

Example: Il me donne *les livres.*/Il me *les* donne.

1. Il lui donne *le paquet.*
2. Il nous montre *les robes.*
3. Ne me donnez pas *ce verre.*
4. Il me montre *des cahiers.*
5. J'y mets *le livre.*

V. Transform the following sentences to the negative. Translate the negative sentences only.

Example: Donnez-le-moi./Ne me le donnez pas.

1. Montrez-la-leur.

2. Vendez-les-lui.

3. Donnez-m'en.

4. Racontez-la-nous.

5. Prête-le-moi.

VI. Translate the following into French; then say them aloud.

1. *Un chapeau?* I prefer that one in silk.

2. *Une robe?* I like this one in rayon.

3. *Des gants?* He likes those in wool.

4. *Des chaussures?* She likes those in linen.

5. *Des chemises?* We prefer these in cotton.

6. *Des bas?* She prefers these in nylon.

7. (for hats, shoes, gloves) What is your size?

8. (for coats, dresses, suits) What is your size?

9. I'd like this one (masc.) in pink.

10. I'd like that one (fem.) in navy blue *(blue marine)*.

11. I'd like these (masc.) in white.

12. I'd like those (masc.) in red.

13. I'd like these (fem.) in yellow.

14. He'd like those (fem.) in gray.

15. The dress with the long sleeves *(manches longues)*.

16. This one (masc.) suits you wonderfully.

17. That one (fem.) suits you (fam.) perfectly.

18. Here is something *(quelque chose de)* beautiful.

19. There is nothing else *(rien d'autre)* here.

20. He's going to send them to you.

21. He's going to wrap them for him.

22. Give them to me.

23. Don't tell them about it. (Lit.: Don't tell it to them.)

24. Could you (would you be able to) tell me where the bus is?

25. Would you know the name of that gentleman?

26. I would like to see him.

27. Would you have the kindness to tell me (to indicate to me) the time?

Answers at back of book.

QUIZ

From among the three choices, select the one which correctly renders the English word or phrase given at the beginning of each sentence. Write the complete sentence, and translate.

1. (*every day*) Je voudrais des gants pour
   _____.
   (a) toujours
   (b) toutes les jours
   (c) tous les jours.

2. (*quite*) Ceux-là sont _____ jolis.
   (a) aussi
   (b) assez
   (c) assis

3. (*sizes*) Les _____ pour les gants sont les mêmes.
   (a) points
   (b) tailles
   (c) pointures

4. (*a silk dress*) Je cherche _____.
   (a) une soie robe
   (b) une robe soie
   (c) une robe de soie

5. (*bargain*) C'est une _____.
   (a) occasion
   (b) opportunité
   (c) marché

6. (*in the shoulders*) Je la trouve large
   _____.
   (a) dans l'épaule
   (b) aux épaules
   (c) sur les épaules

7. (*What*) _____ vous désirez, madame?
   (a) Que
   (b) Qu'est-ce que
   (c) Quoi

8. (*I'm looking for*) _____ des mouchoirs.
   (a) Je regarde pour
   (b) Je cherche
   (c) Je cherche pour

9. (*a dozen*) Ils se vendent à 100 francs
   _____.
   (a) la douzaine
   (b) une douzaine
   (c) par douzaine

10. (*change*) Voici votre _____.
    (a) change
    (b) monnaie
    (c) argent.

Answers at back of book.

LESSON 47

ON SE FAIT COIFFER
WE HAVE OUR HAIR DONE

A. *Chez le coiffeur* At the hairdresser's

1. Coiffeur: **Ah, bonjour, monsieur. Qu'est-ce qu'il y a pour votre service° aujourd'hui?**
   Good day, sir. What can we do for you today?

2. Charles: **Une coupe de cheveux, d'abord. J'ai l'impression qu'ils poussent *plus vite que jamais* ces jours-ci.**
   First a haircut. I have the feeling that my hair is growing faster than ever these days.

3. Coiffeur: *Je vous les coupe°* **comme d'habitude? Pas trop longs sur le dessus, n'est-ce pas?**
   Shall I cut it for you as usual? Not too long on top, right?

4. Charles: **Oui, mais assez courts sur les côtés et sur la nuque. Employez la tondeuse.**
   Yes, but rather short on the sides and on the nape of the neck. Use the clippers.

5. Coiffeur: **Très bien, monsieur... Voilà! Je fais la raie à droite ou à gauche?**
   Very well, sir. There! Shall I part it on the right or on the left?

6. Charles: **A gauche, s'il vous plaît.**
   On the left, please.

7. Coiffeur: **Bien. Encore un coup° de peigne ... Et voilà, monsieur!** *Je peux vous faire* **autre chose?**

Good. Another dash (stroke) with the comb
... And there you are, sir! Can I do anything
else for you?

8. Charles: **Voyons ... Ma femme est à côté,
   au *salon des dames*. Pendant que je
   l'attends ...**
   Let's see ... My wife is next door at the beauty
   salon. While I'm waiting for her ...

9. Coiffeur: **Vous devrez attendre longtemps, si
   je connais les femmes!**
   You will have to wait a long time, if I know
   women!

10. Charles: **Vous avez raison. Eh bien, rasez-
    moi, alors. Mais attention; *j'ai la barbe
    dure,* vous savez.**
    You are right. Well, give me a shave, then. But
    be careful; I have a tough beard, you know.

11. Coiffeur: **Ne vous inquiétez pas, monsieur.
    C'est vite fait.**
    Don't worry, sir. It will be done quickly.

12. Charles: **Quel luxe que de *se faire raser* par
    un autre de temps en temps!**
    What a luxury to have oneself shaved by some-
    one else from time to time!

13. Coiffeur: **A votre service, monsieur. Mainte-
    nant, une serviette chaude ...**
    At your service, sir. Now, a hot towel ...

14. Charles: **Ah! Mais vraiment, vous me gâtez!**
    Ah! But you are really pampering me!

15. Coiffeur: **C'est un plaisir, monsieur. On
    vous reverra la semaine prochaine?**
    It's a pleasure, sir. Will we see you again next
    week?

16. Charles: **Oui**, *je me ferai réserver* **une heure à la caisse.**
    Yes, I'll have an hour reserved for me at the cashier's desk.

17. Coiffeur: *Vous pouvez le faire* **quand vous payerez.**
    You can do it when you pay your bill.

18. Charles: **Très bien. Et voilà quelque chose en plus pour vous.°**
    Fine. And here's something extra for you.

19. Coiffeur: **Merci beaucoup, monsieur. A la semaine prochaine.**
    Thank you very much, sir. See you next week.

B. *Dans la rue*   In the street

20. Charles: **Tiens,° te voilà, chérie!°** *Je venais justement te chercher.*
    Well, there you are, dear. I was just coming to fetch you.

21. Jeanne: **Je vois que** *tu t'es fait couper les cheveux.*
    I see that you had your hair cut.

22. Charles: **Et** *je me suis fait raser* **aussi. Mais toi, tu es** *plus jolie que jamais.* **Qu'est-ce que** *tu t'es fait faire?*
    And I got a shave too. But you are prettier than ever. What did you have done?

23. Jeanne: **Un shampooing° et une coupe, et puis** *je me suis fait faire* **une mise en plis°** comme toujours.**
    A shampoo and cut, and then I had my hair set, as usual.

24. Charles: **Tu ne me dis pas tout. Il y a quelque chose de différent aujourd'hui.**

You aren't telling me everything. There is
something different today.

25. Jeanne: **Tiens, c'est merveilleux! Tu l'as re-
marqué! On m'a éclairci la couleur un tout
petit peu. Ça° te plaît?**
Well, that's wonderful! You noticed it! They
lightened the color for me just a little bit. Do
you like it?

26. Charles: **C'est ravissant. Tu es délicieuse.°
Mais pas de manucure cette fois-ci?**
It's gorgeous. You are (look) delightful. But no
manicure this time?

27. Jeanne: **Si,° bien entendu *je me suis fait faire
les ongles. Et la semaine prochaine...***
Yes, of course I had my nails done. And next
week...

28. Charles: **Assez! En moins de trois heures, tu
es épuisé toutes nos économies!**
Enough! In less than three hours you've ex-
hausted all our savings!

29. Jeanne: **Pas tout à fait. Il nous reste encore
quelques sous.°**
Not altogether. We still have a few pennies
left.

30. Charles: **Allons donc *à la Tour d'Argent.°* Je
veux que tout le monde admire ma femme.**
Let's go to the Tour d'Argent, then. I want
everybody to admire my wife.

NOTES

1. *Qu'est-ce qu'il y a pour votre service?:* one of
   a number of expressions meaning "What can I
   do for you?" Others are *Qu'y a-t-il pour votre*

service?; Qu'est-ce que vous désirez? Madame [Monsieur] désire?; En quoi puis-je vous être utile?

3. *Je vous les coupe:* Note use of the present tense, whereas in English we would use the future. In general, use the present tense when referring to an action that is going to be performed at once. In this phrase, *les* refers to *les cheveux.* Lit.: Do I cut them (*les cheveux*) for you?

7. *un coup de:* a blow or stroke of or with something. Used in expressions such as *un coup de pied* (a kick), *un coup de coude* (a nudge), *un coup de téléphone* (a phone call).

18. A tip of approximately 15 percent is usually given to persons who have performed some service.

20. *Tiens!:* a commonly used expression to introduce sentences or thoughts; similar to the English "Well!" However, "Tiens" always expresses mild and usually pleasant surprise.
   chérie: a common term of endearment similar to the English "darling." The masculine is "chéri."

23. *un shampooing:* an example of "franglais"; that is, English words which are invading the French language more and more.
   une mise en plis: lit.: a putting into folds (French verb "mettre").

25. *ça:* a common abbreviated form for "cela."

26. *délicieuse:* lit. "delicious." A term such as this would not be considered affected in French.

27. *Si:* Note that Jane's *si* ("yes") is in response to a preceding **negative** question. Whenever a question is phrased in the negative, and the answer is "yes," use *si*. Contrast:

Tu ne l'as pas vu? **Si,** *je viens de le voir.*
Haven't you seen him? Yes, I just saw him.

Tu l'as vu? **Oui,** je viens de le voir.
Have you seen him? Yes, I just saw him.

29. *sou:* a penny. Used in expressions such as this but no longer a unit of French currency.

30. *La Tour d'Argent:* one of the most chic and expensive restaurants in Paris, located near Notre Dame. It is noted especially for its pressed duck, which is first chosen by the diner and then prepared to his taste.

GRAMMATICAL ITEMS FOR SPECIAL STUDY

I. *Que jamais*—than ever, *in comparisons*

Study:

	plus/ moins	Adj./Adv.	que	jamais
1. Ils parlent	plus	vite	que	jamais.
2. Tu es	plus	jolie	que	jamais.
3. Il est	moins	aimable	que	jamais.

1. *They are speaking faster than ever.*

2. *You are prettier than ever.*

3. *He is less likeable than ever.*

II. *Pouvoir + infinitive*

Study:

pouvoir	Pronoun Object	Infinitive	Complement
1. Je peux	vous	faire	autre chose.
2. Vous pouvez	le	voir	plus tard.
3. Nous pourrions	lui	parler.	

1. *I can do something else for you.*

2. *You can see it later.*

3. *We could talk to him.*

Note: Notice that the pronoun object comes **after** *pouvoir*, and immediately precedes the infinitive.

III. *Se faire + infinitive*

Study:

Subject	Reflex. Pron.	faire	Infinitive	Complement
1. Je	me	fais	couper	les cheveux.
2. Nous	nous	ferons	bâtir	une maison.
3. Il	s'	est fait	raser.	
4. Je	me	suis fait	faire	les ongles.

1. *I am having my hair cut (for myself).*

2. *We will have a house built (for ourselves).*

3. *He had himself shaved.*

4. *I had my nails done (for myself).*

NOTES:

1. The auxiliary *être* must be used when *se faire* +
   infinitive are used. (See Ex. 3 and 4.)

2. The past participle of *faire* does not agree; i.e.,
   it is invariable when followed by the infinitive.
   (See Ex. 3 and 4.)

IV. The *definite article* with *parts of the body*

Study:

	Def. Art.	Part of Body	
1. Elle a	les	yeux	bleus.
2. Tu t'es fait couper	les	cheveux.	
3. Je me suis coupé	le	doigt.	
4.	La	tête	me tourne.
5. J'ai mal	aux	dents.	

Note: *A* and *les* are contracted and become *aux*. *A* +
le become *au*. See Section V.

1. *She has blue eyes.*

2. *You had your hair cut.*

3. *I cut my finger.*

4. *My head is spinning.*

5. *I have a toothache.*

Note: In general, correct French uses the definite
article (*le, la, les*) with parts of the body, instead of
the possessive adjective (*mon, ton,* etc.). You will,
however, hear the possessive adjective in colloquial
speech.

V. *Contractions:* The prepositions *à* and *de*, when used with the masculine or plural definite article, are contracted. Study the following:

at the, to the, in the	of the, about
à + le = au	de + le = du
à + les = aux	de + les = des
à + la not contracted	de + la not contracted
à + l' used if noun begins with vowel	de + l' used if noun begins with vowel

Examples:

1. Le patron **du** magasin est allé aux Halles.¹
   The owner of the store went to Les Halles.

2. L'histoire **des** pays d'Europe commence à la fine de l'empire romain.
   The history of the countries of Europe begins at the end of the Roman Empire.

3. Au début **de la** pièce, les comediens chantent ensemble.
   At the beginning of the play, the actors sing together.

VI. *Chez* ("at the place of")

Study:

Subject	Verb	*chez*	Complement	
1. Je	vais	chez	lui.	
2.	Venez	chez	moi	demain.
3. Il	a été	chez	le médecin.	
4. Nous	l'avons vu	chez	Dupont	hier soir.

1. *I am going to his place* (or *his home*).

2. *Come to my house tomorrow.*

3. *He has been to the doctor's* (*office* implied)

4. *We saw him at Dupont's yesterday evening.*

Note: *Chez* + *noun or pronoun complement* encompasses the meanings of "at the home of," "at the place of," "at the place of work of," "at the location of" someone.

DRILLS AND EXERCISES

I. Write each of the following sentences in full, say aloud, and translate.

Elle parle (1) au garçon qu'elle a rencontré à la banque.

(2) de l'arbre qui est plein de fleurs.

(3) aux enfants qui se rendent à l'épicerie.

(4) constamment du petit truc[1] qu'elle a vu au magasin.

(5) souvent de la jolie petite fille du professeur.

II. Substitute each word in parentheses for the italicized word in the model sentence. Say and write the entire new sentence.

A. Tu es plus *jolie* que jamais. (intéressante, belle, aimable, charmante, bavarde)

B. Vous pouvez le *voir* plus tard. (faire, demander, dire, chercher, manger, boire, lire)

C. Nous pourrions vous le *montrer*. (donner, demander, dire, expliquer [watch l'], recommander)

[1]*truc:* whatsis, gadget, etc.

III. Transform each sentence below to indicate that the subject is having the action done by somebody else.

Example: Je me coupe les cheveux./Je *me fais couper* les cheveux.

1. Je me lave les cheveux.
2. Je me teins¹ les cheveux.
3. Je me rase.
4. Je me fais une mise en plis.
5. Je me fais les ongles.

IV. Transform each sentence below from present to present perfect. Say and translate each.

Example: Je *me fais* faire les cheveux./Je *me suis fait* faire les cheveux.

1. Je *me fais* raser.
2. Je *me fais* laver les vêtements.
3. Elle *se fait* faire les ongles.
4. Elle *se fait* couper les cheveux.

V. Translate the following sentences into French; then say them aloud.

1. What can we do for you, madame?
2. What do you wish, sir?
3. What does monsieur [madame] desire?
4. I want to have a hair set.
5. She wants to have a shampoo.
6. He wants to have his hair cut.
7. She wants to have her nails done.

¹from *teindre*—to dye, to tint

8. She wants to have her hair lightened (*éclaircir*).

9. Don't cut it too short at the nape of the neck (*la nuque*).

10. What luxury to be at the hairdresser's!

11. What luxury to go to Paris!

12. Would you want a set?

13. I'd like a haircut.

14. She'd like a shampoo.

15. Do it as usual (*d'habitude*).

16. Do it as always.

17. Do it as you wish.

18. She will have a long wait.

19. Will I have a long wait? (use *Est-ce que*)

20. The terrace of the café is always open to the public.

21. Do you (polite) want to go with him to the library in order to (*pour*) speak to the students?

22. The critic of *Le Monde* spoke to me about the films of today.

23. Come (fam.) with me to the school of agriculture.

24. At our place, one will find many (*beaucoup de*) books

Answers at back of book.

QUIZ

From among the three choices, select the one which correctly renders the English word or phrase given at the beginning of each sentence, write the complete sentence, and translate.

1. (*faster*) Ils poussent _____ que jamais.
   (a) vite
   (b) plus vite
   (c) plus rapide

2. (*as usual*) Je vous les coupe _____.
   (a) comme jamais
   (b) comme d'habitude
   (c) comme d'habit

3. (*a long time*) Vous en aurez pour _____.
   (a) un long temps
   (b) un longtemps
   (c) longtemps

4. (*next door*) Ma femme est _____.
   (a) à côté
   (b) du côté
   (c) à la porte

5. (*once in a while*) Quel luxe que de se faire raser
   _____.
   (a) une fois
   (b) de temps en temps
   (c) de quelque temps

6. (*next week*) On vous reverra _____.
   (a) prochaine semaine
   (b) la semaine prochaine
   (c) une semaine prochaine

7. (*something extra*) Voilà _____ pour vous.
   (a) quelque chose plus
   (b) quelque chose mais
   (c) quelque chose en plus

8. (*There you are*) _____, chérie!
   (a) Voilà toi
   (b) Voilà vous
   (c) Te voilà

9. (*something different*) Il y a _____.
   (a) quelque chose de différent
   (b) quelque chose différent
   (c) chose différente

10. (*this time*) Pas de manucure _____?
    (a) cette fois-ci
    (b) ce temps-ci
    (c) cette heure-ci

Answers at back of book.

LESSON 48

AU THÉÂTRE
AT THE THEATRE

A. *Au bureau de location*   At the ticket office

1. Charles: **Est-ce que vous avez quatre places pour ce soir? *Des fauteuils*° d'orchestre, de préférence, et pas trop de côté.**
   Do you have four seats for this evening? Orchestra seats, preferably, and not too far to the side.

2. Employée: **Voyons...*je n'ai que*° des places *séparées* à l'orchestre, sauf quelques-unes qui sont de côté. Mais j'ai encore *de bonnes places* au balcon, tout à fait au centre.**
   Let's see...I have only separate seats left in the orchestra, except a few which are on the side. But I still have good seats in the balcony, right in the center.

3. Charles: **Très bien, alors; je les prendrai.**
Fine, then; I'll take them.

4. Employée: **Cela fait soixante-douze francs,°**
monsieur.
That's seventy-two francs, sir.

5. Charles: **A quelle heure commence la repré-**
sentation, s'il vous plaît?
At what time does the performance begin,
please?

6. Employée: **A 21 heures° précises, monsieur.**
At nine o'clock exactly, sir.

B. *Au Théâtre Français*   At the *Théâtre Français*

7. Charles: **Tiens, voilà Nicole et Michel! Ni-**
cole, Michel, quel plaisir de vous revoir!
Look, there are Nicole and Michael. Nicole,
Michael, what a pleasure to see you again!

8. Michel: **Vous êtes si gentils de nous inviter ce**
soir, et avec cette pluie!
You are so kind to invite us this evening, and
with this rain!

9. Nicole: **Votre robe est ravissante. La**
couleur vous va à merveille.
Your dress is gorgeous. The color becomes
you wonderfully.

10. Jeanne: **Vous êtes très aimable. Je viens de**
l'acheter. Ici, à Paris, naturellement.
You're very kind. I've just bought it. Here in
Paris, of course.

11. Michel: **Assez de politesses, les femmes! Le**
rideau va bientôt se lever.
Enough polite phrases, ladies. The curtain will
be going up soon.

12. Le Vendeur de Programmes: **Programme, messieurs?**
Program-Seller: Program, gentlemen?

13. Michel: *Permettez-moi,* Charles. **Deux programmes, s'il vous plaît.**
Permit me, Charles. Two programs, please.

14. Nicole: (*à Jeanne, en aparté*) *Voyuez-vous,* **en France on achète le programme. On donne un pourboire au vendeur, et aussi à l'ouvreuse.**
(*to Jane, aside*) You see, in France you buy the program. You give a tip to the seller, and also to the usherette.

15. L'Ouvreuse: **Vos billets, messieurs? Par ici, s'il vous plaît. Troisième rang, les quatre premières places.**
Usherette: Your tickets, gentlemen? This way, please. Third row, the first four seats.

16. Michel: **Merci, madame. Et voici quelque chose pour vous.**
Thank you, madam. And here's something for you.

17. Charles: **Ces places sont excellentes. Avec les jumelles, nous verrons très bien la scène.**
These seats are excellent. With the opera glasses, we'll see the stage very well.

18. Nicole: **Que de monde! Cette pièce fait toujours salle comble.**
What a crowd! This play always draws a full house.

19. Michel: **Chut! . . . Voilà les trois coups;° la pièce va commencer.**
Shh! . . . There are the three knocks. The play is about to begin.

C. *A l'entr'acte, au foyer* At the intermission, in
   the foyer

20. Nicole: **Un grand succès, à en juger par ces
    applaudissements! Vous les avez entendus?**
    A great success, judging by that applause! Did
    you hear it?

21. Michel: **En France, vous savez, on n'hésite
    pas à siffler et à huer, si le jeu des acteurs
    est mauvais.**
    In France, you know, people don't hesitate to
    hiss and boo if the acting is bad.

22. Charles: **Les comédiens° sont tout à fait
    extraordinaires. Ils vous font vraiment
    éprouver les sentiments des personnages.
    Voilà pourquoi je me plais à voir°** *des pièces*
    en France.
    The actors are quite extraordinary. They really
    make you feel the emotions of the characters.
    That's why I like to see plays in France.

23. Nicole: **Je trouve aussi que les décors et les
    jeux de lumière illustrent parfaitement l'ac-
    tion.**
    I think too that the sets and the lighting bring
    out the action perfectly.

24. jeanne: **Même mon mari, qui est un fanati-
    que du cinéma, avouera qu'un film n'est pas
    souvent si fort, si émouvant...**
    Even my husband, who's a movie fan, will
    admit that a film is rarely so powerful, so
    moving...

25. Michel: **A vrai dire, je trouve qu'une in-
    trigue me paraît toujours moins intense à
    l'écran.**

Truthfully, I find that a plot always seems to
me to be less intense on the screen.

26. Nicole: **Et puis, après les actualités, les dessins animés et les réclames,° le grand film
semble toujours moins dramatique!**
And then, after the news, the cartoons and the
advertising, the main feature always seems less
dramatic!

27. Charles: **Je voudrais bien revoir cette pièce,
mais nous n'aurons pas le temps de le faire.**
I'd very much like to see this play again, but
we won't have the time to do it.

28. Nicole: **Cette pièce passe souvent à la télévision. Vous aurez sûrement l'occasion de la
revoir.**
This play is often shown on television. You'll
surely have the chance to see it again.

29. Jeanne: **Vraiment? A quelle chaîne?**
Really? On what channel?

30. Nicole: **Je crois que c'est la deuxième.° Mais
vous le° trouverez certainement dans un
journal.**
I think it's the second one. But you'll certainly
find it in the newspaper.

31. Michel: **Et il y a toujours *des compagnies
françaises*° qui font des tournées aux Etats-
Unis.**
And there are always French companies that go
on tour in the United States.

32. Michel: **A propos de spectacles, *êtes-vous
déjà allés* à l'Opéra? Les interprétations
sont toujours excellentes.**

Speaking of entertainment, have you been to the Opera yet? The performances are always excellent.

33. Nicole: **Et si vous aimez les œuvres symphoniques ou la musique de chambre, il y a aussi plusieurs salles de concert à Paris ...**
And if you like symphonic works or chamber music, there are also several concert halls in Paris ...

34. L'Ouvreuse: **Reprenez vos places, mesdames et messieurs. Le quatrième acte commence.**
Return to your seats, ladies and gentlemen. The fourth act is beginning.

35. Charles: *Dépêchons-nous,* **alors! Nous ne voulons pas manquer le dénouement!**
Let's hurry, then! We don't want to miss the ending!

NOTES

1. *fauteuil:* lit., "armchair." Used primarily for a comfortable orchestra seat.

2. *je n'ai que:* In this context, the idea might also be expressed as "il ne reste que" or "il n'y a que."

4. The theatre and opera are subsidized by the government. Seats are therefore relatively inexpensive.

6. Official time is calculated on the basis of twenty-four hours in announcements of starting, ending, departure, and arrival times for activities related to public entertainment, transportation, private invitations, and many other formal events. For example, a 2:00 P.M. train

will be listed in the schedule as leaving at *14 h. (heures)*. But in ordinary speech, the train leaves at *deux heures de l'après-midi,* and the theatre performance (21 h.) really begins at *neuf heures du soir.*

19. *trois coups:* To announce the fact that the curtain is about to rise, three knocks are sounded.

21. French audiences tend to be rather demonstrative.

22. *Les comédiens:* Actors of any kind.

je me plais à voir: I like to see. *Se plaire*—to like (lit.: to please oneself) is followed by the preposition *à* before a complementary infinitive. Other uses of *se plaire* are:

Tu me plais. I like you. (lit.: You please me.)
Il se plaît en France. He has a good time in France.
(Lit.: He please himself in France.)

26. Advertisements for many products are shown on the screen before the main feature begins.

30. French television is owned and operated by the government. At the present time, there are four channels.
le: refers to le renseignement, the information (understood).

31. Excellent French theatre groups (also called *troupes*) such as those of the Comédie Française and the Théâtre National Populaire have delighted American audiences in recent years.

GRAMMATICAL ITEMS FOR SPECIAL STUDY

I. *ne + verb + que = only*
   Study:

Subject	ne	Verb	que	Complement
1. Je	n'	ai	que	des places séparées.
2. Nous	n'	avons	que	dix francs.
3. Elle	ne	fait	que	parler.
4. Je	ne	veux	que	ton bonheur.

1. *I have only separate seats.*

2. *We have only ten francs.*

3. *She only talks. (She does nothing but talk.)*

4. *I want only your happiness.*

II. *The Partitive Article*. In English, we express the concept of **partition** by the words *some* or *any*. For example, "I have some apples." This indicates that, of all the apples in the world, I have only a part. This concept of partition is expressed in French by the use of *de* + the definite article (*le, la, les*). Notice that "some" or "any" may be merely implied in English, whereas it is *always* expressed in French.

   Study the material below, and particularly notice the contrasts in meaning between the sentences using the definite article alone, and those using the partitive article.

A. Before masculine singular nouns:

	Def. Article	Noun		Part. Article	Noun
1. Voici	le	café.	Voulez-vous	du	café?

2. Voici	le	vin.	Voulez-vous	du	vin?
3. Voici	le	fro-mage	Elle veut	du	fro-mage

1. *Here's the coffee.*	*Do you want (some/any) coffee?*
2. *Here's the wine.*	*Do you want (some/any) wine?*
3. *Here's the cheese.*	*She wants (some) cheese.*

Note: "Some" or "any" before a masculine singular noun is *du* (contraction of *de + le*).

B. Before feminine singular nouns:

	Def. Article	Noun		Part. Article	Noun
1. Voici	la	craie.	Voulez-vous	de la	craie?
2. Voilà	la	viande.	Nous mangerons	de la	viande.
3. Voici	la	mon-naie.	Vous avez	de la	mon-naie.

1. *Here's the chalk.*	*Do you want (some/any) chalk?*
2. *There's the meat.*	*We'll eat (some) meat.*
3. *Here's the change.*	*You have (some) change.*

Note: *Some* or *any* before a feminine singular noun is *de + la*.

C. Before singular nouns beginning with a vowel:

	Def. Article	Noun		Part. Article	Noun
1.	L'	argent.	Il me faut	de l'	argent.
2.	L'	eau.	Il lui faut	de l'	eau.
3.	L'	essence.	Il nous faut	de l'	essence.

1. *The money.*   *I need (some) money.*
2. *The water.*   *He needs (some) water.*
3. *The gas.*   *We need (some) gas.*

Note: *Some* or *any* before all singular nouns beginning with a vowel is *de l'*.

D. Before *all* plural nouns:

	Def. Article			Part. Article	
1.	Les	places?	Je vais chercher	des	places à l'orchestre.
2.	Les	pro- grammes?	J'ach- èterai	des	programmes pour tous.
3.	Les	acteurs?	Vous allez voir	des	acteurs qui sont excellents.

1. *The seats?*   *I'm going to get some*
                                   seats in the
                                   orchestra.

| 2. *The programs?* | *I'll buy (some) programs for everybody.* |
| 3. *The actors?* | *You're going to see (some) actors who are excellent.* |

Note: "Some" or "any" before most plural nouns either masculine or feminine, is *des* (contraction of *de + les*). Exceptions to this rule are discussed in Sections E and F below.

E. With negative sentences:

Subject	Negative Verb	Partitive Article	Noun
1.	Ne veut-elle pas	de	fromage?
2. Non, elle	ne veut pas	de	fromage.
3. Nous	ne mangeons pas	d'	escargots.
4. Il	ne nous faut pas	d'	essence.
5. Je	n'acheterai pas	de	programmes.

1. *Doesn't she want some cheese?*

2. *No, she doesn't want any cheese.*

3. *We aren't eating (any) escargots (snails).*

4. *We don't need any gas.*

5. *I won't buy (any) programs.*

Note: "Some" or "any" in a negative sentence is *de (d')* alone, without a definite article. Notice that this holds true before *all* nouns, masculine and feminine, singular and plural.

F. Plural Partitive Nouns Preceded by Adjectives

Study:

Contrast

	de + article	Noun		de	Adjective	Noun
1. J'ai	des	places.	J'ai	de	bonnes	places.
2. Elle à	des	robes.	Elle a	de	belles	robes.
3. J'ai	des	amis.	J'ai	d'	autres	amis.
4. J'ai lu	des	livres.	J'ai lu	de	bons	livres.

1. *I have (some) seats.* *I have (some) good seats.*
2. *She has (some) dresses.* *She has (some) beautiful dresses.*
3. *I have (some) friends.* *I have (some) other friends.*
4. *I've read (some) books.* *I've read (some) good books.*

Note: If the noun, of whatever gender or number, is preceded by an adjective, use only *de* or *d'*.

III. *Imperative forms with pronouns*

Study:

Contrast

1. Pertmettez-moi   1. *Permit me*
2. Excuse-toi   2. *Excuse yourself*
3. Pardonnez-moi   3. *Pardon me*
4. Excusez-nous   4. *Excuse us*
5. Parlons-lui   5. *Let's speak to him*

1. Ne me permettez pas ...	1. *Don't permit me ...*
2. Ne t'excuse pas	2. *Don't excuse yourself*
3. Ne me pardonnez pas	3. *Don't pardon me*
4. Ne nous excusez pas	4. *Don't excuse us*
5. Ne lui parlons pas	5. *Let's not speak to him*

IV. *Verbs conjugated with être*

Auxiliary être	Past Participle
1. Estes-vous	allés?
2. Est-elle	partie?
3. Sont-ils	arrivés?
4. Sont-elles	restées?

1. *Did you go?* (*Have you gone?*)

2. *Did she leave?* (*Has she left?*)

3. *Did they arrive?* (*Have they arrived?*)

4. *Did they stay?* (*Have they stayed?*)

NOTES

1. About fifteen verbs are conjugated with *être* instead of *avoir* in compound tenses. The most important are (a) intransitive verbs of action: aller, *to go;* venir, *to come;* arriver, *to arrive;* partir, *to leave;* entrer, *to enter;* sortir, *to go out;* mounter, *to go up;* descendre, *to go down;* tomber, *to fall;* retourner, *to return;* and (b) verbs which express a change of state: naître, *to be born;* mourir, *to die;* rester, *to remain;* devenir, *to become.*

2. Compounds of the verbs above, e.g., rentrer, *to come back home,* and revenir, *to come back,* are also conjugated with *être.*

3. These verbs agree with the *subject* in number (singular and plural) and gender (masculine or feminine). Remember that **vous** may be singular or plural and masculine or feminine. Examples:

Ah, vous êtes arrivé, M. Lewis.
Ah, vous êtes arrivés, messieurs.

4. Study these contrasts:

   a. Elle *est* montée. *She went up.*
      Elle *a* monté les bagages. *She took up the bags.*
   b. Elle *est* sortie. *She went out.*
      Elle *a* sorti le chien. *She took the dog out.*

5. Verbs conjugated with *avoir* agree *only* with a preceding direct object. Contrast:

   a. Elle a acheté les livres. *She bought the books.*
   b. Elle les a achetés. *She bought them.*
   c. Elle lui a donné les livres. *She gave him the books.*
      (In this example, *livres* is the direct object, whereas *lui* is the indirect object.)

DRILLS AND EXERCISES

I. Replace *seulement* by *ne...que* in each of the following sentences. Write the complete sentence, say aloud, and translate.

Example: J'ai *seulement* des places séparées./Je *n'*ai *que* des places séparées.

1. Elle a *seulement* deux sœurs.

2. Ils ont *seulement* quatre pièces.

3. Elle veut *seulement* ton bonheur.

4. Nous avons *seulement* un peu d'argent.

II. Expand the following sentences by placing *bons* or *bonnes* before the noun. Make the necessary change in the form "des." Say and translate.

   Example: J'ai *des* amis./J'ai *de bons* amis.
   1. Vous avez des idées.
   2. J'ai lu des livres.
   3. Nous avons vu des films.
   4. J'ai mangé des frites.
   5. Elle a écrit des lettres.

III. Transform the following to the *negative*.

   Example: Parlez-moi./Ne me parlez pas.
   1. Pardonne-lui.
   2. Regardons-les.
   3. Ecoutez-nous.
   4. Excusez-la.
   5. Lève-toi.

IV. Substitute each of the words in parentheses for the italicized word in the model sentence. Write and say each new sentence.

   1. Nous sommes *entres*. (partis, arrivés, venus, restés, tombés)

   2. Elle est *sortie*. (partie, devenue riche, restée, née, montée)

V. Transform the following sentences to the *past*. (Make sure the past participle agrees with the subject.) Say and translate the new sentences.

   Example: Nous *arrivons* / Nous *sommes arrivés*.
   1. Elle descend.
   2. Ils viennent.
   3. Elles partent.
   4. Nous restons.
   5. Vous entrez.

VI. Translate the following sentences into French, then say them aloud.

1. We want only seats in the center.

2. There are only seats on the side.

3. We have good plays in (à) Paris.

4. We have fine symphonic works.

5. We have some other seats.

6. Don't show me the program.

7. (*présenter*) Introduce us to Michael.

8. Give him the money. Don't give him the money.

9. Today he is leaving at nine o'clock.
   Yesterday he left at nine o'clock also.

10. Today you are remaining without saying (*sans dire*) a word.
    Yesterday you remained without saying a word also.

11. She is pleased to see the actors.

12. We are happy to go to the theatre.

13. They enjoy watching TV (*regarder la télé*).

} (Use *se plaire*)

14. I'll have the time to do it.

15. Will have have the chance (*l'occasion*) to do it?

16. What interests me is the setting (*le décor*).

17. What interests me is the action.

18. As for him (*Quant à lui*), he likes the cartoons.

19. I'm sorry she has come.

20. Give me some sugar.

21. He has money.

22. We would like some apples.

23. Go to the market, because we don't have any milk.

24. He has bought very good shoes.

Answers at back of book.

QUIZ

From among the three choices, select the one which best renders the English word or phrase given at the beginning of each sentence. Write the complete sentence, and translate.

1. *(on the side)* Quatre places, pas trop _____.
    (a) à côté
    (b) de côté
    (c) du côté

2. *(good seats)* J'ai encore _____.
    (a) bonnes places
    (b) des bonnes places
    (c) de bonnes places

3. *(to)* Quel plaisir _____ vous revoir.
    (a) de
    (b) à
    (c) pour

4. *(suits)* La couleur vous _____ à merveille.
    (a) suit
    (b) complète
    (c) va

5. *(Permit me)* _____, Charles.
    (a) Me permet
    (b) Permettez-me
    (c) Permettez-moi

6. *(This way)* _____, s'il vous plaît.
    (a) Ce chemin
    (b) Cette route
    (c) Par ici

7. *(What a crowd!)* _____
    (a) Que de monde!
    (b) Quel de monde!
    (c) Que monde!

8. *(Truthfully)* _____, il me plaît.
   (a) Le vrai
   (b) A vrai dire
   (c) Vraiment dire

9. *(It's)* _____ la deuxième chaîne.
   (a) C'est
   (b) Elle est
   (c) Est

10. *(Let's hurry)* _____, alors!
    (a) Laissons vite
    (b) Passons rapide
    (c) Dépêchons-nous

Answers at back of book.

LESSON 49

AU MUSÉE DU LOUVRE
AT THE LOUVRE MUSEUM

1. Employé: **Un franc° chacun, s'il vous plaît.**
   One franc each, please.

2. Charles: **Voici, monsieur.** *(En aparté à Jeanne)*
   **Nous aurions dû venir dimanche. L'entrée est
   gratuite le dimanche.**
   Here you are, sir. *(Aside to Jane)* We should
   have come Sunday. Admission is free on Sundays.

3. Guide: **Monsieur, puis-je vous suggérer une
   visite guidée ou une visite-conférence?**
   Sir, may I suggest a guided tour or a lecture
   tour?

4. Jeanne: **Moi, j'aimerais une visite avec guide.
   Mon mari se connaît en peinture, mais...**

I'd like a guided tour. My husband is knowledgeable about painting, but . . .

5. Charles: **Je ne suis qu'un peintre du dimanche.°**

   I'm only a Sunday painter.

6. Guide: **Vous trouverez ici bien de l'inspiration. Le Louvre° est probablement le musée d'art le plus riche du monde. C'est l'ancienne demeure des rois de France.**

   You will find plenty of inspiration here. The Louvre is probably the richest museum in the world. It's the former residence of the kings of France.

7. Jeanne: **Quelles sont les choses les plus intéressantes à voir?**

   What are the most interesting things to see?

8. Guide: *Je vous ferai voir* rapidement les **antiquités, les sculptures, et les objets d'art . . .**

   I'll show you the antiquities, the sculptures, and the art objects quickly . . .

9. Jeanne: **Regardez! Enfin je vois de près la Vénus de Milo. C'est ma statue préférée.**

   Look! At last I'm seeing the Venus de Milo at close range. It's my favorite statue.

10. Guide: **Vous n'êtes pas la seule à l'admirer. Regardez à droite, et vous verrez la Victoire de Samothrace, qui est également bien connue.**

    You are not the only one to admire it. Look to the right, and you will see the Winged Victory, which is equally well known.

11. Charles: **C'est formidable. On voit dans ces salles toute l'histoire de l'antiquité grecque et romaine.**

It's magnificent. You see in these rooms the entire history of Greek and Roman antiquity.

12. Jeanne: **En effet . . . bustes et statues, sarcophages, frises, bas-reliefs . . .**
That's so . . . busts and statues, sarcophagi, friezes, bas-reliefs . . .

13. Guide: **On voit des sculptures de toutes les grandes époques. On voit représentés le Moyen Age, la Renaissance, le dix-septième siècle . . .**
You see sculptures of all the great periods. You see represented the Middle Ages, the Renaissance, the seventeenth century . . .

14. Charles: **Les meubles anciens sont aussi à voir.**
The antique furniture is also worth seeing.

15. Guide: **Oui, on peut admirer les chefs-d'œuvre du mobilier, de l'orfèvrerie, de la tapisserie. Regardez aussi les bronzes, les ivoires, et les bijoux de la couronne de France.**
Yes, you can admire the masterpieces of furniture, goldsmiths' work, tapestry. Look at the bronzes, the ivories, and the French crown jewels, also.

16. Jeanne: **Que de richesses! Mais où sont les salles de peintures?**
What riches! But where are the paintings?

17. Guide: **Par ici. Comme vous allez le voir, *il y a des peintures* classiques et modernes, gouaches, aquarelles, huiles, ainsi que des gravures, des eaux-fortes . . .**

This way. As you will see, there are classical
and modern paintings, gouaches, watercolors,
oils, as well as engravings, etchings...

18. Charles: **Et de tous les genres aussi—
paysages, natures-mortes, nus...**
And of all kinds too—landscapes, still lifes,
nudes...

19. Guide: **Suivez-moi, s'il vous plaît, dans la
Grande Galerie.** *Je vous ferai voir* **une toile
que vous reconnaîtrez...**
Follow me, please, into the Great Gallery. I'll
show you a canvas that you will recognize...

20. Charles: **Ah! La Joconde,° de Léonard de
Vinci! Qu'elle est bien exposée! Que la lumière est extraordinaire!**
Ah! La Gioconda, by Leonardo da Vinci! How
well it is displayed! How extraordinary the
light is!

21. Guide: **C'est une des œuvres maîtresses de
tous les temps.** *Il y a des gens* **qui restent
émerveillés devant cette peinture pendant
des heures entières.**
This is one of the greatest works of all time.
Some people stay for hours before this painting, filled with wonder.

22. Jeanne: **Mais où sont les tableaux de l'école
impressionniste? Je ne les vois nulle part.**
But where are the pictures of the Impressionist
School? I don't see them anywhere.

23. Guide: **Pour les impressionnistes, il faudra
aller au musée du Jeu de Paume,° qui fait
partie du Louvre.**
For the Impressionists, it will be necessary to
go to the Jeu de Paume Museum, which is part
of the Louvre.

24. Jeanne: **Allons-y tout de suite. Nous reviendrons au Louvre un autre jour.**
Let's go there right away. We'll come back to the Louvre another day.

25. Charles: **Dépêchons-nous. Je voudrais surtout voir les tableaux des pointillistes.**
Let's hurry. I'd especially like to see the paintings of the Pointillists.

26. Jeanne: **Moi, je n'aime pas beaucoup les pointillistes. Je préfère les cubistes.°**
I don't like the Pointillists very much. I prefer the Cubists.

27. Guide: **Suivez-moi. Je vous montrerai où se trouve le Jeu de Paume. Il est à deux pas d'ici, dans le Jardin des Tuileries.°**
Follow me. I'll show you where the Jeu de Paume is. It's nearby, in the Tuileries Garden.

28. Charles: **Merci de votre amabilité. Nous vous chercherons la prochaine fois.**
Thank you for your kindness. We'll look for you next time.

29. Jeanne: **Mais, où est-ce qu'on trouve les Toulouse-Lautrec,° les Degas,° les Matisse,° et *les autres peintres dont on entend toujours parler?***
But where does one find the Toulouse-Lautrecs, the Degas, the Matisses, and the other painters whom we hear about so much?

30. Charles: **On en trouverait sûrement ici. Mais ne les cherchons pas maintenant. J'en ai assez de musées pour le moment.**
We'd find some here surely. But let's not look for them now. I've had enough of museums for the time being.

NOTES

1. There is a small admission fee to museums except on Sundayus.

5. *un peintre du dimanche:* lit., a Sunday painter, that is, one for whom painting is a hobby.

6. The Louvre Museum, one of the largest in the world, is on the Right Bank. As will be noted in the dialogue, it is known to most people for its painting of the Mona Lisa and the statues of the Venus de Milo and the Winged Victory, or "Nike."

20. The Mona Lisa is known as La Joconde (in Italian, La Gioconda), because of her famous enigmatic smile.

23. The Jeu de Paume Museum, in the Tuileries Gardens, was formerly a tennis court. It now houses a famous collection of Impressionist paintings.

26. Cubism: a school of modern painting which flourished in France from 1910 to 1930.

27. *Jardin des Tuileries:* part of the former residence of French kings. The formal gardens were designed by Le Nôtre, one of the most famous French landscape architects, who also planned the gardens of Versailles.

29. Toulouse-Lautrec: a nineteenth-century painter noted for his colorful portrayals of Parisian night life.
Degas: Impressionist painter of the late nineteenth and early twentieth century, noted for his paintings of ballet dancers.
Matisse: twentieth-century French artist famous for his decorative paintings and use of color.

GRAMMATICAL ITEMS FOR SPECIAL STUDY

I. *Faire* + *infinitive*

Study:

Subject	Indirect Obj. Pro.	faire	Infinitive	
1. Je	vous	ferai	visiter	le musée.
2. Je	lui	ferai	voir	La Joconde.
3. Il	nous	a fait	connaître	ses amis.
4. Nous	leur	avons fait	savoir	la nouvelle.

1. *I'll show you around the museum. (I'll have you visit the museum).*

2. *I'll show him the Mona Lisa. (I'll have him see the Mona Lisa).*

3. *He had us become acquainted with his friends. (He had us meet his friends.)*

4. *We told them the news. (We had them informed of the news.)*

NOTES:

1. The *indirect object pronoun* is used when the subject is *not* having something done to himself. (Refer to Lesson 47 on the "Coiffeur" for contrasting uses of the reflexive *se faire* followed by an infinitive.)

2. Remember that the reflexive verb *se faire* uses *être* in compound tenses, whereas nonreflexive *faire* takes *avoir*.

II. *Il y a—there is, there are*

Study:

Il y a	Sing. or Plu. Noun	Adjective	Complement
1. Il y a	des gens		qui restent...
2. Il y a	un livre	intéressant	sur la table.
3. Il y a	une peinture		dans la Grande Galerie.

1. *There are people who stay...*
2. *There is an interesting book on the table.*
3. *There is a painting in the Great Gallery.*

Note: *Il y a* is used for singular and plural nouns as an equivalent for *there is* or *there are* in an unstressed statement of fact. Contrast with *voilà* (there is, there are), which is used to point to something or someone. Contrast:

Il y a un livre sur la table.	Voilà le livre de M. Lewis.
There's a book on the table.	**There's** *Mr. Lewis' book.*
Il y a deux comédiens dans la pièce.	Voilà les deux comédiens.
There are two actors in the play.	**There are** *the two actors.*

III. *Aller + y*

Study:

Contrast

Verb-y	N'/y	Verb	pas
1. Allons-y.	N'y	allons	pas.
2. Vas-y.	N'y	va	pas.
3. Allez-y.	N'y	allez	pas.

1. *Let's go there.*   *Let's not go there.*
2. *Go there* (fam.   *Don't go there.*
   sing.)
3. *Go there* (polite and   *Don't go there.*
   plu.)

Note: Vas-y and allez-y are used colloquially as equivalents of "go ahead" and "go to it."

IV. *Dont—about whom, of whom, whose, of which, about which*

Study:

Noun (Sing. or Plu.)	dont	Subject	Clause
1. Les autres peintres	dont	on	entend parler...
2. Le tableau	dont	je	t'ai parlé...
3. La femme	dont	j'	ai fait la connaissance...
4. La femme	dont	le fils	est dans la classe . . .

1. *The other painters whom we hear about (about whom we hear people speak)* ...

2. *The picture about which I spoke to you* ...

3. *The woman whose acquaintance I made* (lit., *of whom I made the acquaintance*) ...

4. *The woman whose son is in the class* ...

Notes:

1. *Dont* precedes the *subject* of the subordinate clause.

2. It is invariable.

3. *Dont* may be replaced by *de qui* (for persons) or *de* plus the appropriate form of *lequel* (for persons or things). Compare the following sentences with examples given in the chart above.

Example 1. Les autres peintres *de qui* (or *desquels*) on . . .
Example 2. L'homme *de qui* (or *duquel*) je . . .
Example 3. La femme *de qui* (or *de laquelle*) . . .

4. *Lequel* and its variants[1] are used to avoid ambiguity when it is not clear which person is referred to. Study and contrast:

Le fils de la femme *auquel* j'ai parlé.
The son of the woman to whom I spoke.
(The masculine *auquel* indicates you spoke to the son.)

Le fils de la femme *à laquelle* j'ai parlé.
The son of the woman to whom I spoke.
(The feminine *à laquelle* indicates you spoke to the woman.)

[1]which, whom	to which, whom	of which, whom, whose
masc. lequel	auquel	duquel
fem. laquelle	à laquelle	de laquelle
plu. lesquel(le)s	auxquel(le)s	desquel(le)s

DRILLS AND EXERCISES

I. Substitute each of the words or expressions in parentheses for the italicized word or expression in the model sentence. Write the complete sentence and say aloud.

   A. Il *me* fera visiter le Louvre. (te, lui, nous, vous, leur)

   B. Nous vous avons fait *voir* le livre. (lire, acheter, comprendre, connaître, apprécier)

   C. Il y a *un livre* sur la table. (un stylo à bille, un cahier, une plume, des assiettes, des four-chettes)

   D. *L'homme* dont j'ai entendu parler... (la femme, les garçons, le livre, la pièce, la pein-ture, le musée)

II. Expand the expressions below by placing *Il y a* in front of each. Say the entire sentence, then write it.

   Example: une femme à la porte/*il y a* une femme à la porte.

   1. quatre peintures au mur

   2. vingt personnes dans la salle

   3. des garçons devant l'école

   4. de la bonne viande chez le boucher

   5. du sucre dans le placard

III. Transform the following sentences from *affirmative* to *negative,* say, write, and translate.

   1. Vas-y.   3. Il y va.
   2. Allez-y.   4. Il y est allé.

5. Nous y sommes   6. Elles y sont allées.
   allés.

IV. Replace *de* + the *relative pronoun* by *dont* in the following sentences, and translate.

1. L'homme *de qui* je t'avais parlé est arrivé.

2. La femme *de laquelle* j'avais fait la connaissance hier s'appelle Mme. Dupont.

3. Les hommes *desquels* j'avais entendu parler sont partis pour Paris.

4. Les femmes *desquelles* vous connaissez les fils ont aussi des filles.

5. Le livre *duquel* vous avez besoin n'est pas à la bibliothèque.

V. Translate the following sentences into French; then say them aloud.

1. She'll have you visit the Louvre.

2. We'll have him see the paintings.

3. I'll have them look at the statues.

4. There's the Opera! There's also a beautiful *(un bel)* Opera in Milan.

5. There's the Place de la Concorde! There's also a beautiful square *(une belle place)* in Rome.

6. There's the Louvre! There's also a beautiful museum in New York.

7. Here are the *objets d'art* of which he spoke to you.

8. Here are the sculptures of which they spoke to him.

9. Here are the paintings of which she spoke to them.

10. Here are the masterpieces of which we spoke to you.

11. There are the painters whom we always hear about.

12. There are the Impressionists whom I always hear about.

13. My wife is knowledgeable about music.

14. I am knowledgeable about books.

VI. Translate the following dialogue:

I'd like to go to the Louvre.
Let's go there right away.
Where are the paintings?
I'd also like to see the statues.
Look! There are the masterpieces!

Answers at back of book.

QUIZ

From among the three choices, select the one which correctly renders the English word or phrase given at the beginning of each sentence, write the complete sentence, and translate.

1. (*each*) un franc _____, s'il vous plaît.
   (a) l'un
   (b) chacun
   (c) chaque

2. (*We should have*) _____ venir dimanche.
   (a) Nous devons
   (b) Nous avons dû
   (c) Nous aurions dû

3. (*knows about*) Mon mari _____ peinture.
   (a) se connaît en
   (b) se connaît autour
   (c) sait de

4. (*One can admire*) _____ les
   chefs-d'œuvre.
   (a) On doit admirer
   (b) On sait admirer
   (c) On peut admirer

5. (*Follow me*) _____, s'il vous plaît.
   (a) Conduisez-moi
   (b) Venex-moi
   (c) Suivez-moi

6. (*How well displayed it is!*) _____ (la
   peinture)
   (a) Comment bien exposée elle est!
   (b) Qu'elle est bien exposée!
   (c) Qu'elle est bien exposé!

7. (*nowhere*) Je ne les vois _____.
   (a) dans aucun lieu
   (b) partout
   (c) nulle part

8. (*right way*) Allons-y _____.
   (a) tout de suite
   (b) à droit
   (c) tout suite

9. (*I prefer*) _____ le cubisme.
   (a) Je préfère
   (b) Je préfére
   (c) Je prefer

10. (*Let's not look for them*) _____
    maintenant.
    (a) Ne laissons chercher
    (b) Ne les regardons pas
    (c) Ne les cherchons pas

Answers at back of book.

LESSON 50

LES PRODUITS DE L'ARTISANAT; LA PEINTURE
HANDICRAFTS; PAINTING

A. *On décide d'aller au Marché aux Puces*
   We decide to go to the Flea Market

1. Jeanne: **Nous avons si souvent entendu parler du Marché aux Puces.° Qu'est-ce que c'est?**
   We've heard about the Flea Market so often. What is it?

2. Michel: **C'est un grand marché en plein air ...c'est-à-dire,° *ce sont plusieurs petits marchés qui se suivent...où l'on*° peut acheter des objets d'occasion,° comme des meubles, des bibelots, ou des antiquités.**
   Of course! It's a large open-air market, that is, several markets one after the other...where you can buy secondhand things like furniture, knickknacks, or antiques.

3. Jeanne: **Il y aura donc *des choses qui pourraient* nous intéresser, et peut-être même *quelque chose que nous pourrions* acheter, n'est-ce pas,° Charles? Tu te connais en objets d'art. Si on y allait, tous les trois?°**
   Then there will certainly be things which could interest us, and perhaps even something we could buy, don't you think so, Charles? You know art objects. Suppose the three of us went?

4. Charles: **Volontiers! Allons-y!**
   Willingly! Let's go!

5. Michel: **Jeanne, il faudra enlever vos bagues, et porter vos habits les plus vieux!**
Jane, you'll have to take off your rings, and wear your oldest clothes.

6. Jeanne: **Pourquoi?**
Why?

7. Michel: **Il ne faut pas avoir l'air trop riche, vous savez.**
One mustn't look too rich, you know.

B. *On arrive au Marché aux Puces*
We arrive at the Flea Market

8. Jeanne: **Ah! Voilà *une cafetière qui est bien jolie*. C'est combien, madame?**
Oh! There's a coffeepot that's very pretty. How much is it, ma'am?

9. Marchande: **Soixante-dix francs. C'est du Limoges,° madame.**
Seventy francs. It's Limoges porcelaine, madam.

10. Michel: *(En aparté)* **N'oubliez pas qu'il ne faut pas tout croire, et qu'il faut marchander.°**
(Aside) Don't forget that you mustn't believe everything, and that you must bargain.

11. Jeanne: **Oui, en effet, c'est du Limoges. Je vous offre cinquante-cinq francs.**
Yes, as a matter of fact, it is Limoges. I'll give you fifty-five francs.

12. Marchande: **Madame, *c'est la plus jolie cafetière* sur l'étagère...Remarquez ce *beau dessin du bord qui est tout fait à la main...***

Madam, it's the prettiest coffeepot on the shelf
. . . Notice this beautiful border design, which
is all done by hand . . .

13. Jeanne: **Vous me la laissez à soixante francs?**
Will you give it to me for sixty francs?

14. Marchande: **Va pour° soixante-cinq francs!
Allez! Prenez-la!**
Sold for sixty-five francs. Go on! Take it!

15. Jeanne: **Michel,** *je me demande où se trouvent* **les stands de bibelots et de faïence . . .**
Michael, I wonder where the knickknack and
pottery stands are . . .

16. Michel: **Là, au bout de cette allée, à gauche,
je crois . . .**
There, at the end of that passage, to the left, I
think . . .

17. Jeanne: **Attendez! Regardez en face! Les
beaux meubles de style!**
Wait! Look across the way! The beautiful
period furniture!

18. Charles: **Regardez cette magnifique bergère
Louis XV . . .** *celle qui est recouverte* **de tapisserie genre Aubusson°** *. . . Elle est de loin la
plus belle* **de toutes . . .**
Look at that magnificent Louis XV easy chair
. . . the one which is upholstered in Aubusson-
style tapestry . . . It's by far the most beautiful
of all . . .

19. Jeanne: **De toutes les bergères, peut-être.
Mais moi, je préfère ce canapé Louis XVI,**
celui qui est sculpté et doré . . .
Of all the easy chairs, maybe. But I prefer the
Louis XVI sofa, the one which is carved and
gilded . . .

20. Charles: **Si on achetait les deux?**
What about buying both of them?

21. Jeanne: **Ne sois pas trop impulsif, Charles. Nous avons à peine assez d'argent pour en acheter une!**
Don't be too impulsive, Charles. We have hardly enough money to buy one (of them)!

C. *Dans une galerie d'art*   In an art gallery

22. Charles: **Pardon, monsieur. Est-ce que vous exposez en ce moment les toiles de Paillac?**
Pardon me, sir. Are you showing the canvases of Paillac at present?

23. Marchand: *Celui qui a gagné* **un diplôme d'honneur l'année dernière?**
The one who won an honor certificate last year?

24. Charles: **Lui-même.°**
That's the one.

25. Marchand: **Oui, monsieur. Il nous en reste encore quelques-unes.[1] Des peintures à l'huile, seulement. Des gouaches, . . . eh bien, nous n'en avons point.**
Yes, sir. We still have a few left. Oil paintings only. Gouaches . . . well, we haven't any at all.

26. Charles: **Nous cherchons un tableau d'assez grande taille.**
We're looking for a rather large picture.

27. Marchand: **En grande taille, nous n'avons que des natures-mortes. Veuillez m'accompagner au fond de la galerie pour que je puisse vous les montrer.**
In a large size, we have only still lifes. Please come with me to the rear of the gallery so that I can show them to you.

[1]Although the masculine form has been used on the recording, the feminine form is properly used here.

28. Charles: **En voilà une¹ aux couleurs brillantes. Le bleu du premier plan contraste avec le rouge du fond.**
Here is one with brilliant colors. The blue of the foreground contrasts with the red of the background . . .

29. Marchand: **La¹ toile de gauche est meilleure que celle de droite. Il y a une harmonie de mouvement qui me plaît beaucoup.**
The canvas at the left is better than the one at the right; there is a harmony of movement which I like very much.

30. Charles: **Et *celle du milieu est la meilleure* de toutes, à mon avis. Elle doit être très chère.**
And the one in the middle is the best of all, in my opinion. It must be very expensive.

31. Marchand: **Les tableaux de Paillac, de cette taille, se vendent à deux mille cinq cents (2500) francs.**
The pictures by Paillac, in this size, sell for 2500 francs [about $500].

32. Charles: **Ah, oui? C'est bien trop cher pour moi.**
Oh, yes? That's much too expensive for me.

33. Marchand: **Vous savez bien dés qu'un peintre a gagné un prix...Je vous conseille d'aller à Montmartre.° Vous y trouverez certainement un peintre encore inconnu qui sera content de vous vendre quelque chose à meilleur marché.**

¹Although the masculine form has been used on the recording, the feminine form is properly used here.

You know how it is, as soon as a painter has
won a prize . . . I advise you to go to Montmartre. You'll certainly find a painter there
who is still unknown and who'll be happy to
sell you something cheaper.

34. Charles: **Merci, monsieur. Vous avez été
    bien aimable.**
    Thank you, sir. You've been very kind.

NOTES

1. *Marché aux Puces:* a tourist attraction (also
   frequented by many Frenchmen) where one
   can find antiques of all kinds.

2. *c'est-à-dire:* lit., "that is to say." Another
   equivalent might be "I mean."
   où l'on: This expression is used in fairly formal French usage. In colloquial French, you
   will more often hear *où on.*
   occasion: may also mean "on sale," when
   referring to new things; a "bargain."

3. *n'est-ce pas:* an expression literally meaning
   "isn't it?" whose actual English equivalent
   changes, depending upon the sentence to
   which it is attached or the utterance which has
   just been made. Examples:

Tu es malade, n'est-ce pas?	You're sick, *aren't you?*
Vous êtes allé au marché, n'est-ce pas?	You went to the market, *didn't you?*

Vous viendrez, n'est-ce pas?	You'll come, *won't you?*
Speaker 1. *C'est très joli.*	It's very pretty.
Speaker 2. *N'est-ce pas?*	It certainly is, *isn't it?*

Si on y allait, tous les trois! could also be translated as "What about the three of us going?"

9. *Limoges:* the name of a famous, expensive porcelain made in the city of Limoges, about 200 miles southwest of Paris. The city of Sèvres, near Versailles, is another well-known center for porcelain.

10. *marchander:* "Bargaining" is part of the fun, and is expected.

14. *Va pour:* an expression to indicate that something (usually a selling price) has been agreed upon or settled for.

18. *Aubusson:* the name of the town well known for the manufacture of tapestries. Other fine tapestries are made at Beauvais and at the Manufacture des Gobelins in Paris.

24. *lui-même:* literally, "he himself."

33. *Montmartre:* a hill on the Right Bank in Paris. The top of the hill is the Butte Montmartre. It is the site of the Sacré-Cœur Basilica as well as a favorite haunt and working place of amateur artists. When people refer to art or artists, they generally use the terms *La Butte* and *Montmartre* interchangeably.

GRAMMATICAL ITEMS FOR SPECIAL STUDY

I. *Relative pronoun—qui: who, which, that, used as subject*

Study:

Relative Subordinate Clause

Sing. or Plu.	Qui as subject	Verb	Comple-ment	
1. La dame	qui	vend	la cafetière	veut trop d'argent.
2. La bergère	qui	est recouverte de soie		est jolie.
3. Les hommes	qui	arrivent		sont mes cousins.
4. Les bateaux	qui	traversent l'océan		sont grands.
5. Je connais la dame	qui	vend	la cafetière.	

1. *The lady (who is) selling the coffeepot wants too much money.*

2. *The easy chair (which is) covered with silk is pretty.*

3. *The men (who are) arriving are my cousins.*

4. *The boats which cross the ocean are big.*

5. *I know the lady (who is) selling the coffeepot.*

NOTES

1. The relative clause may be embedded in a sentence (Ex. 1, 2, 3, 4) or it may come at the end of the sentence (Ex. 5).

2. The relative pronoun must be expressed in French. In English it is often omitted.

II. *Relative pronoun—que: whom, which, that, used as object*

Study:

Relative Subordinate Clause

	Que as Object	Sub.	Verb	Comple-ment	
1. Le marchand	que	vous	voyez	là-bas	est aveugle.
2. Le canapé	que	je	voudrais acheter		est trop cher.
3. Les toiles	que	j'	aime		sont toutes de Degas.
4. Les hommes	que	j'	ai connus		sont tous morts.
5. Je voudrais acheter les choses	que	j'	ai vues	•	hier.

1. *The merchant (whom) you see over there is blind.*
2. *The sofa (which) I'd like to buy is too expensive.*
3. *The canvases (which) I like are all by Degas.*
4. *The men (whom) I knew are all dead.*
5. *I'd like to buy the things (that) I saw yesterday.*

NOTES

1. See notes 1 and 2 above, for *qui*.
2. The past participle of the relative clause agrees with the antecedent of *que* in number and gender. (Study examples 4 and 5 above.)

III. *Relative pronoun—où: on which, in which, at which, where*

Study:

	où	Subject, etc.
1. Le stand	où	on vend la porcelaine . . .
2. La maison	où	je suis né(e) . . .

1. *The stand at which (where) they sell porcelain . . .*

2. *The house in which (where) I was born . . .*

IV. *Superlatives*

Study:
A.

	Deter-miner	plus/moins	Adject-ive	de	
1. C'est[1]	mon	plus	grand		souci.
2. C'est	la	moins	jolie		robe.
3. Elle est de loin	la	plus	belle	de	toutes.
4. C'est	le	plus	vieux	de	tous les hommes.

1. *It's my biggest worry.*

2. *It's the least pretty dress.*

3. *It's by far the most beautiful of all.*

4. *He's the oldest of all the men.*

[1]The contrast between *c'est* and *il (elle) est* is discussed in Lesson 60.

B.

	Noun	Deter-miner	plus/moins	Adject-ive
1. C'est	la peinture	la	plus	intér-essante.
2. C'est	l'homme	le	moins	aimable.
3. Ce sont	mes amies	les	plus	riches.

1. *It's the most interesting painting.*

2. *He's the least amiable man.*

2. *They are my richest friends.*

NOTES

1. The superlative of the adjective is formed by placing a determiner (definite article: le, la, les) or possessive (mon, notre, etc.) before *plus* or *moins*.

2. *De* is placed *after* the superlatives and *in front of* a noun or pronoun to express *in, of, among.* (See Example A.4)

3. Irregulars are:

	Comparative	Superlative
bon *(good)*	meilleur	le meilleur
mauvais *(bad)*	pire	le pire
petit *(small—in importance)*	moindre	le moindre

NOTES

1. Remember that in the superlative, the determiner agrees with the noun in number and gender.

2. As we know, adjectives agree with the nouns they describe (see V below, however).

3. *Pire* is used primarily in a moral sense.

V. *Colors modified by other adjectives or nouns*

Study:

	Color	Modifier
1. Elle avait des yeux	bleu	ciel.
2. Elle avait un manteau	jaune	paille.
3. Elle portait une jupe	vert	foncé.
4. Elle avait deux robes	bleu	vert.
5. Elle a acheté une robe	marron	clair.

1. *She had sky-blue eyes.*

2. *She had a straw-colored coat.*

3. *She was wearing a dark-green skirt.*

4. *She had two blue-green dresses.*

5. *She bought a light-brown dress.*

Note: Adjectives of color modified by another adjective or noun *do not* agree with the nouns they modify or describe.

DRILLS AND EXERCISES

I. Substitute each word in parentheses for the italicized word in the model sentence. Write the complete sentence and say aloud.

A. Ce tableau est le plus *beau* de l'exposition. (recherché, abstrait, surréaliste, remarquable, original, réaliste)

B. Nous voulons acheter vos toiles les plus *récentes*. (originales, brillantes, coûteuses, chères)

C. Sur un fond bleu, le peintre a mis des fleurs *bleues*. (blanches, jaunes, rouges, roses, violettes)

D. L'homme qui arrive est mon *père*. (frère, cousin, fils, ami, oncle, grand-père)

E. La porcelaine que j'ai *achetée* est belle. (vue, admirée, remarquée)

F. *Le magasin* où je vais est près d'ici. (l'école, la maison, l'église, la bibliothèque, le cinéma)

II. In the sentence "La maison qui *j*'ai vendue est belle," replace *je* by the other subject pronouns (tu, il, elle, nous, vous, ils, elles). Make all necessary verb changes.

III. Translate the following sentences into French; then say them aloud.

1. The merchant who sells the coffeepot is nice.

2. The lady who is buying the furniture is my wife.

3. The merchant (whom) you see is nice.

4. The lady (whom) we like is here.

5. The clothes (which) I'm wearing are old.

6. The rings (which) you have are beautiful.

7. It's the longest passage in the market.

8. It's the richest canvas in the gallery.

9. He's the most interesting man in Paris.

10. It's the best design in the collection.

11. It's the oldest picture in the collection.

12. There will be (some) furniture at the market.

13. There will be (some) paintings at the gallery.

14. It will be necessary to bargain.

15. It will be necessary to wear old clothes *(de vieux habits)*.

16. She looks *(a l'air)* elegant.

17. Do I look rich? (use *Est-ce que*)

18. They don't look nice *(sympathique)*.

19. *(se demander)* I wonder if he has a sofa.

20. One wonders if they have any paintings.

21. We wonder if you have any *objets d'art*.

22. I'd like to see it close up.

23. I'd like to see it from far.

24. She wants to see it from here.

25. You'll find it at the end of the passage *(allée,* fem.).

26. You'll find it opposite the gallery.

27. Will I find it at the corner of the street? (use *Est-ce que*)

28. Show me a sky-blue easy chair.

29. There's a dark green sofa.

30. I'd like a light red tapestry.

31. Do you prefer the tapestry on the right?

32. I prefer the canvas in the middle.

33. She prefers the tapestry on the left.

Answers at back of book.

QUIZ

From among the three choices, select the one which correctly renders the English word or phrase given at the beginning of each sentence, write the complete sentence, and translate.

1. *(heard)* Nous avons si souvent _____ du Marché aux Puces.
   (a) entendu
   (b) écouté parler
   (c) entendu parler

2. *(all three of us)* Si on y allait _____?
   (a) tous trois de nous
   (b) les trois nous
   (c) tous les trois

3. *(that we could buy)* Il y aura quelque chose _____.
   (a) que nous pourrions acheter
   (b) que nous pouvions acheter
   (c) que nous avons pu acheter

4. *(look)* Il ne faut pas _____ trop riche.
   (a) regarder
   (b) chercher
   (c) avoir l'air

5. *(bargain)* Il faut _____
   (a) marchander
   (b) marcher
   (c) acheter

6. *(across the way)* Regardez _____
   (a) à travers le chemin
   (b) en face
   (c) en traversant la route

7. *(Don't be)* _____ trop impulsif.
   (a) N'êtes pas
   (b) Ne soyez pas
   (c) Ne faites pas être

8. *(the one who)*[man] _____ a gagné un diplôme . . .
   (a) Le qui
   (b) Il qui
   (c) Celui qui

9. *(a few)* [toiles] Il nous reste encore _____.
   (a) un quelque
   (b) quelques-uns
   (c) quelques-unes

10. *(must be)* Elle _____ très chère.
    (a) doit être
    (b) peut être
    (c) faut être

Answers at back of book.

LESSON 51

ON FAIT DES PHOTOGRAPHIES
WE TAKE PICTURES

A. *On se prépare*   Getting ready

1. Charles: **Tu es prête? Rappelle-toi, c'est aujourd'hui que nous avons décidé de revoir
   nos endroits préférés et *d'en faire des photos.*°**
   Are you ready? Remember, it's today that we
   decided to see our favorite places again and to
   take some pictures of them.

2. Jeanne: **Mais bien sûr!** *Tu as assez de pellicules* **pour les appareils?°**
Of course! Have you enough film for the cameras?

3. Charles: **Oui, je crois, mais je voudrais passer par un magasin de photographie°** *pour 'en°* *acheter davantage°* **et** *pour demander quelques conseils.*°
Yes, I think so, but I'd like to stop by a camera shop to buy still more [of it] and to ask for some advice.

4. Jeanne: **Rappelle-toi qu'il nous faut des inversibles°** **pour les diapositifs et quelques films pour la caméra.**
Remember that we need some slide film for the transparencies and some film for the movie camera.

5. Charles: **Tu préfères les films en couleurs ou en noir et blanc? Les films en couleurs sont tellement chers.**
Do you prefer color film or black and white? Color film is so expensive.

6. Jeanne: *Il nous en faudra* **au moins deux en couleurs.**
We'll need at least two (of them) in color.

7. Charles: **Tu as raison. Je voudrais me souvenir°** **toujours des couleurs vives et gaies des cafés des Champs-Elysées.°**
You're right. I'd like to remember always the bright gay colors of the cafés on the Champs-Elysées.

8. Jeanne: **Et moi, je voudrais fixer° pour toujours les toiles des artistes sur la Place du Tertre.° Je voudrais des films, des diapositifs, et quelques instantanés de tous les endroits que nous aimons.**

And I'd like to capture forever the canvases of
the artists on the Place du Tertre. I'd like some
movie film, some transparencies (slides), and a
few snapshots of all the places we like.

B. *Dans le magasin de photographie*   In the camera
shop

9. Charles: **Avez-vous des pellicules—des
négatifs°—pour cet appareil?**
Do you have any film—print film—for this
camera?

10. Employé: **Laissez voir,° s'il vous plaît . . . En
noir et blanc ou en couleurs?**
Let me see it, please . . . In black and white or
in color?

11. Charles: **Deux rouleaux de chacun, s'il vous
plaît.**
Two rolls of each one, please.

12. Employé: **Les voici. C'est un très bon appareil que vous avez là.**
Here they are. That's a very good camera you
have there.

13. Charles: **Oui. *J'en suis très satisfait.* Donnez-
moi aussi deux rouleaux d'inversibles pour
cet appareil-ci, s'il vous plaît.**
Yes. I'm very happy with it. Let me also have
two rolls of transparency film for this camera,
please.

14. Employé: **De vingt ou de trente-six poses?°**
Twenty or thirty-six exposures?

15. Charles: **De trente-six, s'il vous plaît. Veuillez aussi donner un coup d'œil° à cet appareil allemand?**
Thirty-six, please. Would you also please take
a look at this German camera?

16. Employé: *Qu'est-ce qui ne va pas?*
    What's the trouble? (lit.: What's not going?)

17. Charles: **Quelquefois, quand j'appuie sur le déclencheur, il reste engagé.°**
    Sometimes, when I press on the release, it sticks.

18. Employé: **Je connais bien ce modèle. Il ne faut jamais presser le bouton trop longtemps. Enlevez tout de suite votre doigt.**
    I know this model well. You must never press the button for too long a time. Take your finger off it right away.

19. Charles: **Ah! Merci beaucoup, monsieur. Je voudrais aussi une douzaine de flashcubes° et deux paquets de lampes-éclair.°**
    Ah! Thank you very much, sir. I'd also like a dozen flashcubes and two packages of flash-bulbs.

20. Employé: **Y a-t-il autre chose? Non? Alors, je vais vous envelopper tout cela. Bonne chance!**
    Is there anything else? No? Then I'll wrap all this up for you. Good luck!

C. *A l'Arc de Triomphe*   At the Arch of Triumph

21. Jeanne: **Nous voici à l'Arc de Triomphe.° Je voudrais une vue panoramique de l'Etoile. N'oublie pas de débarrer l'objectif.**
    Here we are at the Arch of Triumph. I'd like a panoramic view of the Etoile. Don't forget to uncap the lens.

22. Charles: **Ne t'en fais pas.° Je reviens tout de suite. Mets-toi là devant le Drugstore.° Ainsi on te verra dans la photo.**

Don't worry. I'll be right back. Stand over
therre, in front of the Drugstore. That way,
you'll be in the picture.

D. *A la Place de la Concorde* At the Place de la
Concorde

23. Jeanne: **Prends maintenant quelques vues
des Champs-Elysées de l'autre bout. Atten-
tion! Ne prends pas les voitures. Attends que
le feu passe au rouge.**
Now take some shots of the Champs-Elysées
from the other end. Watch out! Don't get the
cars in. Wait until the traffic light changes to
red.

24. Charles: **C'est magnifique. Je vois parfaitement tous les cafés, les kiosques, les arbres
jusqu'à l'Arc de Triomphe.**
This is wonderful. I see perfectly all the cafés,
the newspaper stands, the trees, up to the Arch
of Triumph.

E. *A la Place du Tertre* At the Place du Tertre

25. Jeanne: **Charles, mets-toi ici. Je voudrais le
Sacré-Cœur° et ces deux restaurants.**
Charles, stand here. I'd like the Sacré-Cœur
and these two restaurants.

26. Charles: **Bien. Mais attends que je recharge
l'appareil. Ah! La lumière commence à
changer. Je ferais mieux d'employer le pose-
mètre.**
Fine. But wait until I reload the camera. Oh!
The light is beginning to change. I'd better use
the light meter.

27. Jeanne: **Tu ne l'as pas employé pour les
autres prises de vue?**
You didn't use it for the other shots?

28. Charles: **Ne t'en fais pas. Il y a quinze ans que° je fais des photos sans pose-mètre, et je les ai toujours réussies.**
Don't worry. I've been taking pictures for fifteen years without a light meter, and I've always had them turn out well (lit.: I have always succeeded with them).

29. Jeanne: **Sois° sûr de prendre ces artistes. J'aime bien leurs peintures à l'huile.**
Be sure to get these artists into the picture. I like their oil paintings.

30. Charles: **Moi aussi. Et j'espère que nous pourrons faire developper les clichés pendant que nous sommes en route.**
So do I. And I hope we'll be able to have the negatives developed while we're traveling.

31. Jeanne: **Et nous ferons faire plusieurs épreuves des meilleurs *pour envoyer* à nos amis.**
And we'll have several prints made of the best ones to send our friends.

32. Charles: **Peut- être même des agrandissements aussi.**
Maybe even some enlargements too.

33. Jeanne: **Pourvu que tu n'aies pas raté les photos.**
Provided you haven't spoiled the pictures.

34. Charles: **Allons donc! Tu sais bien que je suis un bon photographe.**
Come now! You know very well that I'm a good photographer.

NOTES

1. *photos:* customary short form for *photographies* (fem.)

2. *appareil:* the general term for *appareil photographique,* any still camera. A movie camera is *une caméra* (see 4 in the text) or sometimes *un appareil cinématographique.*

3. Photographic equipment and supplies of all kinds are readily available in France. Those imported from other countries, however, are naturally quite expensive.
   en: of it; of them. In this case, *en* refers to *pellicules.*
   davantage: more, still more of something already mentioned.
   conseils: Notice that "advice," which is always used in the singular in English, can be plural in French.

4. *inversibles:* reversible film for transparencies or slides.

7. *se souvenir: se souvenir* and *se rappeler* both mean "to remember." When you use *se souvenir.* you must use *de* before the object. Example: Je me souviens *de* votre nom. (I remember your name.) But: Je me rappelle votre nom.
   Champs-Elysées: lit., the Elysian Fields. A beautiful wide avenue in Paris extending from the Place de la Concorde to the Place de l'Etoile (where the Arch of Triumph is located).

8. *fixer:* fixer dans la mémoire = to preserve in one's memory.
   la Place du Tertre: a celebrated gay, colorful square in Montmartre where restaurants, painters, and tourists abound.

9. *des négatifs:* refers to film that makes prints only, in contrast to *inversibles* from which transparencies can also be made.

10. *Laissez* [-moi le] *voir:* Note colloquial ommission of *-moi le.*

14. *vingt, trente-six poses:* reference to the number of exposures in a roll of film for still cameras.

15. *un coup d'œil:* a glance. *Donner un coup d'œil à* or *jeter un coup d'œil sur* (to give or to throw a glance upon) means *to glance at.*

16. *ne va pas: aller* and *marcher* are used colloquially for "to work," "to run," "to function." Example: *Mon horloge ne marche pas.* My clock isn't working.

17. *engagé:* or . . . *il reste bloqué.*

19. *flashcubes:* another example of "franglais." *lampes-éclair:* in "franglais" this would be *lampes-flash.*

21. *Arc de Triomphe:* Arch of Triumph. A large arch in the center of the Place de l'Etoile, under which is found the Tomb of the Unknown Soldier.

22. *ne t'en fais pas:* lit., "don't make anything of it." *S'en faire* is used casually for "to worry." *le Drugstore:* an elegant French fantasy of what an American drugstore is like, located on the Champs-Elysées. There are now several American-type drugstores in Paris. Before the influx of American influence, *les pharmacies* sold only drugs.

25. *Sacré-Cœur:* This basilica is a spectacular example of Byzantine style architecture which

dominates Montmartre and can be seen from almost anywhere in Paris.

28. *Il y a quinze ans que:* lit., "it is fifteen years that . . ." This very common time expression is discussed in Lesson 59.

29. *sois:* be. Familiar imperative of *être* (See the *être* forms in the *Irregular Verb Charts*).

GRAMMATICAL ITEMS FOR SPECIAL STUDY

I. *en—some of it; some of them; of it; of them*

Study:

Contrast

1. J'ai acheté *des* robes. — J'*en* ai acheté.

2. Je voudrais *de la* viande. — J'*en* voudrais.

3. J'ai beaucoup *d'argent.* — J'*en* ai beaucoup.

4. Il m'a donné *trois livres.* — Il m'*en* a donné trois.

5. Ne me donnez pas *de pommes.* — Ne m'*en* donnez pas.

6. Donnez-moi *des pommes.* — Donnez-m'*en.*

1. *I bought some dresses.* — *I bought some (of them).*

2. *I'd like some meat.* — *I'd like some (of it).*

3. *I have a lot of money.* — *I have a lot (of it).*

4. *He gave me three books.* — *He gave me three (of them).*

5. *Don't give me any apples.* — *Don't give me any (of them).*

6. *Give me some apples.* — *Give me some (of them).*

NOTES

1. The partitive construction (*de* + definite article + noun), discussed in Lesson 48, is replaced by *en* when the noun, when it is "partitioned," is not specifically mentioned, but is only implied. See examples 1, 2, 5, 6 above. Study, in the above examples, the position of *en* in the sentence.

2. When the sentence ends with a *number* or an *adverb of quantity,* the sentence must contain *en.* (See Examples 3 and 4 above.)

3. *En* is never omitted in French, but in many expressions, *en* need not be translated into English, particularly when the word or expression to which it refers is clear. Examples:

Combien de livres avez-vous?	*How many books do you have?*
J'**en** ai trois.	*I have three.*
Il n'**en** reste que des natures-mortes.	*We only have still lifes left.* (lit.: No more of them [paintings] are left than still lifes.)

4. *En* is invariable.

5. Even when the noun to which *en* refers is feminine or plural, there is *no* agreement of the past participle. (See Examples 1 and 4 above.)

6. *En* precedes the verb of which it is the object, *except* in *affirmative requests,* e.g., Donnez-en à Charles. *Give some to Charles.*

II. *Assez de—enough*

Study:

	assez	de	Noun (Sing. or Pl.)
1. J'ai	assez	de	films.
2. Il a mangé	assez	de	viande.
3. Nous n'avons pas	assez	d'	argent.

1. *I have enough film.*

2. *He ate enough meat.*

3. *We don't have enough money.*

III. *Qu'est-ce qui—what* (lit.: What is it that)

Study:

Qu'est-ce qui	Verb
1. Qu'est-ce qui	ne va pas?
2. Qu'est-ce qui	arrive?
3. Qu'est-ce qui	s'est passé?

1. *What's wrong? (What "isn't going"?)*

2. *What's happening?*   Notice the *two* French
3. *What happened?*   equivalents of
                               "What's
                               happening?" or
                               "What's going on?"

NOTES

1. The interrogative form *qu'est-ce qui* is used as a *subject*.

2. It refers only to *things*.

3. It always *begins* a sentence.

IV. *Pour + infinitive = to; in order to*

Study:

	pour	Pron.	Infinitive
1. Il faut manger	pour		vivre.
2. On doit prendre le train	pour	y	aller.
3. Je suis arrivé de bonne heure	pour	les	voir.
4. Allez au grand magasin	pour	en	acheter.

1. *It is necessary to eat (in order) to live.*

2. *One must take the train (in order) to go there.*

3. *I arrived early (in order) to see them.*

4. *Go to the department store (in order) to buy some.*

DRILLS AND EXERCISES

I. Substitute each of the words in parentheses for the italicized word in the model sentence. Write the complete sentence, say aloud, and translate.

   A. J'en ai *acheté,* (demandé, cherché, trouvé, mangé, regardé)

   B. Il a assez de *films.* (rouleaux, appareils [watch the d'], inversibles, diapositifs, photos)

   C. Allez au magasin pour en *acheter.* (voir, trouver, chercher, admirer, essayer)

II. Expand the expressions below by placing *Qu'est-ce qui* in front of each. Write the complete sentence and say it aloud.

1. _____ se passe?

2. _____ ne marche pas?

3. _____ vous ennuie?

4. _____ est arrívé?

5. _____ l'inquiète?

III. Replace the italicized expression by *en*. Say and write the entire new sentence and translate. Example: Il faut faire *du travail.*/Il faut *en* faire.

1. J'ai acheté *des robes*.

2. Je voudrais *du pain*.

3. Nous avons assez *de viande*.

4. Il m'a donné quatre *livres*.

5. Prêtez-moi *des chaussettes*.

IV. Translate the following sentences into French; then say them aloud.

1. Photos? He took several of them.

2. I'd like four of them.

3. Don't give me any film; I have enough.

4. Do you have enough film for the camera?

5. Yes, but there's not enough light.

6. What's on the table?

7. What's going to happen?

8. What's bothering you? *(ennuyer)*

9. In order to learn, one must understand.

10. I don't have enough money to buy this film.

11. Do you have to take a plane to get there?

Answers at back of book.

QUIZ

From among the three choices, select the one which best renders the English word or phrase given at the beginning of each sentence. Write the complete sentence, and translate.

1. (*enough*) tu as _____ inversibles?
   (a) assez d'
   (b) assez de
   (c) assez des

2. (*in*) Je voudrais des films _____ noir et blanc.
   (a) en
   (b) dans
   (c) dedans

3. (*at least*) Il nous en faudra _____ deux.
   (a) à moins
   (b) moins
   (c) au moins

4. (*remember*) Je voudrais _____ des couleurs.
   (a) se souvenir
   (b) me souvenir
   (c) rappelle-toi

5. (*Here they are*) _____.
   (a) Voici les sont
   (b) Les voici
   (c) Ici ils sont

6. (*in the*) Je l'ai acheté _____ Etats-Unis.
   (a) dans les
   (b) dans l'
   (c) aux

7. (*a glance*) Veuillez aussi donner _____ à
   cet appareil?
   (a) un cherche
   (b) un regard
   (c) un coup d'œil

8. (*anything else*) Y a-t-il _____?
   (a) autre chose
   (b) quoi d'autre
   (c) rien d'autre

9. (*up to*) Je vois _____ l'Arc de Triomphe.
   (a) haut à
   (b) jusqu'à
   (c) monte à

10. (*I'd better*) _____ d'employer le
    pose-mètre.
    (a) Je mieux
    (b) Je fais meilleur
    (c) Je ferais mieux

Answers at back of book.

LESSON 52

AGENCE DE VOYAGES
TRAVEL AGENCY

A. *On demande des renseignements* Asking for
information

   1. Employé: **Bonjour, monsieur, 'dame. En quoi
      puis-je vous être utile?**
      Good day, sir, madam. How can I help you?

   2. Charles: **Nous voudrions voyager un peu *en
      France, en dehors de Paris*. Pourriez-vous
      suggérer quelques itinéraires?**

We'd like to travel a little in France, outside of
Paris. Could you suggest some itineraries?

3. Employé: **Avec plaisir. Comment pensiez-
vous faire le voyage? Je vous conseille de
louer une voiture. C'est de loin le meilleur
moyen de voir notre pays.** *En auto,* **vous
pouvez aller n'importe où,**° *en Bretagne,*° *en
Provence*° ...

With pleasure. How did you intend to make the
trip? I'd advise you to rent a car. It's by far the
best way to see our country. By car you can go
anywhere (lit.: no matter where), to Brittany, to
Provence ...

4. Charles: **Nous pensions faire d'abord quelques petits tours aux alentours de Paris.** *A
Fontainebleau,*° **par exemple.**

We were thinking of taking a few little trips in
the areas surrounding Paris first. To Fontainebleau, for example.

5. Employé: **Il y a un très bon autocar qui part
pour Fontainebleau plusieurs fois par jour.**

There is a very good bus that leaves for Fontainebleau several times a day.

6. Jeanne: **Et pour Chartres° et Versailles?°**

And for Chartres and Versailles?

7. Employé: **Vous pouvez y aller** *en chemin de
fer.* **Il n'y aura pas de problèmes pour les
billets. Et ensuite?**

You can go there by train. There will be no
problem about the tickets. And what else? (lit.:
And then?)

8. Charles: **Nous voudrions voir la Bretagne, les
châteaux de la Loire,° et la Côte d'Azur.**

We'd like to see Brittany, the châteaux of the
Loire, and the Riviera.

9. Employé: **Vous avez parfaitement raison. Comme cela vous verrez un peu de campagne, un peu de plage, et quelques beaux monuments historiques.**

   You are absolutely right. That way you will see a little country, a little beach, and some fine historic monuments.

10. Charles: **Nous traverserons Nîmes,° Arles,° et Aix-en-Provence,° je crois, en allant *à la Côte d'Azur.*°**

    We'll go through Nîmes, Arles and Aix-en-Provence, I believe, on the way to the Riviera.

11. Employé: **Cela fera un très bon voyage. Avec une voiture et une bonne carte routière, vous pourrez vous arrêter où vous voudrez.**

    That will make a very good trip. With a car and a good road map, you'll be able to stop wherever you wish.

12. Jeanne: **Nous voulions aussi voyager *en Italie* et *dans la Suisse française.*° Mais mon mari préfère aller d'abord *en Espagne* et *au Portugal.***

    We also wanted to travel in Italy and French-speaking Switzerland. But my husband prefers to go to Spain and Portugal first.

13. Employé: **Vous ferez ces voyages *en avion,* sans doute. Vous gagnerez° ainsi beaucoup de temps.**

    You'll no doubt make those trips by plane. You will save a lot of time that way.

14. Charles: **Non, je crois que nous préférons prendre le train pour aller *à Madrid.* Demain je passerai au bureau de la S.N.C.F.° pour prendre des renseignements.**

No, I believe we prefer to take the train to go to
Madrid. Tomorrow, I'll stop in at the office of
French Railways to get some information.

15. Employé: **Mais pas du tout. Nous faisons
    tout cela pour vous ici. Voici un horaire.
    Prenez-le pour vérifier les heures de départ
    et d'arrivée. Il y a un très bon train qui part
    à sept heures et demie. Mais il y en a
    d'autres aussi.**
    No, indeed. We do all that for you here. Here's
    a timetable. Take it to check departure and
    arrival times. There's a very good train that
    leaves at seven thirty. But there are others,
    also.

16. Jeanne: **Si vous permettez, nous allons étu-
    dier l'horaire, la carte, et un calendrier ce
    soir, et nous reviendrons demain.**
    If you don't mind, we'll study the timetable,
    the maps, and a calendar this evening, and
    we'll come back tomorrow.

B. *Le lendemain*   The next day

17. Employé: **Ah, bonjour. Alors, qu'est-ce que
    vous avez décidé?**
    Oh, hello. So, what have you decided?

18. Charles: **Voyons. Nous voudrions deux bil-
    lets d'autocar pour Fontainebleau pour de-
    main matin.**
    Let's see. We'd like two bus tickets for Fon-
    tainebleau for tomorrow morning.

19. Jeanne: **Et deux billets de chemin de fer pour
    Versailles pour dimanche matin. On nous a
    dit qu'on peut voir les jeux d'eau seulement
    les dimanches.**

And two railway tickets for Versailles for Sunday morning. We were told that we can see the fountains playing only on Sundays.

20. Employé: **Oui, c'est juste. On peut les voir aussi tous les jours de fête ... Et après?**
Yes, that's correct. You can also see them on all holidays ... And then what?

21. Charles: **Nous avons décidé de louer une voiture mardi matin pour faire le petit tour de France dont nous avons parlé.**
We've decided to rent a car Tuesday morning to take the little trip around France we spoke about.

22. Jeanne: **Voudriez-vous bien nous retenir des chambres d'hôtel? J'ai ici la liste des villes que nous voulons visiter.**
Would you please reserve hotel rooms for us? I have a list here of the cities that we want to visit.

23. Charles: **Nous voulons passer deux jours** *au* **Mont-Saint-Michel°** et **un jour** *à* **Saint-Malo.°**
We want to spend two days in Mont-Saint-Michel and one day in Saint-Malo.

24. Employé: **Vous avez bien choisi. Je vois ici Chambord, Chenonceaux, et Amboise. Où préférez-vous passer la nuit? Vous trouverez Chenonceaux magnifique.**
You've made a good choice. I see here Chambord, Chenonceaux, and Amboise. Where do you prefer to spend the night? You'll find Chenonceaux magnificent.

25. Jeanne: **Chenonceaux, alors.** *Pensez-vous que nous puissions aller* **directement** *à Arles?*

Chenonceaux, then. Do you think we can go
directly to Arles?

26. Employé: **Si vous y tenez absolument, vous
pourriez le faire, mais c'est un peu long.**
If you insist on it, you could do it, but it's a
rather long distance.

27. Charles: **Qu'est-ce que vous suggérez?**
What do you suggest?

28. Employé: **Vous pouvez passer un jour à
Lyon.° Aionsi vous verrez les paysages aux
bords du Rhône.° La campagne là est une
des plus belles de toute la France, à mon
avis.**
You can spend a day in Lyons. That way you'll
see the scenery in the Rhone Valley. The
countryside there is one of the most beautiful
in all France, in my opinion.

29. Charles: **J'ai entendu dire qu'il y a de très
bons vins *dans cette région*.**
I've heard that there are some very good wines
in that region.

30. Jeanne: **Les vins ne m'intéressent pas, mais
la plage, si. Nous voudrions passer au moins
trois jours *à Cannes*.**
Wines don't interest me, but the beach does.
We'd like to spend at least three days in
Cannes.

31. Charles: **Et comme nous voulons passer la
plupart de notre temps sur la plage, nous
voudrions un hôtel qui donne directement
sur la mer.**
And since we want to spend most of our time
on the beach, we'd like a hotel facing the sea
(lit.: that gives directly on the sea).

32. Employé: **Je vais m'occuper de tout cela cet après-midi. J'ai de bons amis à Cannes qui vous trouveront tout ce qu'il vous faut ... Et pour le voyage *en Espagne?***

    I'll take care of all that this afternoon. I have good friends in Cannes who will find you everything you need. And for the trip to Spain?

33. Jeanne: **Nous pensons le faire aussi *en voiture.***

    We intend to do it by car also.

34. Charles: **Comme cela, on verra d'autres régions de la France ... et en route on goûtera aussi les bons vins de Bordeaux.**

    In that way, we'll see other regions of France ... and on the way we'll also taste the good Bordeaux wines.

NOTES

3. *n'importe où:* no matter where; *n'importe quoi,* no matter what; *n'importe qui,* no matter who.

   Bretagne, Provence: former provinces of France. (Although the present administrative unit of France is the *département,* the ancient provinces have kept their identities.) The cities and towns of Bretagne (Brittany), in the northwestern part of France, and Provence, in the southeast, contain many tourist attractions.

4. *Fontainebleau:* a small town near Paris noted for a beautiful château and its surrounding large forests. The art school in Fontainebleau is highly regarded.

6. *Chartres:* a small town near Paris with a Gothic cathedral whose stained glass windows are considered among the most beautiful in the world.

Versailles: the former palace of French kings, built by Louis XIV, noted particularly for its formal gardens, its fountains, and its Hall of Mirrors. The treaty ending World War I was signed there.

8. *Les châteaux de la Loire:* The banks of the Loire River—the longest river in France—are lined with Renaissance castles. The most famous are Chenonceaux, Amboise, Chambord, and Azay-le-Rideau.

10. *Nîmes, Arles, et Aix-en-Provence:* cities in Provence, where one may still see vestiges of Roman architecture.
    la Côte d'Azur: the French Riviera (lit., "the Azure Coast"). This area includes such famous resort cities as Cannes, Nice, and Saint Tropez.

12. *Suisse française:* French-speaking Switzerland is also referred to as *la Suisse romande.*

13. *gagnerez: gagner,* to win, to gain. Also "to earn," as in *gagner de l'argent,* to earn money; *gagner sa vie,* to earn one's living.

14. *S.N.C.F.:* the initials of *Societé Nationale des Chemins de Fer Français,* the French national railway.

23. *Saint-Malo:* a fishing town in Brittany, destroyed during World War II, and now completely restored to its original state.
    Mont-Saint-Michel: a monastery in the northwestern part of France dating from the twelfth century, built on a small island. It has been linked to the mainland by a causeway since 1875.

28. *Lyon:* a large city (the third largest in France) about 300 miles southeast of Paris, noted for silk and related industries.

le Rhône: a river in southeastern France, which the Saône River joins at Lyons. It flows into the Mediterranean.

GRAMMATICAL ITEMS FOR SPECIAL STUDY

I. *Prepositions en, à, dans with place names*

Study:

A.	en	Feminine Countries, Provinces, Continents
Je voudrais voyager	en	France.
	en	Bretagne.
	en	Suisse.
	en	Amérique.

I'd like to travel **to** *or* **in** *France, Brittany, Switzerland, America.*

B.	à + Art.	Masculine Countries and Provinces
1. Il demeure	au	Portugal.
2. Il ira	au	Canada.
	au	Languedoc.
	aux	Etats-Unis.

1. *He is living* **in** *Portugal, Canada, Languedoc* (a province in southeastern France), *the United States.*

2. *He will go* **to** *Portugal, Canada, Languedoc, the United States.*

C.	à	Cities
1. Nous voudrons aller	à	Fontainebleau.
2. Nous resterons	à	Chartres.
	à	New-York.
	à	Londres.

1. *We'll want to go* **to** *Fontainebleau, Chartres, New York, London.*

2. *We'll stay* **in** *Fontainebleau, Chartres, New York, London.*

D.	dans	Place	Modifier
1. Il va	dans	l'Amérique	du Sud.
2. Il travaille	dans	la Suisse	française.
	dans	le Canada	français.

1. *He is going* **to** *South America, French Switzerland, French Canada.*

2. *He is working* **in** *South America, French Switzerland, French Canada.*

NOTES

1. All continents are feminine.

2. Place names ending in *e* are feminine except for *le Mexique.*

3. Cities are preceded by *à* alone. A notable exception is *au* Havre (*to* Le Havre).

4. *En* is used instead of *au* for masculine countries beginning with a vowel. Example: Nous allons *en* Israël. *We are going to Israel.*

II. *Preposition de with place names*

Study:

A.	de	Feminine Countries, Provinces, Continents
Il vient	de	France.
	de	Bretagne.
	d'	Amérique.

He comes **from** *France, Brittany, America.*

B.	de	Cities
Nous arriverons	de	New-York.
	de	Paris.
	de	Londres.

We'll arrive **from** *New York, Paris, London.*

C.	de + Art.	Masculine Countries and Provinces
Il revient	du	Portugal.
	du	Danemark.
	du	Japon.
	du	Languedoc.
	des	Etats-Unis.

He is coming back **from** *Portugal, Denmark, Japan, Languedoc, the United States.*

D.	de + Art.	Place	Modifier
Elle est arrivée	de l'	Amérique	du Nord.
	du	Canada	français.
	de la	Suisse	française.

She arrived **from** *North America, French Canada, French Switzerland.*

Note: Il revient *du* Havre. *He returns from Le Havre.*
Il revient *du* Mexique. *He returns from Mexico.*

III. *Prepositions with means of transportation*

Study:

A.	en	
Il voyage	en	autobus.
	en	avion.
	en	voiture.
	en	chemin de fer.
	en	bateau.

*He travels **by** bus, plane, car, rail, boat.*

B.	à	
Il aime se promener	à	pied.
	à	bicyclette.
	à	cheval.

*He likes to take a walk (to go **on** foot); to take a bicycle ride (**on** a bicycle); to take a horseback ride (**on** horseback).*

IV. *Subjunctive after the interrogative or negative of croire and penser*

Study:

A. Interrogative of croire and penser	que	Subjunctive	Complement
1. Croyez-vous	qu'	il soit	intelligent?
2. Pensez-vous	qu'	elle soit arrivée?	

1. *Do you believe (that) he's intelligent?*

2. *Do you think (that) she has arrived?*

B. Negative of croire and penser	que	Subjunctive	Complement
1. Je ne crois pas	qu'	il soit arrivé.	
2. Je ne pense pas	qu'	elle soit	riche.
3. Il ne croit pas	que	nous ayons	de l'argent.

1. *I don't believe (that) he has arrived.*

2. *I don't think (that) she is rich.*

3. *He doesn't believe (that) we have any money.*

DRILLS AND EXERCISES

I. Substitute each of the words or expressions in parentheses for the italicized word or phrase in the model sentence. Write the complete sentence and say aloud.

A. Il voudrait aller en *France*. (Amérique, Afrique, Provence, Asie, Europe, Angleterre)

B. Il doit aller à *Paris*. (Londres, New-York, Madrid, Buenos Aires, Genève)

C. Elle va toujours dans *l'Amérique du Sud*. (l'Amérique du Nord, l'Amérique Centrale, la Suisse française, l'Afrique du Sud)

D. Il est revenu hier de *New-York*. (Paris, Londres, France, Bretagne, Provence)

E. Elle aime voyager en *avion*. (autobus, voiture, chemin de fer, bateau)

F. Il voudrait faire une excursion à *pied*. (cheval, bicyclette)

II. Replace *je* by the other subject pronouns *(tu, il, elle, nous, vous, ils, elles)*. Make the necessary changes in the verb forms. Say and write the new sentences.

A. Croit-il que *je* sois stupide?

B. Il ne pense pas que *j'*aie de l'argent.

III. Translate the following sentences into French; then say them aloud.

1. They went to Italy last year.

2. There is a beautiful cathedral at Chartres.

3. In France, people *(on)* speak French.

4. We received a letter from French Canada.

5. She came back from Paris yesterday.

6. This wine comes from Portugal.

7. They always travel by car.

8. I returned home on foot.

9. I don't think she is very pretty.

10. Do you believe that he came yesterday?

11. I don't believe that they can do this.

Answers at back of book.

QUIZ

From among the three choices, select the one which correctly renders the English word or phrase given at the beginning of each sentence. Write the complete sentence, and translate.

1. *(outside of)* Je voudrais voyager _____ Paris.
   - (a) hors
   - (b) en dehors de
   - (c) loin de

2. *(anywhere)* Vous pouvez aller _____.
   - (a) n'importe où
   - (b) toute part
   - (c) toujours

3. *(by train)* Vous pouvez y aller _____.
   - (a) à train
   - (b) à chemin de fer
   - (c) en chemin de fer

4. *(road map)* J'ai besoin d' _____.
   - (a) une route carte
   - (b) une carte route
   - (c) une carte routière

5. *(a lot of time)* Vous gagnerez ainsi _____.
   - (a) grand temps
   - (b) un lot de temps
   - (c) beaucoup de temps

6. *(What)* _____ vous avez décidé?
   - (a) Qu'est-ce que
   - (b) Que
   - (c) Quoi

7. *(on Sundays)* On peut voir les jeux d'eau seulement _____
   - (a) dimanches
   - (b) sur dimanches
   - (c) les dimanches

8. *(hotel rooms)* Voudriez-vous bien nous retenir des _____?
   - (a) hôtel chambres
   - (b) chambres d'hôtel
   - (c) pièces d'hôtel

9. *(If you insist)* _____, vous pourrez le
   faire.
   (a) Si vous tenez
   (b) Si vous en tenez
   (c) Si vous y tenez

10. *(There are)* _____ de très bons vins en
    Provence.
    (a) Il y a
    (b) Il y est
    (c) Voilà sont

Answers at back of book.

LESSON 53

VOITURES—LOCATION OU ACHAT
CARS—RENTAL OR PURCHASE

A. *Location d'une voiture*   Renting a car

1. Employé: **Bonjour, monsieur, 'dame. Qu'est-
   ce que vous désirez?**
   Good day, sir, ma'am. May I help you?

2. Charles: *Nous pensions louer une voiture.
   Quels sont les tarifs?*
   We were thinking of renting a car. What are the
   rates?

3. Employé: **Cela dépend du modèle que vous
   choisissez, monsieur. C'est pour vous deux?**
   That depends on the model that you choose, sir.
   It's for the two of you?

4. Jeanne: **Oui, mais nous avons beaucoup de
   bagages.**
   Yes, but we have a lot of baggage.

5. Employé: **La Simca° 1000 fera votre affaire,
   alors. Quatre places, quatre portières...**
   The Simca (model) 1000 will meet your needs,
   then. Four seats, four doors...

6. Charles: **Est-ce qu'un porte-bagages sera
   fourni gratuitement?**
   Will a baggage-rack be furnished free of
   charge?

7. Employé: **Oui, monsieur. Et pour la location, vous pouvez payer *par heure, par jour,*
   ou *par semaine.***
   Yes, sir. And as for the rental, you can pay by
   the hour, by the day, or by the week.

8. Jeanne: **Qu'est-ce qui est inclus dans le tarif?**
   What's included in the rate?

9. Employé: **L'huile, le graissage, les frais
   d'entretien normal—aussi l'assurance et
   toutes les taxes.**
   The oil, the lubrication, the costs of normal
   upkeep—also the insurance and all the taxes.

10. Charles: **L'essence et le kilométrage° ne sont
    pas compris?**
    Gas and mileage are not included?

11. Employé: **Le kilométrage est illimité, mon-
    sieur. Quant à l'essence, le Super ne coûte
    qu'un franc cinq (1,05)° le litre.°**
    Mileage is unlimited, sir. As for gas, "super"
    costs only 1 franc 5 (centimes) a liter.

12. Jeanne: **Et on aura combien de kilomètres
    par litre?**
    And how many kilometers will we get per
    liter?

13. Employé: **Au moins douze, madame. Comme vous voyez, cette voiture est très économique.**
    At least twelve, madam. As you see, this car is very economical.

14. Charles: **Nous payerons[1] quand nous rendrons la voiture, n'est-ce pas?**
    We pay when we return the car, don't we?

15. Employé: **Non, monsieur, le montant est payable à la prise en charge, et il y a aussi un dépôt remboursable de 150 francs.**
    No, sir, the total amount is payable when you take the car (lit., upon taking in charge), and there is also a deposit of 150 francs which is refundable.

16. Charles: **Et pour la livraison et la reprise de la voiture?**
    And for the delivery and pickup of the car?

17. Employé: **A Paris, il n'y a qu'un petit supplément de 5 francs. On vous la livre directement à l'hôtel.**
    In Paris, there's only a small supplementary charge of 5 francs. We deliver it to you right at the hotel.

18. Jeanne: **Mais si on la laisse ailleurs?**
    But if we leave it somewhere else?

19. Employé: **En ce cas-là, les frais de retour dépendent de la distance entre les lieux de location et d'abandon.**
    In that case, the charge for returning the car depends on the distance between the place you hire the car and the place you leave it.

---

[1]On the recording you will hear *payons*. However, *payerons* is correct.

20. Charles: *Qu'est-ce qu'il nous faut* comme papiers?

What do we need in the way of documents?

21. Employé: *Il ne vous faut qu'*un permis de conduire valable, monsieur. Nous fournissons tous les autres documents.

You need only a valid driver's license, sir. We furnish all the other documents.

B. *Achat d'une voiture* The purchase of a car/ Buying a car

22. Jeanne: *Nous pensions* peut-être *acheter* une auto en Europe.

We were thinking perhaps of buying a car in Europe.

23. Employé: Ce serait une bonne idée, madame. Même avec les frais de transport et les droits de douane, cela revient beaucoup moins cher.°

That would be a good idea, madam. Even with the costs of transportation and customs duties, it's much less expensive.

24. Charles: Les prix en Europe sont exempts d'impôts, n'est-ce pas?

The prices in Europe are tax-free (exempt from taxes), aren't they?

25. Employé: Oui, monsieur, et vous pouvez acheter la voiture comptant ou à crédit.

Yes, sir, and you can buy the car for cash or on credit.

26. Charles: Et si nous voulions la revendre plus tard?

And suppose we wanted to sell it later?

27. Employé: Les prix de rachat sont très avantageux, monsieur.

The resale prices are very favorable, sir.

28. Charles: **Est-ce que vous avez une voiture avec changement de vitesses automatique?**
   Do you have a car with automatic transmission?

29. Employé: **Certainement, monsieur. Nous en avons de tous les genres—voitures neuves et d'occasion ... Regardez cette brochure.**
   Certainly, sir. We have all kinds, new and used cars ... Look at this brochure.

30. Jeanne: **Oh, que celle-là est belle, cette décapotable! Et que la garniture d'intérieur est élégante!**
   Oh, how beautiful that one is, that convertible! And how elegant the upholstery is!

31. Employé: **Et elle fait jusqu'à cent cinquante kilomètres à l'heure, si vous aimez la vitesse! Voudriez-vous faire un essai? Je peux vous accompagner tout de suite.**
   And it does up to 150 kilometers an hour, if you like speed. Would you like to try it out? I can go with you right away.

32. Charles: **Il faudra que nous réfléchissions un peu. Nous reviendrons dans quelques jours.**
   We'll have to think it over a bit. We'll come back in a few days.

33. Employé: **Très bien, monsieur. Au revoir, monsieur, 'dame.°**
   Very well, sir. Good bye, sir, madam.

NOTES

5. *Simca:* a brand of French car. Some others are Citroën, Renault, and Peugeot. In France, cars are generally designated, not only by the name, but also by the model number (e.g., Simca 1000).

10. *kilométrage:* Distances are measured in kilometers. A kilometer is five-eighths of a mile.

11. *1,05 NF:* Nouveau Franc. This monetary unit (in 1985 worth about 11¢—nine to the dollar) has been in circulation since 1960. One NF, made up of 100 *centimes,* is equivalent to 100 AF *(Anciens Francs).* In recent years, the franc has been fluctuating between eight and ten francs to the dollar.
    litre: a measure of liquid capacity, a little over a quart. Gasoline is sold by the liter.

23. *revient beaucoup moins cher:* literally, "comes back (to you) much less expensive."

33. *Monsieur, 'dame:* colloquial expression commonly used when addressing a lady and gentleman together, or a group of men and women. You will also hear " *'Sieur 'dame.* "

GRAMMATICAL ITEMS FOR SPECIAL STUDY
I. *The interrogative pronoun quel*

Study:

Quel	être	
1. Quel	est	votre projet?
2. Quelle	est	sa nationalité?
3. Quels	étaient	ses conseils?
4. Quelles	sont	tes intentions?

1. *What is your plan?*

2. *What is his nationality?*

3. *What were his suggestions? (What was his advice?)*

4. *What are your intentions?*

II. *The interrogative adjective quel*

Study:

A. Quel	Noun	Verb
1. Quel	àge	avez-vous?
2. Quelle	heure	est-il?
3. Quels	livres	avez-vous lus?
4. Quelles	maisons	aimez-vous?

1. *How old are you?* (lit., *What age have you?*)

2. *What time is it?*

3. *What books have you read?*

4. *What houses do you like?*

Note: In Example A.3, the past participle agrees with *livres*, which is the preceding direct object. See Lesson 55.

B. Preposition	quel	Noun	
1. A	quel	moment	est-il arrivé?
2. Pour	quelle	raison	est-elle partie?
3. Avec	quels	amis	êtes-vous sortis?
4. De	quelles	histoires	parlez-vous?

1. *At what moment did he arrive?*

2. *For what reason did she leave?*

3. *With what friends did you go out?*

4. *Of what stories are you speaking?*

III. *par in expressions of time*

Study:

	par	Unit of time
1. Il y va deux fois	par	semaine.
2. Nous mangeons trois fois	par	jour.
3. Il paye les impôts une fois	par	an.

1. *He goes there twice a week.*

2. *We eat three times a day.*

3. *He pays (the) taxes once a year.*

IV. *Forms of falloir with indirect object pronoun*

Study:

	Ind. Obj. Pron.	falloir	Noun as Dir. Obj.
1. Il	me	faut	un livre.
2. Il	nous	faudra	deux billets.
3. Il	vous	faudra	de l'argent.
4. Il	lui	fallait	une nouvelle voiture.

1. *I need a book. (For me is necessary a book.)*

2. *We'll need two tickets. (For us will be necessary two tickets.)*

3. *You'll need some money. (For you will be necessary some money.)*

4. *He needed a new car. (For him was necessary a new car.)*

V. *penser + infinitive—to think of, to consider, to
    intend*

   Study:

	penser	Infinitive	
1. Que	pensez-vous	faire	demain?
2.	Je pense	voyager	en Italie.
3.	Nous avons pensé	louer	des chambres.

1. *What do you intend to do (are you thinking of
   doing) tomorrow?*

2. *I intend to travel (am considering traveling) in
   Italy.*

3. *We intended to rent (thought of renting) some
   rooms.*

DRILLS AND EXERCISES

I. Substitute each of the words in parentheses for the
   italicized word in the model sentence. Write the
   complete sentence and say aloud.

   A. Quelle est votre *ambition?* (idée, profession,
      nationalité, adresse, préférence)

   B. Quels livres *as-tu* lus? (a-t-il, a-t-elle, avez-
      vous, ont-ils, ont-elles)

   C. Elle pense *partir* demain. (rentrer, sortir, venir,
      téléphoner, commencer)

II. Complete the sentences below by placing *par jour*
    at the end of each one, and translate.

   A. Il mange trois fois

   B. Ils se voient deux fois

   C. Elles sortent une fois

D. Il me téléphone plusieurs fois

E. Nous les changeons une fois

III. Transform each of the following sentences according to the model:

J'ai besoin de cent francs./*Il me faut* cent francs.

A. *Nous avons besoin de* trois livres.

B. *Il a besoin d'*un ami.

C. *Ils ont besoin d'*argent.[1]

D. *Vous avez besoin de* conseils.[1]

E. *Elle a besoin de* sommeil.[1]

IV. Translate the following sentences into French; then say them aloud.

1. What's her question?

2. What's your problem?

3. What were his reasons?

4. Which dress do you prefer?

5. Which car did he buy?

6. What trip will they take?

[1]Remember that *de* is not followed by the definite article in *avoir besoin de*. However, *de* requires the article after *Il faut*.
Contrast: Il a besoin de médicament.⎫
        Il lui faut du médicament.⎭ He *needs medicine.*

7. I see her once a year.

8. Children go to school five days a week.

9. How many times a day do you eat?

10. I need a car for my work.

11. He needed money.

12. Do you need a new car?

13. She intended to work last night.

14. What do you intend to do Saturday?

15. I intend to go to the movies.

Answers at back of book.

QUIZ

From among the three choices, select the one which correctly renders the English word or phrase given at the beginning of each sentence, write the complete sentence, and translate.

1. (*the two of you*) C'est pour _____.
    (a) les deux de vous
    (b) deux de vous
    (c) vous deux

2. (*What*) _____ est inclus dans le tarif?
    (a) Quel
    (b) Quoi
    (c) Qu'est-ce qui

3. (*As for*) _____ l'essence, c'est trop cher.
    (a) Comme pour
    (b) Quant à
    (c) Quant pour

4. (*return*) Nous payerons quand nous _____ la voiture.
   - (a) rendrons
   - (b) rendons
   - (c) retournons.

5. (*elsewhere*) Mais si on la laisse _____?
   - (a) autre place
   - (b) d'ailleurs
   - (c) ailleurs

6. (*less expensive*) Cela revient _____.
   - (a) bon marché
   - (b) moins cher
   - (c) plus bon marché

7. (*for cash*) Vous pouvez l'acheter _____.
   - (a) cache
   - (b) comptant
   - (c) argent

8. (*secondhand*) Ce sont des voitures _____.
   - (a) d'occasion
   - (b) de deuxième main
   - (c) usées

9. (*try out*) Voudriez-vous _____?
   - (a) essayer le
   - (b) faire essayer
   - (c) faire un essai

10. (*a little*) Il faudra que nous y réfléchissions

    _____.
    - (a) peu
    - (b) un peu
    - (c) un petit

Answers at back of book.

LESSON 54

À LA STATION-SERVICE
AT THE SERVICE STATION

1. Mécanicien: **Bonjour, monsieur. Vous désirez?**
   Mechanic: Good day, sir. What can I do for you?

2. Charles: **Je ne sais pas, au juste. Quand j'appuie sur le démarreur, il y a un drôle de bruit° dans le moteur, un cognement.**
   I don't know exactly. When I press on the starter, there is a funny noise in the motor, a knocking.

3. Mécanicien: **Ce n'est peut-être qu'*une panne° sèche*. Avez-vous vérifilé le niveau d'essence?**
   Perhaps it's only that you're out of gas. Did you check the gas gauge?

4. Charles: **Je croyais en avoir encore quelques litres dans le réservoir.**
   I thought I still had a few liters (of it) in the tank.

5. Mécanicien: **Voyons . . . Non, c'est bien une panne d'essence. Combien de litres voulez-vous que *j'y mette?***
   Let's see . . . No, it really is out of gas. How many liters do you want me to put in?

6. Charles: **Faites le plein. Et donnez-moi aussi un bidon d'essence—en cas d'urgence, vous savez. *Nous allons faire un long voyage* à travers la France.**

Fill it up. And give me a can of gas, too, in case of emergency, you know. We're going to take a long trip through France.

7. Mécanicien: **C'est une excellente idée, monsieur. On ne trouve pas toujours de stations-service en route.**
That's an excellent idea, sir. You don't always find service stations along the way.

8. Charles: **Voudriez-vous aussi vérifier la pression? Je crois qu'il faut gonfler les pneus.**
Would you also check the air pressure? I think it's necessary to put air in the tires (the tires need inflating).

9. Mécanicien: **Volontiers, monsieur. Mais vous semblez avoir une crevaison du pneu avant.**
Gladly, sir. But you seem to have a puncture in the front tire.

10. Charles: **Comment! J'ai un pneu à plat!°**
What? I have a flat tire?

11. Mécanicien: **C'était probablement causé par un clou ou par un morceau de verre. Vous n'avez rien senti au volant?**
It was probably caused by a nail or by a piece of glass. Didn't you feel anything [while you were] at the wheel?

12. Charles: **Par moments, sur la route, je sentais la voiture qui dérapait un peu.**
Occasionally, on the road, I felt the car skid a little.

13. Mécanicien: **C'était ça, alors. *Je vais vous le changer.***
That was it, then. I'll change it for you.

14. Charles: **Il y a un pneu de rechange dans le coffre.**
There's a spare tire in the trunk.

15. Mécanicien: **Ah, bon!** *Je vais remplacer le pneu crevé* **et puis** *je vais le réparer.*
Good. I'll replace the flat tire and then I'll repair it for you.

16. Mécanicien: **Comme vous faites un long voyage,** *je vais vérifier les bougies* **et la batterie, s'il le faut.**
Since you're taking a long trip, I'll check the spark plugs and the storage battery, if necessary.

17. Charles: **Mettez aussi un peu d'eau dans le radiateur. Le moteur chauffait tout à l'heure.**
Also, put a little water in the radiator. The motor was heating up a little while ago.

18. Mécanicien: **Très bien, monsieur. Et si vous voulez faire faire le graissage, et faire changer l'huile°** . . .
Very well, sir. And if you'd like to have a lubrication job, and have the oil changed . . .

19. Charles: **Doucement! Je viens de l'acheter, cette voiture!**
Go easy! I've just bought this car!

20. Mécanicien: *Elle est neuve,* **vous dites? Je vois pourtant qu'il y a plusieurs choses à réparer.**
It's new, you say? I see, however, that there are several things to repair.

21. Charles: **On m'aura vendu un rossignol,°
alors!**

They must have sold me a piece of junk then!

22. Mécanicien: **Pas du tout, monsieur. On a souvent de ces petits ennuis, même au début. Mieux vaut les faire réparer tout de suite.**

Not at all, sir. People often have these little annoyances, even in the beginning. It's better to have them repaired immediately.

23. Charles: **Vous avez raison. Faudra-t-il que je laisse la voiture au garage?**

You're right. Will it be necessary for me to leave the car in the garage?

24. Mécanicien: **Pendant quelques heures, au moins, si vous voulez que je fasse une remise en état.**

For a few hours at least, if you want me to put it into shape.

25. Charles: **Mais j'aurai absolument besoin de la voiture pour le week-end.°**

But I'll absolutely need the car for the weekend.

26. Mécanicien: **J'espère qu'il ne faudra pas commander des pièces de rechange.**

I hope it won't be necessary to order spare parts.

27. Charles: **Faites seulement les choses strictement nécessaires.**

Do only what's absolutely essential.

28. Mécanicien: **Très bien, monsieur. Si vous voulez repasser demain matin, tout sera prêt.**

Very well, sir. If you'll come back tomorrow morning, everything will be ready.

29. Charles: **C'est parfait, alors.**
    That's fine.

30. Mécanicien: **Nous faisons toujours de notre mieux pour plaire à nos clients.**
    We always do our best to please our customers.

31. Charles: **Vous êtes très gentil. A demain.**
    You're very kind. See you tomorrow.

32. Mécanicien: **A votre service, monsieur. Au revoir.**
    At your service, sir. Good-bye.

NOTES

2. *un drôle de bruit.* A funny (kind of) noise; "funny" meaning peculiar, not amusing.

3. *panne:* a breakdown, a term used to indicate mechanical failure, i.e., *être en panne*, to be stuck; *avoir une panne de moteur*, to have engine trouble; *une panne d'allumage*, ignition trouble; *en panne*, out of order.

10. *un pneu à plat:* a flat tire. There are also other ways of saying "flat tire", e.g., *un pneu crevé; une crevaison.*

18. *faire changer l'huile:* A more colloquial expression for an oil change is *la vidange*, as in *Et si vous voulez faire faire le graissage et la vidange.*

21. *un rossignol:* lit., a nightingale. Used colloquially as the equivalent of the English slang "a lemon."

25. *le week-end:* more "franglais"!

GRAMMATICAL ITEMS FOR SPECIAL STUDY

I. *Y—there; in it; in there; about it; etc.* (The equivalent depends on the context.)

Study:

A.	Prep. of Place	Place		y	Verb	Complement
1. Je vais	à	Paris.	J'	y	vais.	
2. Nous sommes	à	l'école.	Nous	y	sommes.	
3. Je mettrai 2 litres	dans	le réservoir.	J'	y	mettrai	2 litres.
4. Il est resté	chez	moi.	Il	y	est resté.	
5. J'ai mis le livre	sur	le bureau.	J'	y	ai mis	le livre.

1. *I'm going to Paris.*   *I'm going there.*
2. *We are at school.*   *We are there.*
3. *I'll put two liters in* *I'll put 2 liters in it.*
   the tank.
4. *He stayed at my*   *He stayed there (in it).*
   house.
5. *I put the book on the*   *I put the book on it.*
   desk.

B. Imperative	Prep.	Place	Imperative	y
1. Va	à	l'école.	Vas-	y.
2. Allez	au	magasin.	Allez-	y.

1. *Go to school.*   *Go there.*
2. *Go to the store.*   *Go there.*

C. Study the following contrasts:

1. Je pense *à Jean.*   Je pense *à lui.*
   Je pense *à mon*   J'*y* pense.
   travail.

2. Je réponds *à Marie.*   Je *lui* réponds.
   Je réponds *à la*   J'*y* réponds.
   lettre.

3. J'obéis *à ma mère.*   Je *lui* obéis.
   J'obéis *à la loi.*   J'*y* obéis.

1. I'm thinking *of*   I'm thinking *of him.*
   John.
   I'm thinking *of my*   I'm thinking *of it.*
   work.

2. I answer *Marie.*   I answer *her.*
   I answer the *letter.*   I answer *it.*

3. I obey *my mother.*   I obey *her.*
   I obey *the law.*   I obey *it.*

Note: Use *y* to replace *à* + an inanimate object. With animate beings, use the indirect object pronoun.

II. *aller + infinitive—going to; will and shall future; immediate future.*

Study:

	aller	Infinitive	
1. Il	va	venir	demain.
2. Nous	allons	sortir	plus tard.
3. Elles	vont	acheter	des robes.

1. *He's going to come tomorrow. (He'll come tomorrow. He's coming tomorrow.)*

2. *We're going to go out later. (We'll go out later.)*

3. *They're going to buy some dresses. (They'll buy some dresses.)*

III. *Forms of irregular adjectives*

Study these contrasts:

Feminine	Masculine
1. une *longue* promenade	un *long* voyage
2. Elle est *gentille.*	Il est *gentil.*
3. Elle est *heureuse.*	Il est *heureux.*
4. Elle est *active.*	Il est *actif.*
5. Elle est *neuve.*	Il est *neuf.*
6. Elle est *fière.*	Il est *fier.*
7. Elle est *étrangère.*	Il est *étranger.*
8. Elle est *belle.*	Il est *beau.*
9. Elle est *italienne.*	Il est *italien.*
10. Elle est *sèche.*	Il est *sec.*

1. *a long walk*	*a long trip*
2. *She is nice.*	*He is nice.*
3. *She is happy.*	*He is happy.*
4. *She is active.*	*He is active.*
5. *It is new.*	*It is new.*
6. *She is proud.*	*He is proud.*
7. *She is foreign.*	*He is foreign.*
8. *She is beautiful.*	*He is handsome.*
9. *She is Italian.*	*He is Italian.*
10. *It is dry.*	*It is dry.*

Note: Depending on the word to which it refers, *il* and *elle* may mean *it* as well as *he* or *she.* Example: J'ai acheté *une robe. Elle* est belle. *I bought a dress. It's beautiful.*

DRILLS AND EXERCISES

I. Replace the italicized phrases in each of the following sentences by *y, lui* or *leur.* Write the complete sentence, say aloud, and translate.

Example: Je vais *à Londres.*/J'*y* vais.

1. Elle restera *à Rome.*

2. Je passerai mes vacances *à la mer.*

3. Il parle *à Jean.*

4. J'ai trouvé mes chaussettes *sous le lit.*

5. Il est entré *dans le magasin.*

6. Elle lit le roman *à l'enfant.*

7. Il a posé une question *aux messieurs.*

8. Il a passé trois semaines *chez sa tante.*

II. Transform the *affirmative* to the *negative.*

Example: J'y vais./Je *n*'y vais *pas.*

1. J'y suis.   6. Allez-y.
2. J'y reste.   7. Vas-y.
3. Il y obéit.   8. Allons-y.
4. Elle y répond.   9. Répondons-y.
5. Nous y pensons.   10. Entrez-y.

III. Transform the *future* sentences below to a verb phrase with *aller,* and translate.

Example: Il *viendra* demain./Il *va venir* demain.

1. Elle *partira* ce soir.

2. Ils *sortiront* plus tard.

3. Elles *arriveront* à sept heures.

4. Nous *ferons* une promenade.

5. Elle *vera* sa sœur demain.

IV. Translate the following sentences into French; then say them aloud.

1. I'm going there in three weeks.

2. We stayed there for *(pendant)* a month.

3. Her trip? She thinks about it every day.

4. We're going to leave tomorrow.

5. Is she going to come later?

6. I'm going to replace the flat tire.

7. It's a long story.

8. What a beautiful car!

9. He isn't very happy today.

Answers at back of book.

QUIZ

From among the three choices, select the one which correctly renders the English word or phrase given. Write the complete sentence, and translate.

1. *(exactly)* Je ne sais pas _____.
   (a) justement
   (b) juste
   (c) au juste

2. *(funny)* Il y a _____ bruit.
   (a) un amusant
   (b) un drôle de
   (c) un drôle

3. *(still)* Je croyais en avoir _____ quelques litres.
   (a) tranquille
   (b) chaque
   (c) encore

4. (*through*) Nous allons faire un voyage
   _____ la France.
   (a) à travers
   (b) en face
   (c) par

5. (*a spare tire*) Il y a un _____ dans le
   coffre.
   (a) un pneu maigre
   (b) un rechange pneu
   (c) un pneu de rechange

6. (*if necessary*) Je vais vérifier les bougies
   _____.
   (a) s'il faut
   (b) s'il nécessaire
   (c) s'il le faut.

7. (*new*) [*the car*] Elle est _____.
   (a) neuf
   (b) nouvelle
   (c) neuve

8. (*Not at all*) _____, monsieur.
   (a) Pas du tout
   (b) Pas à tout
   (c) Pas tout

9. (*I'll need*) _____ la voiture.
   (a) J'aurai besoin de
   (b) J'aurai faut de
   (c) J'aurai besoin

10. (*our best*) Nous faisons _____.
    (a) notre meilleur
    (b) notre mieux
    (c) de notre mieux

Answers at back of book.

LESSON 55

LA DOUANE
CUSTOMS

A. *On approche de la frontière espagnole*
Approaching the Spanish frontier

1. Jeanne: **Regarde donc cette queue de voitures devant le poste de douane!**
   Just look at that line of cars in front of the customs station!

2. Charles: **C'était à prévoir. Hendaye° est la douane principale entre la France et l'Espagne.**
   It was to be expected. Hendaye is the principal customs (station) between France and Spain.

3. Jeanne: **En effet!** *J'en ai souvent entendu parler.* **Nous en aurons pour longtemps,° sans doute.**
   Indeed! (You're right.) I've often heard about it. We'll undoubtedly have a long wait.

4. Charles: **Au contraire,** *j'ai entendu dire* **que cette douane n'est pas trop difficile à passer.**
   On the contrary, I've heard that this customs station is not too difficult to get through.

5. Jeanne: **Espérons que la visite des bagages ne sera pas trop minutieuse.** *Commençons à manger* **des bonbons pendant que nous attendons.**
   Let's hope that the baggage examination will not be too thorough. Let's begin to eat some candy while we wait.

6. Charles: **Je ne crois pas qu'ils soient très stricts pour les touristes; d'ailleurs, nous n'avons rien à cacher!**
I don't think they're very strict with tourists. Anyway, we have nothing to hide.

B. *A la frontière*   At the frontier

7. Jeanne: **Nous voici enfin à la frontière.** *Je vois venir* **le douanier.**
Here we are at last at the border. I see the customs officer coming.

8. Douanier: **Bonjour, monsieur, 'dame. Vous resterez longtemps en Espagne?**
Customs Officer: Good day, sir, madam. Will you be staying in Spain for a long time?

9. Charles: **Non, monsieur, ce ne sera qu'une courte visite. Nous sommes touristes.**
No, sir. It will be only a short visit. We're tourists.

10. Douanier: **Avez-vous quelque chose à déclarer?**
Do you have anything to declare?

11. Jeanne: **Pas que je sache.**°
Not that I know of.

12. Douanier: **Alcool? Tabac? Bijoux? Parfum?**°
Alcohol? Tobacco? Jewels? Perfume?

13. Charles: **Non, monsieur, nous n'avons rien à déclarer.**
No, sir, we have nothing to declare.

14. Jeanne: **Alors, il ne faudra pas ouvrir les bagages...**
Then it will not be necessary to open the baggage...

15. Douanier: **Si, madame, c'est une formalité. Veuillez ouvrir cette valise bleue.**
    Yes, madam, it's a formality. Please open this blue valise.

16. Charles: *Voulez-vous que j'ouvre* **aussi les autres?**
    Do you want me to open the others too?

17. Douanier: **Pas pour le moment. Est-ce que** *ces effets° ont été portés?*
    Not for the moment. Have these clothes been worn?

18. Charles: **Oui, monsieur. Tout ce que nous avons est pour notre usage personnel.**
    Yes, sir. Everything we have is for our personal use.

19. Jeanne: **Donc, pas de déclaration à faire, pas de droits à payer...**
    Therefore (So), no declaration to make, no customs duties to pay...

20. Douanier: **C'est ça, madame. Mais puis-je voir les papiers pour la voiture? Votre carnet?°**
    That's right, madam. But may I see the documents for the car? Your customs permit (for the car)?

21. Charles: **Le voici et voici les autres documents, monsieur. Comme vous voyez, la voiture est immatriculée° en France.**
    Here it is, sir, and here are the other documents. As you see, the car is registered in France.

22. Douanier: **Très bien. Et maintenant, vos passeports, s'il vous plaît.**
    Very good. And now, your passports, please.

23. Jeanne: **Est-ce qu'un visa° spécial est exigé?**
    Is a special visa required?

24. Douanier: **Non, simplement ce visa d'entrée.**
    (Il vise les passeports.) **Voilá. Maintenant,**
    tout est en règle.
    No, simply this entrance visa. *(He visas the*
    passports.) There. Now, everything is in or-
    der.

25. Jeanne: **On peut passer, alors?**
    We can go through, then?

26. Douanier: **Certainement, madame. Et je**
    vous souhaite bon séjour° en Espagne.
    Certainly, madam. And I wish you a pleasant
    stay in Spain.

C. *Plus tard* Later

27. Jeanne: **Tu avais raison. On ne nous a pas**
    fait attendre trop longtemps.
    You were right. They didn't make us wait too
    long.

28. Charles: **Heureusement. Te souviens-tu de**
    notre dernier voyage? C'était bien pire!
    Fortunately. Do you remember our last trip? It
    was much worse.

29. Jeanne: **Comment puis-je l'oublier?** *L'a-*
    gent° **de l'immigration** *a examiné nos passe-*
    ports **comme si nous étions des criminels!**
    How can I forget it? The immigration officer
    examined our passports as though we were
    criminals.

30. Charles: **J'ai vraiment cru qu'on ne nous**
    laisserait pas entrer!
    I really believed they wouldn't let us enter!

31. Jeanne: **Et on nous a fait ouvrir toutes nos valises!**
    And they made us open all our valises!

32. Charles: **Oui, et *on les a fouillées* comme si nous étions des contrebandiers!**
    Yes, and they searched them as though we were smugglers!

33. Jeanne: **Et les formalités! On nous a fait remplir tant de fiches et de formulaires— une feuille de débarquement, une déclaration en douane, ...**
    And the red tape! They made us fill out so many slips and forms—a debarkation sheet, a customs declaration, ...

34. Charles: **En fin de compte, *nous y avons mis*° presque deux heures.**
    In the end (All in all) it took us almost two hours.

35. Jeanne: **Mais, comme on dit, tout est bien qui finit bien.°**
    But, as they say, all's well that ends well.

NOTES

2. *Hendaye:* a city in the southwest of France. It is a seaside resort, as well as one of the main cities through which one crosses into Spain.

3. *Nous en aurons pour longtemps: en avoir pour longtemps* is a colloquialism meaning "to have a long wait" or "to have a long siege of" or "bout with." Example: *Elle en aura pour longtemps.* (She'll be ill for a long time.)

11. *Pas que je sache:* not that I know (of); a commonly used formula.

12. Each country has its own list of articles which may not be imported—either without the payment of a duty, or not at all.

17. *effets:* personal effects, clothing. Generally, clothing which is for personal use, or clothing which has been worn, is not taxed.

20. *carnet:* a form, usually prepared in triplicate, which is required of every motorist when crossing a border.

21. *immatriculée:* Cars are required to have a metal shield or plaque (usually placed near the license plate) indicating the country in which they are registered. Each country, of course, has its own system of symbols or letters on the license plates.

23. *un visa:* In addition to the passport, some countries require an entrance visa. Information about visas may be procured from the agency of the country or, in the case of American citizens, from the Consular Service of the Department of State, or from reputable travel agencies.

26. *Je vous souhaite bon séjour:* a commonly used expression or formula. Notice the omission of *un* in front of *bon*.

29. *agent:* The word *agent [de police]* is also used for uniformed policemen working within the larger metropolitan areas, such as Paris, Marseilles, etc. Outside the cities, the police are called *gendarmes*. A "cop" is *un flic*.

34. *mis:* literally, "placed" or "put" (past participle of the verb *mettre*).

35. *Tout est bien qui finit bien:* All's well that ends well. A common proverb.

GRAMMATICAL ITEMS FOR SPECIAL STUDY

I. *entendre, voir* + *infinitive*

Study:

Subject	Entendre/ Voir	Infinitive	Complement
1. J'	ai entendu	parler	de cela.
2. Il	a entendu	dire	cela.
3. Elle	a entendu	dire	qu'il était malade.
4. Nous	avons vu	venir	le douanier.

1. *I heard that spoken of.* (Lit.: *I've heard speak of that.*)

2. *He heard that (said).*

3. *She heard (it said) that he was sick.*

4. *We saw the customs officer come.*

II. *vouloir* + *the subjunctive*

Study:

Vouloir	que	Subject	Sub-junctive	Comple-ment
1. Voulez-vous	que	j'	ouvre	les valises?
2. Je veux	qu'	elle	vienne	me voir.
3. Il ne veut pas	que	vous	soyez	en retard.
4. Ne voulez-vous pas	qu'	il	sache	la vérité?

1. *Do you want me to open* (lit., *that I open*) *the valises?*

2. *I want her to come* (lit., *that she come*) *to see me.*

3. *He doesn't want you to be* (lit., *that you be*) *late.*

4. *Don't you want him to know* (lit., *that he know*) *the truth?*

But

Note: The infinitive (*not* the subjunctive) is used when the subject of the *main* verb and of the *subordinate* verb are the *same*. Contrast the following:

Je veux venir vous voir. *I want to come to see you.*
Je veux *qu'il* vienne vous voir. *I want him to come to see you.*

III. *The forms of the past participle.*
   Study:

A. With *avoir*

1. Nous avons vu les hommes.	*We saw the men.*
2. Nous les avons vus.	*We saw them.*
3. Les hommes que nous avons vus sont nos frères.	*The men whom we saw are our brothers.*
4. Les femmes que nous avons vues sont nos sœurs.	*The women whom we saw are our sisters.*
5. Quels hommes avez-vous vus?	*What men have you seen?*
6. Quelles femmes avez-vous vues?	*What women have you seen?*
7. Combien d'hommes avez-vous vus?	*How many men have you seen?*
8. J'en ai vu trois.	*I've seen three of them.*
9. Combien de femmes avez-vous vues?	*How many women have you seen?*
10. J'en ai vu trois.	*I've seen three of them.*

11. Je les lui ai *I gave them to him.*
 donné*(e)s.*

Note: Past participles of verbs conjugated with *avoir* agree in number and gender with the *preceding direct* object *only.* There is never any agreement with *en,* however.

B. With *être*

1. Nous sommes *We arrived yesterday.*
 arrivés hier.
2. Elles étaient sort*ies* *They had gone out very*
 de très bonne heure. *early.*
3. Ils sont restés *They stayed a long*
 longtemps. *time.*

Note: Past participles of verbs conjugated with *être* (except reflexive verbs) agree in number and gender with the *subject.* Refer to Lesson 48 to review material on use of *être.*

C. Reflexive and reciprocal verbs

1. Nous *nous* sommes *We washed ourselves.*
 lavés.
2. Nous nous sommes *We washed our hands*
 lavé *les mains.* (lit.: *We washed the*
 hands for ourselves.)

Note: Past participles of reflexive verbs, although conjugated with *être*, agree with the *preceding direct* object.

1. Nous *nous* sommes *We saw each other.*
 vus.
2. Nous nous sommes *We spoke to each other.*
 parlé.

Note: Past participles of reciprocal verbs (verbs expressing "each other"), although conjugated with *être*, agree with the *preceding direct* object.

IV. *Verbs ending in -cer*

Study:

je commence	nous commençons
tu commences	vous commencez
il elle } commence	ils elles } commencent

NOTES

1. For other tenses, see *Regular Verb Charts*.

2. *commencer à*—to begin to

3. Similarly conjugated are: *avancer, menacer, annoncer, placer, prononcer, remplacer.*

V. *Verbs ending in -ger*

Study:

je mange	nous mangeons
tu manges	vous mangez
il elle } mange	ils elles } mangent

NOTES

1. For other tenses, see *Regular Verb Charts*.

2. Similarly conjugated are: *arranger, corriger, songer, changer, nager, partager.*

DRILLS AND EXERCISES

I. Substitute each of the words in parentheses for the italicized word or expression in the model sentence. Write the complete sentence and say aloud.

A. Nous avons entendu parler de *cela*. (Jean, Marie, cette pièce, ce film, ces livres, ces histoires, ceux-là, M. Dupont)

B. Il a vu ɣenir *le douanier.* (le mécanicien, l'employé, le professeur, la femme, les ouvreuses)

C. Il ne veut pas que vous soyez *en retard.* (malade, paresseuse, fatiguée, triste, malheureuse, active)

D. Ils sont *partis* hier. (rentrés, arrivés, venus, sortis, tombés, retournés, morts)

E. (les livres) Nous les avons lu*s.* (vus, écrits, achetés, regardés, cherchés, admirés)

F. (les femmes) Il les a vu*es.* (regardées, cherchées, admirées, aimées, chassées)

II. Expand the clauses listed below in the manner specified:

A. Place *J'ai entendu dire* in front of each of the following, write, say, and translate:
 1. qu'elle est arrivée.
 2. que vous étiez malade.
 3. qu'ils sont très pauvres.
 4. que tu étais parti hier.
 5. qu'il ne veut pas venir.

B. Place *Il ne veut pas* in front of each of the following, write, say, and translate.
 1. que vous ayez de la peine.
 2. qu'elle sache la vérité.
 3. que nous parlions trop fort.
 4. que je fasse ce voyage.
 5. qu'ils aillent à Paris.
 6. que je finisse ce travail.
 7. qu'elles apprennent cette nouvelle

III. Translate the following sentences into French; then say them aloud.

1. Have you heard of this book?

2. I heard that she will leave tomorrow.

3. I see the usherette coming.

4. He doesn't want me to be sad.

5. Do you want me to come at three o'clock?

6. I want you to leave immediately!

7. The books I read were excellent.

8. I read them last year.

9. She arrived late.

10. We met each other, but we didn't write to each other.

11. Let's eat together.

12. I was beginning to read when he came in.

13. We are beginning to get tired (lit.: to tire ourselves).

14. She was eating slowly.

Answers at back of book.

QUIZ

From among the three choices, select the one which correctly renders the English word or phrase given, write the complete sentence, and translate.

1. *(line)* Regarde cette _____ devant le poste de douane.
   (a) ligne
   (b) queue
   (c) quelle

2. *(between)* C'est la douane _____ la France et l'Espagne.
   (a) entre
   (b) contre
   (c) à travers

3. *(are)* Je ne crois pas qu'ils _____ stricts.
   - (a) sont
   - (b) seront
   - (c) soient

4. *(at last)* Nous voici _____ à la frontière.
   - (a) à fin
   - (b) enfin
   - (c) derniers

5. *(will only be)* Ce _____ une courte visite.
   - (a) ne sera qu'
   - (b) ne va être qu'
   - (c) ne soit qu'

6. *(Not that I know of)* _____.
   - (a) Ne pas que je sais.
   - (b) Ne pas que je sache.
   - (c) Pas que je sache.

7. *(Everything)* _____ nous avons est pour nous.
   - (a) Tout le monde
   - (b) Chaque chose
   - (c) Tout ce que

8. *(in order)* Tout est _____
   - (a) en ordre
   - (b) dans la règle
   - (c) en règle

9. *(Do you remember)* _____ notre dernier voyage?
   - (a) Te souviens-tu de
   - (b) Te souviens-tu
   - (c) Souviens-toi

10. *(searched)* [les valises] On les a _____.
    - (a) cherchées
    - (b) fouillé
    - (c) fouillées.

Answers at back of book.

LESSON 56

À LA BANQUE
AT THE BANK

A. *Au guichet de change*   At the exchange window.

1. Charles: **Est-ce que je peux changer ici un chèque de voyage° de cent dollars?**
   Can I change a hundred-dollar traveler's check here?

2. Caissier: *Certainement,* **monsieur. Vous n'avez qu'à le contresigner.**
   Certainly, sir. You have only to countersign it.

3. Charles: **C'est à combien le dollar,° monsieur?**
   How much is the dollar, sir?

4. Caissier: **Le cours du change est à quatre francs quatre-vingt-cinq aujourd'hui. Et maintenant, votre passeport, s'il vous plaît.**
   The exchange rate is four francs eighty-five today. And now, your passport, please.

5. Charles: **Mon passeport? Pourquoi faire?**
   My passport? What for?

6. Caissier: **Il me faut le numéro de votre passe-port,° votre nom, et votre adresse, pour pouvoir remplir cette fiche.**
   I need the number of your passport, your name, and your address, in order to fill out this form.

7. Charles: **Ah! Je comprends! Le voici, monsieur.**
   Ah! I understand! Here it is, sir.

8. Caissier: **Comment voulez-vous que je vous donne votre argent?**
   How do you want me to give you your money?

9. Charles: **Donnez-le moi en gros billets, avec un peu de petite monnaie aussi, s'il vous plaît.**
Give it to me in large bills, with some small change as well, please.

10. Caissier: **Voilà, monsieur, quatre cent quatre-vingt-cinq francs. Et n'oubliez pas de garder cette fiche.°**
Here you are, sir. Four hundred eighty-five francs. And don't forget to keep this form.

11. Charles: **Merci bien, monsieur. Pour un envoi commercial à l'étranger, à qui dois-je m'adresser?**
Thank you very much, sir. For a commercial shipment to a foreign country, to whom should I speak?

12. Caissier: **Adressez-vous au directeur, M. Lemaître.**
Speak to the manager, Mr. Lemaître.

B. *Au bureau du directeur* In the manager's office

13. M. Lemaître: **En quoi pourrais-je vous servir, monsieur?**
How can I help you, sir?

14. Charles: **Je voudrais expédier aux Etats-Unis une caisse de cadres pour tableaux, et je voudrais faire payer les frais par ma banque à New York.**
I'd like to ship a case of picture frames to the United States, and I'd like to have the costs paid by my bank in New York.

15. M. Lemaître: **Vous avez donc trois questions à régler. La première est celle du montant**

de vos achats. *Si vos achats reviennent* à plus
de mille dollars, *il vous faudra* une licence
d'exportation°.

Then you have three matters to consider. The
first is the matter of the total sum of your
purchases. If your purchases come to more
than a thousand dollars, you'll need an export
license.

16. Charles: **Et la deuxième question?**
    And the second matter?

17. M. Lemaître: **Celle de l'expédition.** *Après
    avoir fait emballer la marchandise,* **vous
    pourrez l'envoyer soit par la gare, soit par
    messagerie.**
    The problem of shipment. After having the
    merchandise packed, you can send it either by
    railway or by a transport service.

18. Charles: **Par la gare on est limité à vingt
    kilos,° n'est-ce pas?**
    By railway, you're limited to twenty kilos
    (forty-four pounds), aren't you?

19. M. Lemaître: **C'est exact.** Donc *avant de
    décider,* il faudra d'abord savoir le poids de
    la caisse. *Si la caisse pèse* audessus de vingt
    kilos, *il faudra* l'envoyer par messagerie, ou
    par un transitaire.
    That's right. Then before deciding, you'll first
    have to know the weight of the case. If the case
    weighs more than forty-four pounds, you'll
    have to send it by a transport service or a
    forwarding agent.

20. Charles: **Pourquoi un transitaire?**
    Why a forwarding agent?

21. M. Lemaître: **Le transitaire vous fera un
    prix global: le coût de la marchandise, l'em-**

ballage, et l'envoi, y compris les droits de douane.° Il s'occupe, en somme, de tout.
The forwarding agent will make you a total price: the cost of the merchandise, the packing, and the shipment, including customs duties. In a word, he takes care of everything.

22. Charles: **Que c'est compliqué! Et la troisième question?**
How complicated it is! And the third matter?

23. M. Lemaître: **Il s'agit° du paiement, ce qui est** *réellement* **une chose très simple ces jours-ci...**
It's a question of payment which is actually a very simple thing these days...

24. Charles: **Mais pour moi, ça c'est un vrai problème. Je n'ai pas assez d'argent sur moi pour payer le transitaire.**
But for me, that's a real problem. I don't have enough money with me to pay the forwarding agent.

25. M. Lemaître: **Vous n'avez qu'à écrire un chèque personnel.° N'importe quel chèque sur n'importe quelle banque américaine peut être changé** *instantanément* **en France!**
All you have to do is write a personal check. Any check drawn on any American bank can be cashed at once in France!

26. Charles: **C'est-à-dire que je dois simplement verser à mon compte aux Etats-Unis suffisamment d'argent pour couvrir mon chéque?**
You mean to say that I have only to put enough money into my account in the U.S.A. to cover my check?

27. M. Lemaître: **Oui, et après, pour toucher votre chèque, il faudra que quelqu'un vous connaisse ... votre marchand, par exemple ...**
Yes, and afterwards, to cash your check, it will be necessary for someone to know you ... your dealer, for example ...

28. Charles: **Naturellement! Comme cela se fait partout!°**
Naturally! As is customary everywhere!

29. M. Lemaître: *Si vous voulez, vous pourrez* **vous arranger avec le transitaire pour payer le tout° quand la caisse arrivera aux Etats-Unis.**
If you wish, you can arrange [yourself] with the forwarding agent to pay the entire amount when the case reaches the U.S.A.

30. Charles: **Quels seront les impôts à payer?°**
What taxes will have to be paid?

31. M. Lemaître: **Pour vous, puisque vous êtes étranger, il n'y a pas d'impôts en France.**
For you, since you are a foreigner, there are no taxes in France.

32. Charles: **Heureusement! Et autre chose encore.** *Si j'en avais besoin, pourrais-je* **louer un coffre-fort ou bien ouvrir un compte ici?°**
Fortunately! And another thing. If I needed to, could I rent a safe-deposit box or open an account here?

33. M. Lemaître: **Bien sûr. Nous sommes à votre disposition.**
Of course. We are at your service.

NOTES

1. Traveler's checks are accepted nearly everywhere in the world. They can be changed in banks and in many stores and other commercial establishments.

3.-4. The value of the franc fluctuates slightly from day to day. The rate of exchange is clearly posted in all banks, and will be found in many newspapers.

6. *passeport:* Travelers should always carry their passports or other identification.

10. *fiche:* It is a good idea to save the receipts for all business transactions and especially for the exchange of money. In some countries these must be shown upon leaving.

15. *licence d'exportation:* For large purchases, an export license may be required. In order to export art objects such as paintings in quantity, a French customs examination may be required.

18. *kilo:* the spoken abbreviation of *kilogramme* (*kg.* in writing). The measure of weight equivalent to 2.2 pounds. This abbreviation is commonly used, whereas *kilomètre* is never abbreviated in speech but may be written as *km.*

21. Merchandise which is shipped (in excess of the amount permitted the traveler) is subject to customs duties. The duty varies according to the merchandise.

23. *Il s'agit de:* It's a question (or matter) of, it's about, it concerns. Example: *Il s'agit de lui.* It's about him. *Il s'agit de* is a very frequently used expression.

25. Personal checks are not generally honored unless the client is very well known to the receiver of the check.

28. *Cela se fait partout:* "It's done everywhere."
    Cela ne se fait pas is "That's not done."

29. *le tout:* literally, the whole thing.

30. *les impôts à payer:* Foreigners do not pay taxes on certain transactions.

32. Opening a bank account is not necessarily an easy matter. It is desirable to find out what formalities are required and to have a letter form one's home bank establishing identity and credit. American banks usually have correspondent banks in foreign countries, and some large banks have branches abroad. It is preferable to handle large transactions with these banks.

GRAMMATICAL ITEMS FOR SPECIAL STUDY

I. *avant de + infinitive = before -ing*

Study:

	avant de	Infinitive	
1. Mangez	avant de	partir.	
2.	Avant de	décider,	vous devriez réfléchir.
3. Réfléchissez	avant de	décider	de partir.

1. *Eat before leaving.*

2. *Before deciding, you should think.*

3. *Think before deciding to leave.*

Note: *Avant de* + *infinitive* may start or end a sentence or may be embedded in a sentence (Example 3).

Perfect Infinitive

II. *après* + $\begin{Bmatrix} avoir \\ or \\ être \end{Bmatrix}$ + *past participle* = $\begin{Bmatrix} after\ -ing \\ after\ having— \\ after\ being— \end{Bmatrix}$

Study:

après	Obj. Pro.	avoir/ être	Past Part.	
1. Après		avoir	reçu	le chèque, il est parti.
2. Après	m'	avoir	changé	le chèque, elle est sortie.
3. Après	les	avoir	vu*es*	je m'en suis allé(e).
4. Après		être	rentré	il est venu me voir.
5. Après		être	arrivé*s*	ils ont dit, "Bonjour."
6. Après		être	arrivé*es*	elles ont changé de robe.
7. Après	s'	être	lavée	elle s'est habillée.
8. Après	m'	être	levé(e)	je me suis lavé(e).

1. *After receiving the check, he left.*

2. *After changing the check for me, she went out.*

3. *After having seen them* (fem.), *I went away.*

4. *After having returned home, he came to see me.*

5. *After arriving* (masc. plu.), *they said, "Good day."*

6. *After arriving* (fem. plu.), *they changed their dresses.*

7. *After getting washed, she got dressed.*

8. *After getting up, I got washed.*

III. *The conditional perfect*

A. Formation: The conditional perfect is formed by using the conditional of *avoir* or *être*, plus the past participle of the verb.

Study:

Cond. of *avoir* + Past Part. of *faire* Complement

(I would have	done	that, etc.)
J'aurais	fait	cela.
Tu aurais	fait	cela.
Il aurait	fait	cela.
Elle aurait	fait	cela.
Nous aurions	fait	cela.
Vous auriez	fait	cela.
Ils auraient	fait	cela.
Elles auraient	fait	cela.

Cond. of *être* + Past Part. of *entrer*

(I would have	entered, etc.)
Je serais	entré(e).
Tu serais	entré(e).
Il serait	entré.
Elle serait	entrée.
Nous serions	entré(e)s.
Vous seriez	entré(e)(s).
Ils seraient	entrés.
Elles seraient	entrées.

B. Use:

1. The conditional perfect is generally used in French as it is in English. Examples:

a. Je *serais parti(e)* à l'heure.
   I <u>would have left</u> on time.

b. Elle *aurait acheté* deux robes.
   She <u>would have bought</u> two dresses.

For the use of the conditional perfect in sentences with "if" clauses, see Section IV in this lesson.

2. Note the special use of the conditional perfect of *devoir. Il aurait dû* payer l'addition.
   He <u>should have paid</u> the check.

IV. *Sentences with if*

Study:

A.	If	Present		Present/ Imperative/ Future
	1. Si	vous *avez*	de l'argent	vous le dépens*ez.*
	2. Si	vous *avez*	de l'argent	dépens*ez*-le.
	3. Si	vous *avez*	de l'argent	vous le dépens*erez.*

1. *If you have some money, you spend it.*

2. *If you have some money, spend it.*

3. *If you have some money, you will spend it.*

B.	If	Imperfect		Conditional
	1. Si	elle av*ait*	de l'argent	elle ach*èterait* une robe.
	2. Si	nous av*ions*	le temps	nous viendr*ions* vous voir.

1. *If she had some money, she would buy a dress.*

2. *If we had the time, we would come to see you.*

C.

If	Past Perfect			Past Conditional
1. Si	j'*avais eu*	le temps	je *serais allé(e)* au cinéma.
2. Si	vous *étiez sorti*		vous *auriez vu* l'accident.

1. *If I had had the time, I would have gone to the movies.*

2. *If you had gone out, you would have seen the accident.*

V. *Forms of adverbs*

Study:

A. *Feminine form of adjective*   *Adverb*

heureuse	heureuse*ment*	*fortunately*
certaine	certaine*ment*	*certainly*
réelle	réelle*ment*	*really, actually*

B. *Feminine form of adjective*   *Adverb (with added accent)*

précise	préci*sément*	*precisely*
énorme	énor*mément*	*enormously*
profonde	profon*dément*	*profoundly*

C. *Masc.*
   adjective
   ending in
   vowel   *Adverb*

poli	poli*ment*	*politely*
vrai	vrai*ment*	*really*
absolu	absolu*ment*	*absolutely*
véritable	véritable*ment*	*truly*
instantané	instantané*ment*	*immediately, at once.*

D. *Masc.*
   adjective
   ending in ent
   or
   ant   *Adverb*

const*ant*	const*amment*	*constantly*
suffis*ant*	suffis*amment*	*sufficiently*
prud*ent*	prud*emment*	*prudently*
évid*ent*	évid*emment*	*evidently*
intellig*ent*	intellig*emment*	*intelligently*

DRILLS AND EXERCISES

I. Substitute each of the words or expressions in parentheses for the italicized word or expression in the model sentence. Write the complete sentence and say aloud.

   A. Mangez avant de *partir.* (sortir, travailler, commencer, téléphoner, boire, y aller [note: *d'*])

   B. Après avoir *mangé,* elle est partie. (étudié, travaillé, changé de robe, lu le livre, dit "Au revoir")

   C. Après être *rentrée,* elle m'a téléphoné. (arrivée, revenue, retournée, entrée, descendue, montée)

D. Si nous avons de l'argent, nous achèterons *une voiture.* (un rouleau de film, une maison, un canot, une télévision)

E. S'il avait *une voiture,* il vous la donnerait. (une plume, une cigarette, une allumette, une radio)

F. S'il avait fait beau (temps), je serais *sorti.* (allé à la plage, parti plus tôt, resté encore trois jours, arrivé à l'heure)

II. Expand the following expressions by placing *avant de commencer* in the position indicated by the line. Say, write, and translate.

1. Reposez-vous _____.

2. Il faut réfléchir _____.

3. Vous devez manger _____.

4. Il pourrait vous parler _____.

5. _____ je viendrai vous voir.

6. _____ elle a téléphoné à son amie.

7. Pensez bien _____ ce travail.

8. Réfléchissez bien _____ ce que vous allez faire.

III. Expand the following by placing *Il parle* in front of each. Say and write each sentence.

1. _____ constamment.

2. _____ prudemment.

3. _____ poliment.

4. _____ intelligemment.

5. _____ suffisamment.

IV. Translate the following sentences into French; then say them aloud.

1. She said good-bye before leaving.

2. Before saying "no," make an effort.

3. I wash my hands before eating.

4. After reading them, I returned [*rendre*] the books to Mary.

5. After returning home, she went to bed.

6. After washing our hands, we sit down to eat.

7. If she has enough money, she'll buy that coat.

8. I'd write to you more often if I had the time.

9. If it had snowed, I'd have stayed home.

10. Fortunately, we have enough money.

11. She's evidently very intelligent.

12. You're absolutely right.

13. I should have spoken to him.

14. They would have left.

Answers at back of book.

QUIZ

From among the three choices, select the one which correctly renders the English word or phrase given, write the complete sentence, and translate.

1. (*You need only to*) _____ le contresigner.
   (a) Vous seulement besoin de
   (b) Vous avez à
   (c) Vous n'avez qu'à

2. (*show me*) Il faudra que vous _____ une
   pièce d'identité.
   (a) montrez-moi
   (b) me montriez
   (c) moi montrez.

3. (*Give it to me*) _____ en gros billets.
   (a) Donnez-le-moi
   (b) Donnez-le-me
   (c) Donnez-moi-le

4. (*I'd like to*) _____ expédier une caisse.
   (a) Je voudrais
   (b) Je voulais
   (c) Je me plais à

5. (*second*) Et la _____ question?
   (a) prochaine
   (b) deuxième
   (c) deux

6. (*right*) C'est _____.
   (a) raison
   (b) droite
   (c) exact

7. (*He takes care*) _____ de tout.
   (a) Il soigne
   (b) Il prend cure
   (c) Il s'occupe

8. (*It's a question of the*) _____ paiement.
   (a) Il s'agit du
   (b) Il s'agit de
   (c) C'est agit

9. (*enough*) Je n'ai pas _____ d'argent.
   (a) suffisantement
   (b) suffisantément
   (c) suffisamment

10. (*What*) _____ seront les impôts à payer?
    (a) Quels
    (b) Quel
    (c) Quelles

Answers at back of book.

LESSON 57

À LA POSTE
AT THE POST OFFICE

A. *Au guichet "Affranchissements"*
   At the "Stamps" window

1. Charles: **Pardon, madame, je voudrais envoyer ces trois lettres aux Etats-Unis. Quel est l'affranchissement, s'il vous plaît?**
   Excuse me, ma'am, I'd like to send these three letters to the United States. What's the postage, please?

2. Employée: **Par avion° ou ordinaire, monsieur?**
   Airmail or regular, sir?

3. Charles: **Par avion, s'il vous plaît.**
   Airmail, please.

4. Employée: **Je dois d'abord les peser. Voyons ... il vous faudra trois timbres de quatre-vingt-cinq centimes.°**
   I'll have to weigh them first. Let's see ... you'll need three eighty-five-centime stamps.

5. Charles: **Je voulais aussi envoyer une lettre par exprès.**
   I also wanted to send a special-delivery letter.

6. Employée: **Si c'est pour Paris, pourquoi n'envoyez-vous pas un pneumatique?**° Ainsi **la lettre parviendra au destinataire** *en une heure ou deux.*
   If it's for Paris, why don't you send an express letter? That way the letter will reach the addressee in one or two hours.

7. Charles: *J'ai aussi à envoyer* **un télégramme, chercher mon courrier à la poste restante,**° **et envoyer un colis. Est-ce ici . . .**
   I also have to send a telegram, pick up my mail at the general delivery, and send a package. Is it here . . .

8. Employée: **Non, monsieur, ces guichets-là sont tous là-bas, en face.**
   No, sir. Those windows are all over there, on the other side.

B. *Au guichet "Poste Restante"*
   At the "General Delivery" window

9. Charles: **Y a-t-il du courrier pour moi, s'il vous plaît? Je m'appelle Charles Lewis.**
   Is there any mail for me, please? My name is Charles Lewis.

10. Employée: **Oui, je vois que vous avez plusieurs cartes postales, un mandat-poste, et une lettre recommandée; aussi quelques imprimés. J'aurai besoin d'une pièce d'identité, monsieur.**
    Yes, I see you have several postcards, a postal money order, and a registered letter; also some printed matter. I'll need some identification, sir.

11. Charles: **J'ai mon passeport. Cela suffit?**
    I have my passport. Will that be sufficient?

12. Employée: **Oui. Merci beaucoup, monsieur. Voici votre courrier.**
Yes. Thank you very much, sir. Here's your mail.

C. *Au guichet "Télégrammes"*
At the "Telegraph" window

13. Charles: **Pardon, mademoiselle, comment fait-on pour envoyer un télégramme, s'il vous plaît?**
Excuse me, miss, how does one go about sending a telegram, please?

14. Employée: **Eh bien, monsieur, vous prendrez° un formulaire dans cette petite boîte-là, vous écrirez votre télégramme là-dessus, et puis vous me le remettrez ici.**
Well, sir, you take a form from that little box there, you write out your telegram on it, and then you give it back to me here.

15. Charles: **En effet, c'est très simple...Et voilà! Combien est-ce?**
Really, it's quite simple...There! How much is it?

16. Employée: **Ça dépend du nombre de mots. Je dois compter aussi l'adresse et le nom de l'expéditeur.**
That depends on the number of words. I must also count the address and the name of the sender.

17. Charles: *J'ai aussi un colis à expédier.* **Ce serait quel guichet?**
I have also a package to send. Which window would that be?

18. Employée: **A gauche, au numéro onze.**
To the left, at number eleven.

D. *Au guichet "Colis"*
   At the "Parcel Post" window

19. Charles: **Je voudrais envoyer ce colis aux Etats-Unis.**
    I'd like to send this parcel to the United States.

20. Employée: **Je regrette, monsieur, mais ce colis pèse au-dessus° d'un kilo. Effectivement, il pèse presque trois kilos. Pour la France, ça va,° mais pour les Etats-Unis on permet un maximum d'un kilo.**
    I'm sorry, sir, but this parcel weighs more than one kilo. Actually, it weighs almost three kilos. It's all right for France, but a maximum of one kilo is allowed for the United States.

21. Charles: **Alors, comment devrais-je faire pour expédier ce colis?**
    Then how should I go about shipping this parcel?

22. Employée: **Mais c'est bien simple. *Il faudra l'envoyer* par la gare. Allez à cette adresse. C'est le bureau le plus proche de la S.N.C.F.**
    But that's very simple. It will be necessary to send it by railway. Go to this address. It's the nearest office of French Railways.

23. Charles: **Mais, pardon. Pourquoi aller à un bureau de chemin de fer quand c'est par bateau que je l'enverrai?**
    But, pardon me. Why go to a railway office when it's by boat that I'm going to send it?

24. Employée: **Mais, monsieur, le colis doit aller jusqu'au Havre° par chemin de fer. C'est du Havre que partira le bateau.**
    But sir, the parcel must go to Le Havre by railway. It's from Le Havre that the boat leaves.

E. *Au bureau de la S.N.C.F.*
   At the office of French Railways

25. Charles: **Je voudrais envoyer ce colis.**
    I'd like to send this parcel.

26. Employé: **Très bien. Remplissez cette fiche
    et ces deux Déclarations en Douane.°**
    Very well. Fill out this form and these two
    Customs Declarations.

27. Charles: *Je voudrais aussi le faire assurer.*
    I'd like also to have it insured.

28. Employé: **Quelle en est la valeur?**
    What is the value of it?

29. Charles: **Je dirais cinq cents° francs.**
    I'd say five hundred francs.

30. Employé: **Bien. Passez à la caisse avec ça° et
    revenez ici pour votre reçu.**
    O.K. Go to the cashier with this and come back
    here for your receipt.

NOTES

2. Airmail letters should be weighed before mail-
   ing. Some post offices are rather strict about
   weight.

4. *centimes:* There are one hundred centimes in a
   franc.

6. *un pneumatique:* commonly referred to as a
   pneu or *un petit bleu*. A *pneu* reaches its
   destination within about two hours. The term
   derives from the fact that the letter is propelled
   by compressed air through a pneumatic tube.

7. *poste restante:* general delivery. Many travelers to the larger cities abroad have their mail sent care of large travel services such as American Express or Thomas Cook & Son.

14. *vous prendrez:* The present tense may also be used if the action is going to occur immediately.

20. *ça va:* lit., "that goes," and generally used to indicate approval, as "O.K.," "it's O.K.," or "all right," "it's all right." It can also mean "that's enough."
   au-dessus: plus may also be used to signify "more weight." Thus, . . . *ce colis pèse plus d'un kilo.*

24. *au Havre:* to Le Havre. Le Havre is the maritime port for Paris, and often the port of arrival and departure of transatlantic liners.

26. *Déclaration en Douane:* A description of the contents and a statement of the value of anything being sent out of the country are required on this form.

29. *cinq cents:* Notice the *-s* when *cent* is not followed by another number.

30. *ça: cela*—that, is often used to replace *ceci*—this.

GRAMMATICAL ITEMS FOR SPECIAL STUDY
I. *en and dans in time expressions*

Study these contrasts:

1. La lettre lui parviendra *en deux heures.*
   The letter will reach him within two hours
   [before the end of two hours].

2. Venez prendre votre colis *dans deux heures*.
   Come get your package in two hours [after two
hours have elapsed or at the end of two hours].

II. *avoir à—to have to*

Study these contrasts:

A. Subj.	avoir	Obj. of Inf.	à	Infinitive	
1. J'	ai	un colis	à	expédier.	*I have a package to send.*
2. Elle	a	une lettre	à	écrire.	*She has a letter to write.*

B. Subj.	avoir	à	Infinitive	Object	
1. J'	ai	à	écrire	une lettre.	*I have to (must) write a letter.*
2. J'	ai	à	expédier	un colis.	*I have to (must) send a package.*

Note: The difference in position of the object noun
(colis, lettre) is simply a question of emphasis. The
examples in A, above, would be in response to *"What*
do you have to send or write?" that is, "What is to be
sent or written?" In these cases the object to be sent
or written—a package, a letter— is emphasized. The
statements in B, on the other hand, are in response to
"What do you *have to do?"* in which case *avoir*
emphasizes the obligation to do something.

III. *Position of pronouns before complementary infinitives*

Study:

Main Verb	Prep.	Direct Obj. Pro.	Complementary Infinitive
1. Je dois		le	peser.
2. Il faut		le	faire.
3. Elle voudrait		la	voir.
4. Je ne peux pas		les	expliquer.
5. Elles veulent		nous	accompagner.
6. Je refuse	de	l'	acheter.
7. Vous devrez		vous	dépêcher.
8. Nous apprenons	à	le	dire.

1. *I must weigh it.*

2. *It's necessary to do it.*

3. *She would like to see it* (fem.).

4. *I cannot explain them.*

5. *They want to go with (accompany) us.*

6. *I refuse to buy it.*

7. *You'll have to hurry (yourself).*

8. *We are learning to say it.*

DRILLS AND EXERCISES

I. Substitute each of the words in parentheses for the italicized word or expression in the model sentence. Write the complete sentence and say aloud.

A. Nous avons *une lettre* à écrire. (un livre, un billet, une invitation, une note)

B. J'ai à *faire* ce travail. (commencer, finir, terminer, voir, chercher)

C. Il faut le *faire*. (voir, commencer, comprendre, lire, dire, chercher)

D. Elles *veulent* nous parler. (doivent, peuvent, savent, vont)

II. Expand the following by placing *la voir* at the end of each. Say, write, and translate.

A. Il veut _____.

B. Il voulait _____.

C. Il voudra _____.

D. Il voudrait _____.

E. Il a voulu _____.

F. Il avait voulu _____.

G. Il aurait voulu _____.

III. Translate the following sentences into French; then say them aloud.

1. I'll see you again in three weeks.

2. Can you finish the work within an hour?

3. I have something to tell you.

4. Do you have a telegram to send?

5. We have to write several letters.

6. I can't talk to you now.

7. She's going to do it later.

8. I'd like to see him soon.

Answers at back of book.

QUIZ

From among the three choices, select the one which correctly renders the English word or phrase given, write the complete sentence, and translate.

1. (*I'd like*) _____ envoyer ces lettres.
   (a) Je voulais
   (b) Je plais
   (c) Je voudrais

2. (*Airmail?*) _____?
   (a) Avion courrier
   (b) En avion
   (c) Par avion

3. (*within*) Il lui parviendra _____ une heure.
   (a) en
   (b) dans
   (c) dedans

4. (*me*) Y a-t-il du courrier pour _____?
   (a) me
   (b) moi
   (c) je

5. (*How does one go about*) _____ envoyer un télégramme?
   (a) Comment fait-on autour de
   (b) Comment se fait
   (c) Comment fait-on pour

6. (*is it*) Combien _____?
   (a) est-ce
   (b) est-il
   (c) est-elle

7. (*to send*) J'ai aussi un colis _____.
   (a) expédier
   (b) pour expédier
   (c) à expédier

8. *(more than)* Ce colis pèse _____ un kilo.
   (a) plus qu'
   (b) au dessus d'
   (c) sur d'

9. *(nearest)* C'est le bureau _____.
   (a) le plus proche
   (b) le plus prochain
   (c) plus près

10. *(have it insured)* Je voulais aussi _____.
    (a) faire le assuré
    (b) le faire assuré
    (c) le faire assurer

Answers at back of book.

LESSON 58

LES VÊTEMENTS
CLOTHING

A. *Blanchissage et dégraissage*   Laundering and dry cleaning

1. Blanchisseuse:° **Bonjour, Mme Lewis. Je vois que vous avez plusieurs choses à faire laver.**
   Good day, Mrs. Lewis. I see you have a number of things to have washed.

2. Jeanne: **Oui, j'ai une assez longue liste. Pour commencer, ces trois chemises° de mon mari.**
   Yes, I have a rather long list. To begin with, these three shirts of my husband's.

3. Blanchisseuse: **Voulez-vous les faire empeser?**
   Do you want to have them starched?

4. Jeanne: **Seulement un peu d'amidon au col et aux manchettes, s'il vous plaît.**
Only a little starch on the collar and on the cuffs, please.

5. Blanchisseuse: **En effet, je me rappelle qu'*il ne les aime pas très empesées*.**
That's right, I remember that he doesn't like them very stiff.

6. Jeanne: **Et ce bouton vient de sauter; *puis-je vous demander de le recoudre?***
And this button has just come off; may I ask you to sew it back on?

7. Blanchisseuse: **Certainement, madame. C'est tout ce que vous avez?**
Certainly, madam. Is that all you have?

8. Jeanne: **Mais non! Voici un chemisier, une chemise de nuit, une combinaison, un slip,° un pyjama, des mouchoirs, et des chaussettes. Vous allez tout laver à la main, n'est-ce pas?**
No indeed! Here are a blouse, a nightgown, a slip, a pair of shorts, a pair of pajamas, some handkerchiefs, and some socks. You're going to wash everything by hand, aren't you?

9. Blanchisseuse: **Bien sûr. Pour faire laver du linge à la machine, il faudrait aller à une laverie,° une blanchisserie automatique. Vous voulez tout faire repasser, n'est-ce pas?**
Of course. To have clothes washed by machine, you'd have to go to a machine laundry. You want to have everything ironed, don't you?

10. Jeanne: **Décidément! Merci. Je reviendrai dans trois jours. Au revoir.**
Definitely! Thank you. I'll come back in three days. Good-bye.

B. *Nettoyage* Cleaning

11. Jeanne: **Monsieur, je voudrais faire nettoyer à sec cette robe de soie et faire dégraisser ces gants.**
Sir, I'd like to have this silk dress dry-cleaned and (to have) these gloves cleaned.

12. Concierge: **Il faudra les envoyer au pressing.°**
It will be necessary to send them to the cleaner's.

13. Jeanne: **Combien de temps faudra-t-il?**
How long will it take?

14. Concierge: **Vous les aurez dans la journée. On fait tout sur place maintenant.**
You will have them the same day. Everything is done on the premises now.

15. Jeanne: **Faudra-t-il les porter au pressing soi-même?°**
Does one have to take them to the cleaner's oneself?

16. Concierge: **Mais non, madame. On vient les chercher et *on les ramène* à l'hôtel. Je m'en occuperai.**
Certainly not, madam. They come to get them and they bring them back to the hotel. I'll take care of it.

C. *Chez le tailleur*   At the tailor's

17. Charles: **Je voudrais commander un complet-veston.°**
I'd like to order a business suit.

18. Tailleur: **Certainement, monsieur. Il faut prendre vos mesures: la taille, la longueur des manches, la largeur du pantalon,° la longueur du veston . . .**
Certainly, sir. I must take your measurements: the waist, the length of the sleeves, the width of the trousers, the length of the jacket . . .

19. Charles: **Est-ce qu'il faut venir pour un essayage?**
Do I have to come for a fitting?

20. Tailleur: **Naturellement, monsieur. Il vous faudra au moins trois essayages. Voulez-vous *le bas du pantalon retroussé?°***
Naturally, sir. You'll need at least three fittings. Do you want cuffs on the trousers?

21. Charles: **Oui, et je voudrais un veston à deux boutons.**
Yes, and I'd like a two-button jacket.

22. Tailleur: **Très bien, monsieur. Voulez-vous choisir l'étoffe? Voici des échantillons en alpaga, en laine, et en tweed.**
Very well, sir. Do you want to choose the fabric? Here are some samples in alpaca, in wool, and in tweed.

23. Charles: ***Je préfère* ce tissu-ci, en laine. A propos, je voudrais deux fentes latérales au veston.**
I prefer this cloth, in wool. By the way, I'd like two side slashes on the jacket.

D. *Chez la couturière*   At the dressmaker's

24. Jeanne: **J'aime bien le tailleur que vous m'avez fait, mais il me faut quelques petits changements, quelques petites retouches.**
   I like the suit you made me very much, but I need a few little changes, some minor alterations.

25. Couturière: **Mais non, madame, le tailleur vous va à la perfection.**
   Oh, no, madam, the suit fits you perfectly.

26. Jeanne: **Non, je regrette, mais je veux la jupe raccourcie de quelques centimètres.°**
   No, I'm sorry, but I want the skirt shortened a few centimeters.

27. Couturière: **Si vous voulez, madame. Est-ce que vous trouvez la jaquette à votre gré?**
   If you wish, madam. Do you find the jacket to your liking?

28. Jeanne: **Effectivement, non. Non, je la trouve *un peu trop serrée* à la taille, et un peu trop large aux épaules.**
   As a matter of fact, I don't. No, I find it a little too tight at the waist and a little too wide in the shoulders.

29. Couturière: **Je m'en occuperai, madame. Revenez dans deux jours.**
   I'll take care of it, madam. Come back in two days.

NOTES

1. *la blanchisseuse:* lit., "the whitener." The *blanchisseuse* is a hand laundress whose establishment is *une blanchisserie,* a hand laundry. See Note 9 below.

2. *chemise:* shirt in French—not to be confused with English "chemise" which has a number of meanings. Note also 8—*chemise de nuit*—nightgown.

8. *un slip:* an example of "franglais." Notice that *un slip* is a pair of shorts or bathing trunks and *une combinaison* is a slip.

9. *une laverie:* a laundry where the work is done by machine.

Note: machine à laver—washing machine
machine à écrire—typewriter
machine à coudre—sewing machine

12. *un pressing:* still another example of "franglais," and a commonly used term for a dry-cleaning establishment.

15. *soi-même:* oneself.

17. *complet-veston:* The general term for a man's suit is *un complet*. A lady's suit is *un tailleur*. See dialogue, 24.

18. *un pantalon:* Certain nouns, such as *le pantalon, le pyjama* are always used in the singular since they refer to a pair of trousers or a pair of pajamas.

20. *le bas du pantalon retroussé:* lit., the bottom of the trousers turned up.

26. *un centimètre:* $1/100$ of a meter. A meter (*un mètre*) is the unit of measurement for short distances. A meter is a little longer than a yard.

GRAMMATICAL ITEMS FOR SPECIAL STUDY

I. *Prepositions before infinitives* (review)

Study:

A.

Verb	de	Obj. Pron.	Infinitive
1. Il a *décidé*	de	le	faire.
2. Il a *fini*	de	les	manger.
3. Il m'a *dit*	de		partir.
4. Il m'a *demandé*	de	l'	aider.
5. Il m'a *prié*	de		ne pas parler.
6. *Essayez*	de		venir.

1. *He decided to do it.*
2. *He finished eating them.*
3. *He told me to leave.*
4. *He asked me to help him.*
5. *He begged me not to speak.*
6. *Try to come.*

B.

Verb	à	Infinitive	
1. Elle a *commencé*	à	pleurer.	
2. Elle m'a *invité*	à	venir.	
3. Il m'a *aidé*	à	faire	le travail.
4. J'ai *appris*	à	conduire.	
5. Elles ont *réussi*	à	finir	les devoirs.
6. Nous *tenons*	à	voir	Marie.

1. *She began to cry.*
2. *She invited me to come.*
3. *He helped me to do the work.*

4. *I learned to drive.*
5. *They succeeded in finishing the homework.*
6. *We are anxious to see Marie.*

C.

Verb	sans	Infinitive	
1. Elle est partie	sans	dire	un mot.
2. Tu parles toujours	sans	réfléchir.	

1. *She left without saying a word.*
2. *You always talk without thinking.*

Notes:

1. The verbs in A and B above constitute only a brief list of the more common verbs governing *à* and *de*. You should learn whether any given verb is followed by *à* or *de* before an infinitive or whether the infinitive follows directly, as in *Il faut partir.* See Lesson 41.

2. It is important to remember that *sans* plus the infinitive is the equivalent of *without* ____ -*ing.*

II. *The present tense of verbs mener, to lead, and préférer, to prefer*

Study:

A. je mène   nous menons
   tu mènes   vous menez
   il   } mène   ils   } mènent
   elle}   elles }

NOTES

1. Compounds of mener (e.g., *amener,* to bring, lead to, *emmener,* to take [someone somewhere], *ramener,* to bring back) have the same forms.

2. For other tenses, see *Regular Verb Charts*.

3. The common verb *acheter,* to buy, is also formed like mener.

B. je préfère   nous préférons
   tu préfères   vous préférez
   il ⎫   ils ⎫
   elle⎭ préfère   elles⎭ préfèrent

NOTES

1. Some other common verbs formed like *préférer* are *espérer,* to hope, *protéger,* to protect, *répéter,* to repeat.

2. For other tenses, see *Regular Verb Charts*.

III. *Past participles used as adjectives*

   Study:
   Infinitive:

empeser   1. Il n'aime pas ses chemises très
retrousser   empes*ées.*
serrer   2. Le bas du pantalon est retrouss*é*
cuire   3. Ces souliers sont très serr*és*
                 4. J'aime la viande bien cui*te.*

                 1. *He doesn't like his shirts very stiff*
                    (starched).
                 2. *The bottoms of his trousers are*
                    turned up.
                 3. *These shoes are very tight.*
                 4. *I like meat well done (well*
                    cooked).

Note: Past participles used as adjectives agree in number and gender with the nouns they modify.

DRILLS AND EXERCISES

I. Substitute each of the words or expressions in parentheses for the italicized word or expression in the model sentence. Write the complete sentence and say aloud.

  A. Il a décidé de *partir*. (rentrer, étudier [note: d'], m'aider, venir, le faire)

  B. J'ai appris à *conduire*. (danser, chanter, jouer aux cartes, jouer au tennis, jouer du violon, jouer du piano)

  C. Ils sont *partis* sans dire un mot. (entrés, sortis, arrivés, venus, revenus, rentrés)

  D. Ce *veston* est trop serré. (soulier, manteau, complet, chapeau, pantalon)

II. Transform these sentences to the negative. Say, write, and translate.

  A. Je préfère ce livre-ci.

  B. Ils préfèrent les autres chemises.

  C. Nous répétons la leçon.

  D. La mère protège ses enfants.

  E. Elle mène une vie heureuse.

  F. Il ramène les enfants de l'école.

  G. Nous achetons les robes les plus chères.

III. Translate the following sentences into French; then say them aloud.

  1. I'll ask her to come.

  2. They began to walk quickly.

  3. Don't leave without speaking to me.

  4. She brings her child back from school at noon.

  5. Which fabric do you prefer?

  6. The collar is too starched.

  7. The bottoms of the trousers are too tight.

  8. The steak is well done.

Answers at back of book.

QUIZ

From among the three choices, select the one which correctly renders the English word or phrase given, write the complete sentence, and translate.

1. *(to have washed)* Vous avez plusieurs choses
   _____.

   (a) à se laver
   (b) à faire lavé
   (c) à faire laver

2. *(long)* J'ai une assez _____ liste.
   (a) longe
   (b) longue
   (c) long

3. *(I remember)* _____ qu'il ne les aime pas
   empesées.
   (a) Je rappelle
   (b) Je me rappele
   (c) Je me rappelle

4. *(has just)* Ce bouton _____ sauter.
   (a) vient de
   (b) vient à
   (c) a juste

5. *(by hand)* Vous allez tout laver _____.
   (a) à main
   (b) par main
   (c) á la main

6. *(will it take)* Combien de temps _____?
   (a) prendra-t-il
   (b) faudra-t-il
   (c) sera-t-il

7. *(the same day)* Vous l'aurez _____.
   (a) dans la journée
   (b) dans le jour
   (c) la même jour

8. *(the width)* Il faut mesurer _____ du
    pantalon.
    (a) la largeur
    (b) la grandeur
    (c) le large
9. *(By the way)* _____, je voudrais deux
    fentes latérales.
    (a) Par le chemin
    (b) A propos
    (c) En route
10. *(to your liking)* Est-ce que vous trouvez la
    jaquette _____?
    (a) à votre aimant
    (b) à votre plaisir
    (c) à votre gré

Answers at back of book.

LESSON 59

LE DENTISTE,
LE MÉDECIN,
ET LE PHARMACIEN

THE DENTIST
THE DOCTOR,
AND THE PHARMACIST

A. *Chez le dentiste*   At the dentist's
  1. Dentiste: **Qu'est-ce qui ne va pas, Madame
     Lewis?**
     What's wrong, Mrs. Lewis?
  2. Jeanne: **J'ai une dent *qui me fait terriblement
     mal depuis deux jours*. Elle m'a fait mal aussi
     il y a trois semaines.**
     I have a tooth that's been hurting me terribly for
     two days. It also hurt me three weeks ago.

3. Dentiste: **Il se peut que le nerf soit à vif, puisque vous en souffrez tant.**
It's possible that the nerve is exposed, since you're suffering so much from it.

4. Jeanne: **Croyez-vous que ce soit simplement un nerf exposé? Mes gencives sont tout enflées°...**
Do you believe that it's just an exposed nerve? My gums are all swollen...

5. Dentiste: **Est-ce qu'elles saignent?**
Do they bleed?

6. Jeanne: **Oui, un peu.**
Yes, a little.

7. Dentiste: **Eh bien, je vais les radiographier. Rejetez la tête en arrière et *ouvrez la bouche,* s'il vous plaît... Voilà!**
Well then, I'm going to X-ray them. Put your head back and open your mouth, please... There!

8. Jeanne: **Les radios seront prêtes aujourd'hui même?**
Will the X rays be ready today?

9. Dentiste: **Oui, en quelques minutes. En attendant, *je vais examiner la dent.***
Yes, in a few minutes. In the meantime, I'm going to examine the tooth.

10. Jeanne: **Aïe!° Arrêtez! Ne pouvez-vous pas me donner un anesthésique?**
Ouch! Stop! Can't you give me an anesthetic?

11. Dentiste: **Volontiers, madame. Voulez-vous que je vous fasse une piqûre de novocaïne, ou préférez-vous le gaz?**
Gladly, madam. Do you want me to give you an injection of novocaine, or do you prefer gas?

12. Jeanne: **De la novocaïne, s'il vous plaît. Je ne peux pas supporter la douleur.** *Il y a deux ans* **je me suis évanouie chez le dentiste.**
Novocaine, please. I can't stand pain. Two years ago I fainted at the dentist's.

13. Dentiste: **Ah! Je vois maintenant ce dont vous vous plaignez. C'est une des molaires inférieures, à gauche. Je ne pense pas que ce soit très grave.**
Oh! I see now what you are complaining about. It's one of the lower left molars. I don't think it's very serious.

14. Jeanne: **Pourriez-vous au moins conserver la dent?**
Could you at least save the tooth?

15. Dentiste: **Allons regarder la radiographie. Mmmm . . . La racine paraît saine. Non, il ne faudra pas l'arracher.**
Let's look at the X-ray picture. Mmmm . . . the root seems healthy. No, it won't be necessary to pull it.

16. Jeanne: **Ce n'est qu'une dent cariée, alors?**
It's only a decayed tooth, then?

17. Dentiste: **Justement, c'est une assez grande cavité. Je vais la creuser et la plomber.**
Exactly, it's a rather large cavity. I'm going to drill it and fill it.

B. *La visite du médecin*   The doctor's visit

18. Charles: **Jeanne, je ne vais bien pas du tout.° J'ai mal partout—*à la gorge, à la tête, à l'estomac, aux yeux* . . . J'ai aussi mal *au cœur.***
Jane, I don't feel well at all. Everything hurts me—my throat, my head, my stomach, my eyes . . . I also feel nauseated.

19. Jeanne: **En effet, tu as mauvaise mine.°** Je
    vais faire venir le médecin.
    As a matter of fact, you look bad. I'm going to
    send for the doctor...

20. Docteur: *Ouvrez la bouche,* **monsieur. Je vais**
    prendre votre température.° Ah! Vous avez
    justement un peu de fièvre, et *vous avez la*
    gorge toute rouge.° **Toussez, maintenant.** *Je*
    veux écouter les poumons.
    Open your mouth, sir. I'm going to take your
    temperature Ah! You do have a little fever, and
    your throat is all red. Now, cough. I want to
    listen to your lungs.

21. Jeanne: **Qu'est-ce qu'il faut faire, docteur?**
    What must I do (What must be done), Doctor?

22. Docteur **Votre mari doit garder le lit pen-**
    dant deux ou trois jours, jusqu'à ce qu'il°
    n'ait plus de fièvre.
    Your husband must stay in bed for two or three
    days until he has no more fever.

23. Jeanne: **Est-ce qu'il peut manger de tout?**
    Can he eat everything? (lit.: Is he able to eat
    [something] of everything?)

24. Docteur: **Mais non. Il doit faire des repas**
    légers et boire beaucoup de jus de fruits. Il
    devra aussi prendre les pilules° que je vais
    lui prescrire maintenant.
    No, indeed. He must take light meals and drink
    a lot of fruit juice. He'll also have to take the
    pills that I'm going to prescribe for him now.

25. Jeanne: **Quels sont vos honoraires, docteur?**
    What is your fee, doctor?

26. Docteur: **Vingt-cinq francs, madame. Mais
    ça ne presse pas. Je voudrais revoir votre
    mari demain dans l'après-midi.**
    Twenty-five francs, madam. But there's no
    hurry. I'd like to see your husband again to-
    morrow during the afternoon.

C. *A la pharmacie* At the pharmacy

27. Jeanne: **Je voudrais faire préparer cette or-
    donnance, s'il vous plaît**
    I'd like to have this prescription filled, please.

28. Pharmacien: **Je vous la prépare tout de suite
    ... Le malade doit prendre deux pilules
    trois fois par jour, avant les repas.**
    I'll fill it for you right away ... The patient has
    to take two pills three times a day, before
    meals.

29. Jeanne: **Ah! J'avais presque oublié ... J'ai
    besoin d'une bonne lotion** *pour les cheveux,*
    **des lames de rasoir, et de la crème à déma-
    quiller ...**
    Oh! I'd almost forgotten ... I need a good hair
    lotion, some razor blades, and some cleansing
    cream.

30. Pharmacien: **Voici un grand assortiment de
    crèmes. Si madme permet, je suggère celle-
    ci. Nos clientes en achètent beaucoup.**
    Here is a large assortment of creams. If madam
    will permit me, I suggest this one. Our cus-
    tomers buy a lot of it.

NOTES

4. *tout enflées:* all swollen. *Tout(e)(s)*, in this
   adverbial context, is used as an intensifier (the
   equivalent of *entirely, all, very, awfully,
   quite*). Notice that, although the adjective,

enflées, is feminine plural, *tout* has not changed its form. This is true before feminine adjectives beginning with a vowel. See also 20 below.

10. *aïe:* "ouch" is expressed in different ways in all languages of the world.

18. *pas du tout:* not at all. The phrase *du tout* is very commonly used to express the negative "at all." Examples: *Rien du tout.* Nothing at all. *Il ne peut pas manger du tout.* He can eat nothing at all. *or* He can't eat at all. Note the difference between *du tout* and *de tout,* which is used in 23 of the text.

Notice that, for parts of the body, the definite article is often used, rather than the possessive. See Grammatical Items, IV, A and B.

19. *tu as mauvaise mine:* lit., you have a bad appearance. Note the omission of the article.

20. *température:* temperature is measured in degrees Centigrade. 37°C is normal body temperature.

toute rouge: lit., "entirely red." *Toute* is again used as an intensifier, as in Note 4 above. Notice, however, that here *tout* changes its form to agree with a feminine adjective beginning with a consonant.

22. *jusqu'à ce que:* until (with following verb).

24. *pilule:* a general word for "pill." The words *un comprimé* and *un cachet* are synonymous with *une pilule.*

GRAMMATICAL ITEMS FOR SPECIAL STUDY

I. *The present tense with depuis*

Study:

Present of Verb	Complement	depuis	Time Expression
1. J'ai	mal aux dents	depuis	deux jours.
2. Elle lit		depuis	trois heures.
3. Nous sommes	en France	depuis	six ans.
4. Ils étudient	le français	depuis	sept mois.

1. *I've had a toothache for two days.*

2. *She's been reading for three hours.*

3. *We've been in France for six years.*

4. *They've been studying French for seven months.*

NOTES

1. The time expression with *depuis* always comes at the of the sentence.

2. Another way of expressing the same idea is to use *il y a* + time + *que* + the present tense. Examples:

   a. Il y a deux jours que j'ai mal aux dents.
      I've had a toothache for two days.

   b. Il y a deux heures que j'étudie
      I've been studying for two hours.

II. A. *il y a* + *time* + *que* + *past tense* = *ago*

Study these sentences and their meanings:

Il y a	Time	que	Past Tense
1. Il y a	deux heures	que	je l'ai vu.
2. Il y a	deux jours	que	je l'ai vue.
3. Il y a	huit jours	que	nous l'avons vu.
4. Il y a	quinze jours	que	vous l'avez reçu.
5. Il y a	trois semaines	que	tu y es allé(e).
6. Il y a	un an	qu'	ils y sont allés.

1. *I saw him two hours ago.*

2. *I saw her two days ago.*

3. *We saw him a week ago.* (Notice the use of *huit jours* to mean "a week.")

4. *You received it two weeks ago.* (Notice the use of *quinze jours* to mean "two weeks.")

5. *You went there three weeks ago.*

6. *They went there a year ago.*

B. *Past tense + il y a + time = ago*

Study these sentences and their meanings. Compare the word order with the sentences in A, above.

Past Tense	il y a	Time	
1. Je l'ai vu	il y a	deux ans.	*I saw him two years ago.*
2. Tu l'a reçu	il y a	huit jours.	*You received it a week ago.*
3. Il y est allé	il y a	plus d'un an.	*He went there more than a year ago.*

NOTES

1. When you wish to express *time ago,* you can use either a) *Il y a* + time + *que* + past tense, as in Section A; or b) past tense + *il y a* + time, as in Section B.

2. All the above sentences denote action *completed in the past.*

III. *il se peut + subjunctive* (subjunctive of possibility)

Study:

Il se peut		que	Subject	Sub-junctive	Comple-ment
1. Il se peut		qu'	elle	soit	malade.
2. Il se peut		que	vous	ayez	raison.
3. Il se peut		qu'	il	ne puisse pas	venir.
4. Il se peut		que	nous	finissions	le travail.
5. Il se peut		qu'	ils	aient vendu	la maison.

1. *It's possible that she is sick.*

2. *It's possible that you are right.*

3. *It's possible that he may not be able to come.*

4. *It's possible that we may finish the work.*

5. *It's possible that they have sold the house.*

IV. *Definite article with parts of the body*

Study:

A.

	à + Def. Art.	Part of Body
1. J'ai mal	à l'	estomac.
2. Elle a mal	au	foie.
3. Elle a mal	aux	dents.
4. Il a mal	à la	gorge.

1. *I have a stomachache.*
2. *She has a liver complaint.*
3. *She has a toothache.*
4. *He has a sore throat.*

B.

	Def. Art.	Part of Body	
1. Il a	les	yeux	bleus.
2. Elle a	les	cheveux	noirs.
3. Elle a	les	lèvres	rouges.
4. Elle a	le	nez	retroussé.
5. Elle a	l'	oreille	fine.

1. *He has blue eyes.*
2. *She has black hair.*
3. *She has red lips.*
4. *She has a turned-up nose.*
5. *Her hearing is acute. [She has sharp ears.]*

DRILLS AND EXERCISES

I. Substitute each of the words or expressions in parentheses for the italicized word or expression in the model sentence. Write the complete sentence and say aloud.

A. Ils étudient *le français* depuis sept mois. (l'italien, l'espagnol, l'anglais, l'allemand, le japonais)

B. J'étudie le français depuis *sept mois.* (trois ans, huit jours, quinze jours, six semaines, cinq ans)

C. Il y a *trois ans* que je demeure ici. (deux ans, six mois, quinze jours, huit semaines, une quinzaine d'années)

D. Il y a *une heure* que je l'ai vu. (huit jours, un mois, deux mois, un an, longtemps)

E. Il se peut qu'elle soit *malade.* (fâchée, fatiguée, triste, malheureuse, morte)

F. Il se peut que nous *partions* demain. (arrivions, sortions, revenions, rentrions, venions)

G. Elle a les cheveux *noirs.* (blonds, blancs, gris, roux, châtains)

II. Transform the sentences with *Il y a* to sentences with *depuis.* Say, write, and translate.

Example: *Il y a un an* que je suis ici./Je suis ici *depuis un an.*

1. Il y a deux jours que j'attends.

2. Il y a un mois qu'elle est malade.

3. Il y a trois semaines que je veux vous parler.

4. Il y a quartre ans qu'il conduit.

5. Il y a une quinzaine de jours que je demeure dans cet hôtel.

III. Translate the following sentences into French; then say them aloud.

1. She's been working since four o'clock.

2. He's been waiting for me since noon.

3. I've been living here for five years.

4. It's possible that she doesn't know the answer.

5. It's possible that he's hungry.

6. It's possible that they arrived too late.

7. Do you have a headache?

8. She has blond hair.

9. It's possible that he has a sore throat.

10. They arrived an hour ago.

11. She studied two hours ago.

12. We have been waiting for a day.

13. I spoke to him a week ago.

Answers at back of book.

QUIZ

From among the three choices, select the one which correctly renders the English word or phrase given, write the complete sentence, and translate.

1. (*What*) _____ ne va pas?
   (a) Quoi
   (b) Qu'est-ce que
   (c) Qu'est-ce qui

2. (*It may be*) _____ que le nerf soit à vif.
   (a) Il se peut
   (b) Il peut
   (c) Il laisse être

3. (*back*) Rejetez la tête _____.
   (a) au dos
   (b) derrière
   (c) en arrière

4. (*I'm not well*) _____, Jeanne.
   (a) Je ne vais pas bon
   (b) Je ne vais pas bien
   (c) Je ne suis pas bon

5. (*stay in bed*) Votre mari doit _____.
   (a) garder couché
   (b) se coucher
   (c) garder le lit.

6. (*light meals*) Il doit faire des _____.
   (a) lumière à manger
   (b) repas légers
   (c) légers dîners

7. (*your fee*) Quels sont _____?
   (a) votre prix
   (b) vos honoraires
   (c) votre honoraire

8. (*everything*) Vous pouvez manger _____.
   (a) de tout
   (b) tous
   (c) du tout

9. (*in the afternoon*) Je voudrais revoir votre mari
   _____.
   (a) en après-midi
   (b) à l'après-midi
   (c) dans l'après-midi

10. (*immediately*) Je vous la prépare _____.
    (a) tout de suite
    (b) tout à fait
    (c) tout à l'heure

Answers at back of book.

LESSON 60

LES CULTES°
RELIGIONS

A. *Les offices divins* Religious services.

1. Charles: **Y a-t-il une église protestante près de l'hôtel? Ma femme et moi,** *nous avons l'habitude d'aller à l'église le dimanche.*
   Is there a Protestant church near the hotel? My wife and I are in the habit of going to church on Sunday.

2. Concierge: **A Paris, monsieur, comme dans toutes les grandes villes de France, on célèbre tous les cultes, y compris le culte protestant. Pour aller à l'office, vous n'avez qu'à vous rendre au temple,° quai d'Orsay.° C'est tout près.**
   In Paris, sir, as in all the big cities of France, all religions are practiced, including the Protestant religion. To go to the service, you only have to go to the temple on the Quai d'Orsay. It's quite near here.

3. Charles: **Vous avez dit "au temple" et non pas "à l'église . . ."**
   You said "to the temple" and not "to the church . . ."

4. Concierge: *C'est exact.* **Les maisons du culte protestant s'appellent "temples."**
   That's right. The houses of worship of the Protestant religion are called "temples."

5. Charles: **A quelle heure commence l'office?**
   At what time does the service begin?

6. Concierge: **Généralement à onze heures. Et tout se passera comme chez vous. Le pasteur prêchera un sermon, vous chanterez vos hymnes favoris, on fera la quête...**
Generally at eleven o'clock. And everything will be as it is in your country. The minister will preach a sermon, you'll sing your favorite hymns, they'll take up a collection...

7. Charles: *C'est tout en français,* **bien entendu.**
It's all in French, of course.

8. Concierge: **A Paris, vous pouvez choisir entre l'office en anglais ou en français. Voici une liste d'églises, de temples, et de synagogues...**
In Paris, you can choose between the service in English or in French. Here's a list of churches, temples, and synagogues.

9. Charles: *Il serait très intéressant d'assister aussi à un service* **de l'église catholique... à la cathédrale de Notre-Dame,° ou à la Madeleine.°**
It would be very interesting to attend a Catholic service also... at Notre Dame Cathedral, or the Madeleine.

10. Concierge: **Sans doute.** *Le dimanche matin on célèbre toujours* **au moins deux messes, at souvent trois.**
Undoubtedly. On Sunday morning at least two masses, and often three, are celebrated.

11. Charles: **L'office de la messe est partout pareil, n'est-ce pas?**
The celebration of the Mass is the same everywhere, isn't it?   •

12. Concierge: **Bien sûr. Comme partout au monde, le prêtre dit la messe aidé par les enfants de chœur.**
Of course. As everywhere in the world, the priest says the Mass, assisted by the altar boys.

13. Charles: **Je note ici que la Grande Synagogue se trouve rue de la Victoire.**
I notice here that the Great Synagogue is located on the rue de la Victoire.

14. Concierge: *Les offices du culte israélite°* ont *lieu le vendredi soir et el samedi matin,* **comme vous devez le savoir. Le rabbin et le chantre seraient heureux de vous accueillir si vous vouliez assiter à un office.**
The services of the Jewish religion take place on Friday night and Saturday morning, as you must know. The rabbi and the cantor would be glad to welcome you if you wished to attend a service.

15. Charles: **Y a-t-il aussi des mosquées à Paris?**
Are there also mosques in Paris?

16. Concierge: **Oui, naturellement, pour le culte islamique.**
Yes, naturally, for the Islamic religion.

17. Jeanne: **Où étais-tu, Charles? Je te cherchais partout.**
Where were you, Charles? I was looking for you everywhere.

18. Charles: **Je parlais au concierge au sujet des cultes. Il m'a dit où se trouve[1] le temple protestant le plus près.°**

---

[1]In the recording you will hear *se trouvait*. However, *se trouve* is correct.

I was talking to the concierge about religions. He told me where the nearest Protestant church is located.

19. Jeanne: **Nous aurons bientôt l'occasion d'assister à un service catholique aussi.**
We'll soon have the opportunity to attend a Catholic service also.

B. *Un mariage français*   A French wedding

20. Jeanne: **Nous venons de recevoir une carte d'invitation.° Regarde.**
We've just received an invitation. Look.

21. Charles: **Tiens!** *C'est le neveu* **de Michel qui se marie!**
Say! It's Michael's nephew who is getting married!
(Lisant)
M. et Mme Dupuy
M. et Mme Bernard
ont la joie de vous annoncer le mariage de leurs enfants Georgette et Paul qui recevront le sacrement de mariage le 3 juillet à 11 heures en l'église Saint-François-Xavier.

Les fiancés et leurs parents seraient heureux si vous pouviez participer à la cérémonie religieuse à laquelle ils vous invitent cordialement.
(Reading)
Mr. and Mrs. Dupuy, Mr. and Mrs. Bernard are happy to announce the marriage of their children Georgette and Paul who will receive the sacrament of marriage on July 3 at 11 o'clock at the church of Saint Francis Xavier.

The betrothed couple and their parents would be happy if you would take part in the religious ceremony to which they cordially invite you.

Je vais donner un coup de fil à Michel tout de suite. On pourrait peut-être y aller ensemble.
I'm going to give Michael a ring right now. Perhaps we might be able to go there together.

C. *Charles parle au téléphone avec Michel*
Charles speaks to Michael on the phone

22. Charles: **Nous n'avons jamais assisté à un mariage en France, et nous avons pensé que, si cela vous convient, on irait ensemble.**
We've never attended a wedding in France, and we thought that, if it's all right with you, we would go together.

23. Michel: **Je regrette, Charles, mais, malheureusement, *ce ne sera pas possible. Il faut que je sois* témoin au mariage civil° de Georgette et Paul qui aura lieu à la mairie du XVI° arrondissement° le même jour à neuf heures et demie du matin.**
I'm sorry, Charles, but unfortuantely it will not be possible. I have to be a witness at Georgette and Paul's civil marriage which will take place at the town hall of the sixteenth arrondissement the same day at nine thirty in the morning.

24. Charles: **Pensez-vous que nous puissions assiter aussi à ce mariage civil?**
Do you think we might also attend this civil marriage?

25. Michel: **Oh, oui, certainement. Ma sœur sera enchantée de vous voir.**

Oh, yes, certainly. My sister will be delighted to see you.

26. Charles: *A samedi, alors, à neuf heures quinze, à la mairie du XVI°* ...
Until Saturday, then, at nine fifteen, at the town hall of the XVIth ...

NOTES

Title. *les cultes:* There is complete religious freedom in France.

2. *vous rendre au temple:* literally, to render yourself to the church. *Se rendre à* + place name is equivalent to *aller à* + place name. Examples:

Je me rends à l'école ⎫
Je vais à l'école. ⎬ I'm going to school.
⎭

Se rendre is also used as "to make oneself," "to drive oneself." Examples:

Ça me rend fou	That's driving me crazy.
Elle se rend malade.	She's making herself sick.

quai d'Orsay: one of the many quays along the Seine. The Ministry of Foreign Affiars is located on this quay.

9. *cathédrale de Notre-Dame:* La Cathédrale Notre-Dame de Paris is one of the world's most magnificent works of Gothic architecture. Construction was begun in 1163, and was not completed until 1245. Notre-Dame has been the site of many of the greatest events in French history, including the coronation of Napoleon and, more recently, the great Te Deum celebrating the Liberation of Paris. The

cathedral is referred to in conversation as *la cathédrale de Notre-Dame,* or, most often, simply as *Notre-Dame.*

la Madeleine: A Greek-style church on the Right Bank of the Seine, not far from the Operá. The Madeleine is the site of many fashionable weddings.

14. *culte israélite:* literally, Israelite cult. Other words associated with Judaism:

juif (m.)
juive (f.) } Jew *and* Jewish;

l'hébreu (m.), Hebrew; *Israël,* Israel.

18. *le plus près:* It is equally correct to say *le plus proche.*

20. *carte d'invitation:* an invitation. An announcement is *une carte* or *une lettre de faire-part.* Lit., *faire-part* means "to make a party to," and is used for announcements of births, deaths, marriages, and other events of this nature.

23. *mariage civil:* A civil marriage is required. The religious marriage ceremony is optional and follows the civil ceremony. The priest, minister, or rabbi must have the civil marriage certificate before performing the religious ceremony.

arrondissement: Administratively, France is divided into 94 *départements* and la Ville de Paris. Each *département* is subdivided into *arrondissements.* Like a *départment,* Paris is divided into *arrondissements,* each of which is headed by a *maire* whose offices are in the *mairie.* There are 20 *arrondissements* in Paris.

26. *XVIᵉ arrondissement:* the arrondissement of Passy, a fashionable residential district of Paris. Notice that the number is in Roman numerals. The little ᵉ is an abbreviation for *-ième,* equivalent to English th, nd, rd, as in 16th, 2nd, 3rd.

GRAMMATICAL ITEMS FOR SPECIAL STUDY

I. *falloir* + *the subjunctive*

Study:

Falloir	que	Subjunctive	Complement
1. Il faut	que	j'aille	à la bibliothèque.
2. Il faut	qu'	il garde	le lit.
3. Il fallait	qu'	il prenne	ses pilules.
4. Il faudra	que	nous fassions	de notre mieux.
5. Il faudrait	qu'	ils viennent	à trois heures.

1. *I have to go [It is necessary that I go] to the library.*

2. *He has to stay [It is necessary that he stay] in bed.*

3. *He had to take [It was necessary that he take] his pills.*

4. *We will have to do [It will be necessary that we do] our best.*

5. *They would have to come [It would be necessary that they come] at three o'clock.*

NOTE

1. *Falloir* is used only impersonally, that is, with the subject *il.*

2. Refer to Lesson 53 for *falloir* with indirect object pronouns, and to Lesson 44, for review of subjunctive.

II. *Time expressions with days of the week*

Study these contrasts:

1. Il vient *dimanche* à trois heures.
   He is coming Sunday at three o'clock.

   Il vient *le dimanche* (or *les dimanches*).
   He comes on Sundays.

2. Il n'est pas allé à l'école *mercredi*.
   He didn't go to school Wednesday.

   Il ne va pas à l'école *le jeudi* (or *les jeudis*).
   He doesn't go to school on Thursdays.

III. *Some uses of il est and c'est*

Study these contrasts:

A. Il (Elle) est	Prof., etc.	C'est	Indef.	Modifier	Prof., etc.
1. Il est	médecin.	C'est	un	bon	médecin.
2. Il est	catholique.	C'est	un		catholique.
3. Il est	Français.	C'est	un		Français.
4. Elle est	royaliste.	C'est	une		royaliste.

1. *He is a doctor.*   *He is a good doctor.*

2. *He is Catholic.*   *He is a Catholic.*

3. *He is French.*   *He is a Frenchman.*

4. *She is a royalist.*   *She is a royalist.*

NOTES

1. Use *il est* without an article; use *c'est* with an article.

2. A modifier cannot be used with *Il est*. Contrast:

C'est un bon médecin.   *He's a good doctor.*
Il est médecin.   *He's a doctor.*

B.

Il est	Adjective	de	Inf.	Comp.	C'est	Adjective	à Inf.
1. Il est	facile	de	voir	Paris.	C'est	facile	à voir.
2. Il est	difficile	de	faire	cela.	C'est	difficile	à faire.
3. Il est	important	de	savoir	son nom.	C'est	important	à savoir.

1. *It is easy to see Paris.*   *It is easy to see.*

2. *It is difficult to do that.*   *It is difficult to do.*

3. *It is important to know his name.* *It is important to know.*

NOTES

1. When there is a complement to the infinitive, use *il est* + adjective + *de* + infinitive + complement.

2. When there is **no** complement, use *c'est* + adjective + *à* + infinitive.

C.

Il est	Adjective	que + verb	C'est	Adjective
1. Il est	vrai	qu'elle est venue.	C'est	vrai.
2. Il est	probable	qu'elle est arrivée.	C'est	probable.
3. Il est	certain	que vous avez tort.	C'est	certain.
4. Il est	possible	qu'elle soit venue.	C'est	possible.

1. It is true that she came. *It's (That's) true.*
2. It is probable that she arrived. *It's probable.*
3. It is certain that you are wrong. *It is certain.*
4. It is possible that she came. *It is possible.*

Note: Use *Il est* when the adjective is followed by a clause; use *C'est* when the adjective is used alone.

D.

C'est/ Ce sont	Noun/Pronoun	
1. C'est	Jean.	*It's John.*
2. C'est	une table.	*It's a table.*
3. C'est	une petite fille.	*It's a little girl.*
4. C'est	moi.	*It's I.*
5. C'est	le mien.	*It's mine.*
6. C'est	celui-là.	*It's that one.*
7. C'est	tout.	*It's everything. (That's all.)*
8. Ce sont	mes amis.	*They are my friends.*
9. Ce sont	ceux de mon frère.	*They are my brother's.*

DRILLS AND EXERCISES

I. Substitute each of the words or expressions in parentheses for the italicized word or expression in the model sentence. Write the complete sentence and say aloud.

A. Il faut que j'aille à *la bibliothèque*. (au magasin, à l'opéra, à la banque, à la poste, au garage)

B. Il faut qu'il apprenne *le français*. (les mathématiques, l'histoire, les sciences, la biologie, la chimie)

C. Il est *médecin*. (avocat, professeur, banquier, chirurgien, dentiste, pharmacien, tailleur, coiffeur)

D. C'est *le mien*. (le tien, le sien, le vôtre, le nôtre, le leur)

E. Ce sont les *miennes*. (les tiennes, les vôtres, les leurs, les siennes, les nôtres)

F. C'est facile à *voir*. (faire, comprendre, dire, apprendre, lire)

G. Il est *possible* qu'elle soit malade. (regrettable, triste, étonnant, douteux, incroyable)

II. Translate the following sentences into French; then say them aloud.

1. I have to go to the bank now.

2. We have to do our work now.

3. She'll have to take the plane.

4. On Sundays, they go to church.

5. She went to church on Sunday.

6. He's a teacher.

7. He's a good teacher.

8. It's not easy.

9. That's not easy to say.

10. It's possible that she can't come.

11. That pen? It's mine.

Answers at back of book.

QUIZ

From among the three choices, select the one which correctly renders the English word or phrase given, write the complete sentence, and translate.

1. *(near)* Y a-t-il une temple _____ l'hôtel?
   (a) voisin
   (b) près de
   (c) près

2. *(including)* On célèbre tous les cultes, _____ le culte protestant.
   (a) y compris
   (b) incluant
   (c) ci-inclus

3. *(naturally)* C'est tout en français, _____.
   (a) nature
   (b) entendu
   (c) bien entendu

4. *(take place)* Les offices _____ le vendredi soir.
   (a) prennent place
   (b) prennent lieu
   (c) ont lieu

5. *(attend)* Si vous voulez _____ un service, allez-y.
   (a) assister à
   (b) attendre
   (c) aller

6. *(about)* Je parlais _____ de temples.
   - (a) autour
   - (b) au sujet
   - (c) vers

7. *(telephone)* Je vais _____ à Michel.
   - (a) donner un téléphone
   - (b) donner un coup
   - (c) donner un coup de fil

8. *(If that's all right with you)* _____, on irait ensemble.
   - (a) Si c'est juste avec vous
   - (b) Si cela a raison
   - (c) Si cela vous convient

9. *(in the morning)* Il se marie à 9 h 30 _____.
   - (a) du matin
   - (b) dans le matin
   - (c) en matin

10. *(could)* Pensez-vous que nous _____ assister à ce mariage civil?
    - (a) pouvons
    - (b) pourrions
    - (c) puissions

Answers at back of book.

SUMMARY OF
FRENCH GRAMMAR

About the Sounds

Very few sounds are exactly alike in both English and French. The pronunciation equivalents given below can therefore be only approximate. Although exceptions exist for almost every pronunciation rule, the guidelines in this section should prove useful to the student.

The Consonants. French consonant sounds are generally softer than those of English. A number of them are produced by bringing the tongue in contact with different parts of the mouth cavity than for the equivalent English consonant, or by changing the pressure of the airstream. For example, the English speaker produces the sound of *d, t,* or *n* by placing the tip of the tongue *against the gum ridge behind* the upper teeth. The French speaker produces these sounds by placing the tip of the tongue *against the back* of the upper teeth.

In pronouncing a *p* at the beginning of a word such as "pat" or "pen," the English speaker produces a puff of air, whereas the French speaker does not. Try holding your hand in front of your mouth and say the words "pit," "pack," and "punch." You will feel the puff of air each time you say the *p* at the beginning of each of these words. The French speaker, on the other hand, produces the *p* at the beginning of words *without* the puff of air. The French *p* is close in sound to the English *p* in words like "speak" or "spot."

The pronunciation of the sound *l* also varies in the two languages. American English has two *l* sounds—one which is used at the beginning of a word (the "light" *l*), and another which is used in the middle or at the end of a word (the "dark" *l*). Contrast the *l* sound in the words "like" and "beautiful." The *l* in "like" is a "light" *l*, and this is the *l* sound pronounced in French.

The Vowels. Some of the vowel sounds of French resemble the vowels in English. Many vowel sounds, however, are quite different, and some do not exist in English at all. For example, the sound represented by *é* resembles the English *ay* in the word "day," but the two sounds are not the same. When an English speaker says "day," he is actually pronouncing two sounds: an *a* and a *y*, which glide together to form a diphthong. Try holding your hand on your jaw and saying the words listed below. As you do so, notice how your jaw closes up a bit toward the end of the *ay* sound:

> day   say   may   ray   nay   tray   jay

In French, however, the jaw does not move as you say the *é* sound; it remains steady. Pronounce the following French words, while holding the jaw still.

> des   bébé   faché   mes   réalité

A similar phenomenon occurs with the sound *o*. Say the following words in English:

> bow   tow   know   so

Note that the jaw rises at the end of the sound as though to close on the sound *w*. Hold your hand on your jaw and say the above words "in slow motion." Now, leaving off the *w* sound at the end by holding the jaw steady, say the following words in French:

beau   tôt   nos   sot   (the final consonants are silent)

Space does not permit us to compare every English sound with its French counterpart, but the charts below will help to clarify the sounds. Repeated imitation of the speakers on the recordings will be most important in your learning to pronounce French correctly.

1. THE ALPHABET

Letter	Name	Letter	Name	Letter	Name
a	a	j	ji	s	esse
b	be	k	ka	t	te
c	ce	l	elle	u	u
d	de	m	emme	v	ve
e	e	n	enne	w	double ve
f	effe	o	o	x	iks
g	ge	p	pe	y	i grec
h	ache	q	ku	z	zede
i	i	r	erre		

2. THE CONSONANTS

The letters *b, d, f, k, l, m, n, p, s, t, v,* and *z* are pronounced approximately as in English when they are not in final position, but with the differences indicated above. Note however:

c   before *a, o, u, l,* and *r* is like the *c* in "cut."
        Ex., *carte, coeur, cuisine, clarté, croire*
        before *e* and *i,* is like *s* in "see." Ex.,
        centre, cinéma

ç   (*c* with cedilla) is like *s* in "see."   Ex.,
      français, garçon

ch is like *sh* in "ship." Ex., *chéri, cheval*. But:
      chr is pronounced like English *kr*. Ex.,
      chrétien

g   before *a, o, u, l, r* is like *g* in "go." Ex.,
      gare, goût, guerre, glace, grand
      before *e* and *i*, is like the *s* sound in "mea-
      sure." Ex., *genre, voyageur, Gigi*

gn is like *ni* in "onion" or *ny* in "canyon."
      Ex., *oignon, soigner*

h   is not pronounced. Ex., *heure*

j   is like the *s* sound in "measure."   Ex.,
      bonjour, joie

l   is always "light" (as explained above)
      when it is pronounced as *l*. However, in
      the following combinations it is pro-
      nounced like the *y* in "yes": -*ail*, -*eil*,
      -*eille*, -*aille*, -*ille*, -*ill*. Ex., *chandail, ver-
      meil, oreille, grisaille, vieillard*. But: in
      mille, ville the *l*'s are pronounced as *l*.

qu before *a, e, i, o, u* is like *k*. Ex., *qui,
      quotidien*
      before *oi* is like *kwa*. Ex., *quoi*

r   is made farther back in the throat than the
      English *r;* almost like a gargle. There is
      also the *trilled r,*which is used by some
      people in various parts of the country,
      particularly in the South. The *trilled r* is
      formed by the tip of the tongue against
      the gum ridge back of the upper teeth in a
      rapid succession of taps. Both ways of
      pronouncing *r* are considered correct.

s   is generally like the *s* in "see." Ex., *soir,
      estimer*
      between vowels is like the *s* in "rose." Ex.,
      rose, vase

w   (occurring only in foreign words) is generally pronounced *v*. Ex., *wagon*
is sometimes pronounced *w*. Ex., *whisky*

final   As a general rule, final consonants are si-
conso-   lent. However, words ending in *c, f, l,*
nants   and *r* often do pronounce the final consonant. Ex.:

-c: parc, sac, trafic
-f: bref, chef, oeuf
-l: moral, Noël, journal
-r: sur, erreur, manoir

There are several cases in which the final
r is generally silent:

1) The infinite ending of *-er* verbs. Ex.,
parler, aller, jouer
2) Names of certain tradespeople. Ex.,
le boucher, le boulanger, le plombier
3) Nouns ending in *-er*. Ex., *verger,*
soulier, tablier

There are many common words ending
in *c, l,* and *f* in which the final consonant is silent. Ex., *estomac, banc,*
blanc, gentil, pareil, clef

3. SIMPLE VOWELS

a   as in "ah!" or "father." Ex., *pâté, mâle,*
Jacques
as in "marry." Ex., *ami, mal*
e   as in "let." Ex., *belle, cher, cette*
as in "day," without the *y* sound at the
end (as explained above). This occurs
in monosyllables or words ending in *-
er, -et,* or *-ez,* and is the same sound as
é. Ex., *les, des, laver, filet, allez*
as in "the" (the "mute" *e* between two
single consonants or in monosyllabic

words). Ex., *depuis, le, petit, tenir, besoin*

The unaccented *e* is silent ("mute") at the end of a word. Ex., *parle, femme, limonade*

é   (*accent aigu*) as in "day," without the *y* sound at the end. Ex., *église, école, fâché, réalité*

è   (*accent grave*) as in "let." Ex., *père, mètre, Agnès*

ê   (*accent circonflexe*) as in "let." Ex., *tête, être*

i   as in "machine." The letter *y*, when it acts as a vowel, is pronounced the same way. Ex., *machine, lycée, qui, bicyclette*

o   (closed o) as in "go" (without the *w* sound at the end, as explained above). Ex., *tôt, mot, dos*

(open o) as in "north." Ex., *robe, alors, bonne, gosse*

u   has no equivalent in English. To approximate the sound, say *ee*, keep the tongue in the position of *ee* (with the tip of the tongue against the bottom teeth), and then round the lips. Ex., *lune, nuit, assure*

ai   as in "day" (without the *y* sound at the end). Ex., *mais, caisson, lait*

ei   as in "let." Ex., *reine, peine*

au   as in "go" (without the *w* sound at the end). Ex., *auprès, pauvre, eau, eau(x)*

eu   has no equivalent in English. To approximate the sound, place the tongue as if for *é*, but round the lips as for *o*. Ex., *deux, feu, peu, ceux*

œ   has no equivalent in English. It is more "open" than *eu*. To form the sound, place the tongue as if for the *e* of "let," but round the lips. This sound is usually followed by a consonant, as in *sœur, cœur*

oi pronounced *wa*. Ex., *moi, voilà*

ou as in "too." Ex., *nous, vous, cousin, rouge, amour*

4. THE NASALIZED VOWELS

When the consonants *n* and *m* are preceded by a vowel, the sound is generally nasalized; that is, the airstream escapes partly through the nose. The four categories of nasalized vowels are as follows:

1. *an, am, en* and *em* are like the vowel in *father* pronounced through the nose:

an	year
ample	ample
en	in
enveloppe	envelope
temps	time

2. *on* and *om* are like the vowel in *north* pronounced through the nose:

bon	good
tomber	to fall

3. *in, im, ein, eim, ain* and *aim* are like the vowel in *at* pronounced through the nose:

fin	end
simple	simple
faim	hunger
plein	full

4. *un* and *um* are like the vowel in *burn* pronounced through the nose:

un	one
chacun	each one
humble	humble

Vowels are nasalized in the following cases:

1. When the *n* or *m* is the final consonant or one of the final consonants:

fin	end
pont	bridge
champ	field
temps	time

2. In the middle of a word, when the *n* or *m* is not followed by a vowel:

NASALIZED

chambre	room	*impossible*	impossible

NOT NASALIZED

inutile	useless	*inoccupé*	unoccuied
initial	initial	*imitation*	imitation

Note: *mm* and *nn* do not cause the nasalization of the preceding vowel:

flamme	flame	*innocent*	innocent
donner	to give	*immense*	immense

Note: Most of the grammatical material outlined in the following pages is treated fully in the lessons.

5. THE APOSTROPHE

Certain one-syllable words ending in a vowel drop ("elide") the vowel when they come before words beginning with a vowel sound.

This dropping of the vowel or "elision" is marked by an apostrophe. Common cases are:

1. The *a* of *la:*

je l'aime	I like her (or it)	*l'heure*	the hour
l'amande	the almond		

2. The vowel *e* in one-syllable words (*le, je, se, me, que,* etc.):

l'argent	the money	*j'habite*	I live
j'ai	I have		

3. the vowel *i* in *si* "if," when it comes before *il* "he" or *ils* "they":

s'il vous plaît   please ("if it pleases you")

4. *moi* and *toi* when they come before *en* are written *m'* and *t':*

Donnez-m'en   Give me some of it (of them).

5. A few words like *aujourd'hui* today, *entr'acte* interlude, etc.

6. THE DEFINITE ARTICLE

	SINGULAR	PLURAL
Masculine	*le*	*les*
Feminine	*la*	*les*

SINGULAR

le garçon   the boy
la jeune fille   the young girl

PLURAL

les garçons   the boys
les jeunes filles the young girls

1. *Le* and *la* become *l'* before words beginning with a vowel sound:

This contraction takes place before most words beginning with *h* (this *h* is called "mute" *h*). There are a few words where this contraction does not occur (this *h* is called "aspirate" *h*):

l'ami	the friend	*l'heure*	the hour
le héros	the hero	*la hache*	the axe

2. Unlike English, the definite article is used in French before a noun used in a general

sense, before titles, days of the week, parts
of the body, etc.:

l'avocat	the lawyer
l'avion	the airplane
le dimanche	Sunday (*or* Sundays)
le Comte . . .	Count . . .
J'aime les livres	I like books
Le fer est utile.	Iron is useful.
L'avarice est un vice.	Avarice is a vice.
Je vais me laver les mains.	I'm going to wash my hands.

3. The definite article is used with names of languages, unless preceded by *en:*

Le français est difficile.	French is difficult.

But—

Elle ranconte l'histoire en français.	She tells the story in French.

Note: The article is usually omitted with the
name of a language used immediately after the
verb *parler:*

Elle parle français.	She speaks French.

4. Unlike English, the definite articles must be
   repeated before each noun they modify.

les portes et les fenêtres	the doors and windows

7. THE INDEFINITE ARTICLE

	SINGULAR	PLURAL
Masculine	*un*	*des*
Feminine	*une*	*des*

SINGULAR	
un homme	a man
une femme	a woman

PLURAL	
des hommes	men; some men; a few men
des femmes	women; some women; a few women

1. The indefinite article is omitted before an un-modified statement of profession, national-ity, rank, etc.:

Je suis médicin.	I am a doctor.
Elle est américaine.	She is an American.
Il est capitaine.	He is a captain.

2. The indefinite articles are repeated before each noun:

un homme et une femme	a man and woman

8. THE POSSESSIVE

The possessive is expressed in the following way: state the thing possessed + *de* ("of") + the possessor:

le livre de Marie	Mary's book ("the book of Mary")
la plume de l'élève	the pupil's pen ("the pen of the pupil")

9. CONTRACTIONS

1. The preposition *de* "of" combines with the definite articles *le* and *les* as follows:

de + le = du:	*le livre du professeur*	the teacher's book
de + les = des:	*les plumes des élèves*	the pupil's pens

2. The preposition *a* "to" combines with the articles *le* and *les* as follows:

a + le = au:	*Il parle au garçon.*	He's talking to the boy.
a + les = aux:	*Il parle aux garçons.*	He's talking to the boys.

10. GENDER

All English nouns take the articles *the* or *a(n)*. Adjectives modifying English nouns do not

change their form. In French, however, all nouns
show gender *(masculine or feminine)*, and adjectives agree with nouns in gender and number
(singular or plural).

Masculine nouns: Take the definite article *le* in
the singular and *les* in the plural, and the indefinite artcile *un*. They are modified by the
masculine form of an adjective.

Ex., *le costume brun*   the brown suit
     les costumes   the brown suits
       bruns

Feminine nouns: Take the definite article *la* in
the singular and *les* in the plural, and the indefinite article *une*. They are modified by the
feminine form of an adjective.

Ex., *la robe brune*   the brown dress
     les robes brunes   the brown dresses

The gender of each noun must be learned with
the noun. The following tables describing which
noun classes are masculine and which are feminine provide a general rule of thumb. There are a
number of exceptions to each statement.

*The following classes of nouns are generally
masculine*.

1. Nouns naming a male person. Ex., *le père*
   father, *le roi* king.
   But: *la sentinelle* sentinel
2. Nouns ending in a consonant. Ex., *le parc*
   park, *le pont* bridge, *le tarif* rate, tariff
   But: Nouns ending in *-ion* and *-son* are generally feminine. Ex., *l'action* action, *la conversation* conversation, *la raison* reason
3. Nouns ending in any vowel except "mute"
   e. Ex., *le pari* bet, wager, *le vélo* bicycle, *le
   menu* menu

4. Nouns ending in -*ment*, -*age*, -*ege* (note that -*age* and -*ege* end in "mute" *e*). Ex., *le ménage* household, *le manège* riding school, *le document* document, *l'usage* usage

5. Names of days, months, seasons, metals, colors, trees, shrubs. Ex.:

le jeudi Thursday	*le bleu* blue
(le) septembre September	*le chêne* oak
le printemps spring	*l'olivier* olive tree
l'or gold	*le genêt* broom (a shrub)
le plomb lead	

6. The names of parts of speech when used as nouns. Ex., *le nom* noun, *le verbe* verb, *le participe* participle

7. Decimal weights and measures. Ex., *le mètre* meter, *le litre* liter, *le kilogramme* kilogram. Note the contrast with a nondecimal measure: *la livre* pound

8. The names of the cardinal points. Ex., *le nord* north, *l'est* east, *le sud* south, *l'ouest* west.

The following classes of nouns are generally feminine:

1. Nouns naming a female person. Ex., *la mère* mother, *la reine* queen.
   But: *le professeur* teacher (m. or f.)

2. Nouns ending in -*te*, -*son*, -*ion*. Ex., *la détente* détente, *la raison* reason, *la conversation* conversation
   But: *le camion* truck, *l'avion* airplane, *le million* million

3. Names of qualities or states of being ending in:

-*nce*	*la distance* distance
-*esse*	*la gentilesse* niceness
-*eur*	*la eur* width
	la douceur sweetness

But: *le bonheur* happiness, *le malheur* un-
happiness, pain
-ude   *la gratitude* gratitude

4. Most nouns ending in mute *e*. Ex., *la blague*
   joke, *la voiture* car
   But: See exceptions mentioned in item 4,
   page 283, under nouns of masculine gender.
5. Names of moral qualities, sciences, and arts.
   Ex., moral qualities: *la bonté* kindness,
   l'avarice greed
   science: *l'algèbra* algebra, *la chimie* chem-
   istry
   art: *la peinture* painting, *la musique* music
   But: *l'art* (m.), art
6. Most names of fruits. Ex., *la pomme* apple,
   la cerise cherry
   But: *le pamplemousse* grapefruit, *le raisin*
   grapes
7. Nouns ending in -té (very few exceptions, if
   any). Ex., *l'activité* activity, *la générosité*
   generosity, *la proximité* proximity, *la pri-
   orité* priority

11. PLURAL OF NOUNS

1. Most nouns add -*s* to form the plural:

la ville	the city	*les villes*	the cities
l'île	the island	*les îles*	the islands

2. Nouns ending in -*s*, -*x*, -*z* do not change:

le fils	the son	*les fils*	the sons
la voix	the voice	*les voix*	the voices
le nez	the nose	*les nez*	the noses

3. Nouns ending in -*au* or -*eu* add -*x*:

le chapeau	the hat	*les chapeaux*	the hats

| *l'eau* | water | *les eaux* | waters |
| *le jeu* | the game | *les jeux* | the games |

4. Nouns ending in *-al* and *-ail* for the plural with *-aux*.

| *l'hôpital* | the hospital | *les hôpitaux* | the hospitals |
| *le travail* | work | *les travaux* | works |

Some Irregular Plurals:

| *le ciel* | the sky | *les cieux* | the heavens |
| *l'œil* | the eye | *les yeux* | the eyes |

12. FEMININE OF ADJECTIVES

1. The feminine of adjectives is normally formed by adding *-e* to the masculine singular, but if the masculine singular already ends in *-e*, the adjective has the same form in the feminine:

MASCULINE

| *un petit garçon* | a little boy |
| *un jeune homme* | a young man |

FEMININE

| *une petite fille* | a little girl |
| *une jeune femme* | a young woman |

2. Adjectives ending in *-er* change the *e* to *è* and then add *-e:*

étranger m.   *étrangère f.*   foreign

3. Adjectives ending in *-eux* change this ending to *-euse:*

| *heureux m.* | *heureuse f.* | happy |
| *sérieux m.* | *sérieuse f.* | serious |

4. Some adjectives double the final consonant and add *-e:*

bon m.	*bonne f.*	good
ancien m.	*ancienne f.*	former, ancient
gros m.	*grosse f.*	fat

5. There are a number of irregular feminines:

blanc m.	*blanche f.*	white
doux m.	*douce f.*	sweet, gentle, soft
faux m.	*fausse f.*	false
actif m.	*active f.*	active

13. PLURAL OF ADJECTIVES

1. The plural of adjectives is regularly formed by adding *-s* to the singular, but if the masculine singular ends in *-s* or *-x,* the masculine plural has the same form:

SINGULAR	PLURAL
un petit garçon	*deux petits garçons*
a little boy	two little boys
une petite fille	*deux petites filles*
a little girl	two little girls
un mauvais garçon	*deux mauvais garçons*
a bad boy	two bad boys

2. Adjectives ending in *-au* add *-x:*

un nouveau livre	*de nouveaux livres*
a new book	new books

3. Adjectives ending in *-al* change to *-aux:*

un homme loyal	*des hommes loyaux*
a loyal man	loyal men

14. AGREEMENT OF ADJECTIVES

1. Adjectives agree with the nouns they modify
   in gender and number; that is, they are masculine if the noun is masculine, plural if the
   noun is plural, etc.:

Marie et sa soeur sont petites.	Mary and her sister are little.

2. An adjective that modifies nouns of different
   gender is in the masculine plural:

Marie et Jean sont petits.	Mary and John are little.

15. POSITION OF ADJECTIVES

1. Adjectives usually follow the noun:

un livre français	a French book
un homme intéressant	an interesting man
une idée excellente	an excellent idea

2. When they describe an inherent quality or
   when they form a set phrase, etc., they precede the noun:

une jeune fille	a young girl
le savant auteur	the learned scholar
une étroite amitié	a close friendship
une éclatante victoire	a striking victory

3. The following common adjectives usually
   precede the nouns they modify:

autre	other	*jeune*	young
beau	beautiful	*joli*	pretty
bon	good	*long*	long
court	short	*mauvais*	bad
gentil	nice, pleasant	*nouveau*	new

| *grand* | great, large, tall | *petit* | small, little |
| *gros* | big, fat | *vieux* | old |

4. The following common adjectives differ in meaning depending on whether they come before or after the noun.

	BEFORE THE NOUN	AFTER THE NOUN
ancien	former	ancient
grand	great	tall
brave	worthy	brave
cher	dear (beloved)	dear (expensive)
pauvre	poor (wretched)	poor (indigent)
propre	own	clean
même	same	himself, herself itself, very

5. The following adjectives have two forms for the masculine singular:

MASCULINE SINGULAR		FEMININE SINGULAR	
Before a consonant	Before a vowel or "mute" *h*		
beau	*bel*	*belle*	beautiful, fine, handsome
nouveau	*nouvel*	*nouvelle*	new
vieux	*vieil*	*vieille*	old

Examples:

un beau livre	a beautiful book
un bel arbre	a beautiful tree
une belle femme	a beautiful woman

16. COMPARISON OF ADJECTIVES

Most adjectives form the comparative and superlative by placing *plus* and *le plus (la plus)* before the adjective:

POSITIVE

petit	small
grand	large

COMPARATIVE

plus petit	smaller
plus grand	larger

SUPERLATIVE

le plus petit	the smallest
le plus grand	the largest

Common exceptions:

POSITIVE

bon	good
mauvais	bad

COMPARATIVE

meilleur	better
{ *plus mauvais* *pire*	worse

SUPERLATIVE

le meilleur	the best
{ *le plus mauvais* *le pire*	the worst

17. POSSESSIVE ADJECTIVES

1. Possessive adjectives agree in gender and number with the thing possessed:

BEFORE SINGULAR NOUNS:		BEFORE PLURAL NOUNS:	
		MASCULINE AND	
MASCULINE	FEMININE	FEMININE	
mon	*ma*	*mes*	my
ton	*ta*	*tes*	your (*fam.*)
son	*sa*	*ses*	his, her, its
notre	*notre*	*nos*	our
votre	*votre*	*vos*	your
leur	*leur*	*leurs*	their

Examples:

mon chien	my dog
sa mère	his (or her) mother
ma robe	my dress
votre livre	your book
leurs crayons	their pencils

2. Notice that these adjectives agree in gender not with the possessor as in English, but with the noun they modify. *Son, sa* and *ses* may therefore mean "his," "her," or "its.":

Jean parle à sa mère.	John is talking to his mother.
Marie parle à son père.	Mary is talking to her father.

3. Possessive adjectives are repeated before each noun they modify:

mon père et ma mère	my father and mother
leurs livres et leurs plumes	their books and pens

4. Before a feminine word beginning with a vowel or "mute" *h*, the forms *mon, ton, son* are used instead of *ma, ta, sa:*

son histoire	his story, his history
son école	his (or her) school

5. In speaking of parts of the body, the definite article is usually used instead of the possessive adjective (except where it might be ambiguous):

J'ai mal à la tête.	I have a headache.

18. POSSESSIVE PRONOUNS

MASCULINE		FEMININE		
Singular	Plural	Singular	Plural	
le mien	*les miens*	*la mienne*	*les miennes*	mine
le tien	*les tiens*	*la tienne*	*les tiennes*	your (fam.)
le sien	*les siens*	*la sienne*	*les siennes*	his, hers, its
le nôtre	*les nôtres*	*la nôtre*	*les nôtres*	ours
le vôtre	*les vôtres*	*la vôtre*	*les vôtres*	yours
le leur	*les leurs*	*la leur*	*les leurs*	theirs

Examples:

Voici le mien.	Here's mine.
Quel est la vôtre?	Which is yours? (fem. sing.)
Apportez les vôtres; j'apporterai les miens.	Bring yours; I'll bring mine.
J'ai mal à la tète.	I have a headache.

19. DEMONSTRATIVE ADJECTIVES

MASCULINE SINGULAR

ce (before a consonant)	*ce livre*	this (that) book
cet (before a vowel or "mute" *h*)	*cet arbre* *cet homme*	this (that) tree this (that) man

FEMININE SINGULAR

cette	*cette femme*	this (that) woman

PLURAL

ces	*ces hommes*	these (those) men
	ces femmes	these (those) women

1. The demonstrative adjectives agree with the nouns they modify in gender and number. They must be repeated before each noun:

cet homme et cette femme	this man and this woman

2. The demonstrative adjective in French stands for both "this" and "that" (plural "these" and "those"). When it is necessary to distinguish between "this" and "that," *-ci* and *-là* are added to the noun.

Donnez-moi ce livre-ci.	Give me this book.
Voulez-vous cette robe-là?	Do you want that dress (over there)?
J'aime ce livre-ci mais je n'aime pas ce livre-là.	I like this book but I don't like that book.

20. DEMONSTRATIVE PRONOUNS

Masculine Singular	*celui*	this one, that one, the one
Feminine Singular	*celle*	this one, that one, the one
Masculine Plural	*ceux*	these, those, the ones
Feminine Plural	*celles*	these, those, the ones

Examples:

J'aime celui-ci.	I like that one.
Donnes-moi celle de ton frère.	Give me your brother's (pen, for example).

21. PERSONAL PRONOUNS

The forms of the pronouns will depend on whether they are:

1. the subject of a verb
2. the direct object of a verb
3. the indirect object of a verb
4. the object of a preposition
5. used as a reflexive pronoun
6. used in affirmative requests or commands

1. As the subject of a verb:

je	I
tu	you (fam.)
il	he, it
elle	she, it
nous	we
vous	you
ils	they
elles	they

a. *Vous* is the pronoun normally used in talking to one person or several perople. *Tu* is used in addressing people you know very well (whom you call by their first name in English

—a member of one's family or a close friend; also children, pets, etc.).

b. *Il, elle, ils* and *elles* are used as pronouns referring to things as well as to persons. They have the same number and gender as the nouns to which they refer. *Ils* is used to refer to nouns of different genders:

Où est le livre?	Where's the book?
Il est sur la table.	It's on the table.
Où est la lettre?	Where's the letter?
Elle est sur la table.	It's on the table.
Où sont les livres et les lettres?	Where are the books and letters?
Ils sont sur la table.	They're on the table.

2. As the direct object of a verb:

me	me
te	you
le	him, it
la	her, it
nous	us
vous	you
les	them
en	some, any

3. As the indirect object of a verb:

me	to me
te	to you
lui	to him, to her
nous	to us
vous	to you
leur	to them
y	to it, there

4. As the object of a preposition:

moi	I, me
toi	you (fam.)
soi	himself, oneself
lui	he, him

elle	she, her
nous	we, us
vous	you
eux	they, them (masc.)
elles	they, them (fem.)

5. As a reflexive pronoun:

me	myself
te	yourself
se	himself, herself, itself, oneself
nous	ourselves
vous	yourself, yourselves
se	themselves

6. In affirmative requests and commands:

Direct Object	*Indirect Object*
le ⎫	*moi/toi*[1] ⎫
la ⎬ before	*nous* ⎪
les ⎭	*vous* ⎬ before *y*
	lui ⎪ before *en*
	leur ⎭

22. POSITION OF PRONOUNS

The direct and indirect pronoun objects generally precede the verb except in affirmative commands and requests.

---

[1] When *moi* or *toi* are used with *en*, they become *m'* and *t'* and precede *en*.

Examples: Donnez-
le-moi.   BUT: Donnez-*m'en*.
Lève-*toi*.   BUT: Va-t'en.

1. Position before a verb:

$$\begin{cases} me \\ te \\ se \\ nous \\ vous \end{cases} \text{come before} \begin{cases} le \\ la \\ les \end{cases} \text{before} \begin{cases} lui & \text{before } y \\ leur & \text{before } en \end{cases}$$

Examples:

Il me le donne.	He gives it to me.
Il le lui donne.	He gives it to him (to her, to it).
Je l'y ai vu.	I saw him there.
Je leur en parlerai.	I'll speak to them about it.

2. Position after a verb:

$$\begin{cases} le \\ la \\ les \end{cases} \text{come before} \begin{cases} me \ (moi) \\ te \ (toi) \\ lui \\ nous \\ vous \\ leur \end{cases} \text{before } y \text{ before } en$$

Examples:

Donnez-le-lui.	Give it to him.
Donnez-leur-en.	Give them some.
Allez-vous-en.	Go away. Get out of here.

3. In affirmative commands, both the direct and indirect object pronoun follow the verb, the direct preceding the indirect:

Donnez-moi-le livre.	Give me the book.
Donnez-le-moi.	Give it to me.
Montrez-moi les pommes.	Show me the apples.
Montrez-m'en.	Show me some.
Ecrivez-lui une lettre.	Write him a letter.
Ecrivez-la-lui.	Write it to him.

4. The pronoun objects precede *voici* and *voilà*:

Où est le livre?	Where's the book?
Le voici.	Here it is.

23. RELATIVE PRONOUNS

1. As the subject of a verb:

qui	who, which, that
ce qui	what, that which

2. As the object of a verb:

que	whom, which, that
ce que	what, that which

3. As the object of a preposition:

qui (for a person)	whom
lequel (for a thing)	which

Note: *dont* means whose, of whom, of which:

le problème dont je connais la solution. . .	The problem whose solution I know. . .
Le professeur dont je vous ai parlè. . .	The teacher about whom I talked to you. . .

24. INDEFINITE PRONOUNS

quelque chose	something
quelqu'un	someone
chacun	each (one)
on	one, people, they, etc.
ne . . . rien	nothing
ne . . . personne	no one

25. NOUN USED AS INDIRECT OBJECT

A noun used as an indirect object is always preceded by the preposition *à*:

Je donne un livre à la jeune fille.	I'm giving the girl a book.

26. REPETITION OF PREPOSITIONS

The prepositions *à* and *de* must be repeated before each of their objects:

Je parle au deputé et à son secrétaire.	I'm speaking to the deputy and his secretary.
Voici les cahiers de Jean et ceux de Marie.	Here are John's and Mary's notebooks.

27. THE PARTITIVE

1. When a noun is used in such a way as to express or imply quantity, it is preceded by the article with *de*. This construction very often translates the English "some" or "a few."

J'ai de l'argent.	I have some money.
Il a des amis.	He has a few friends.

In many cases, however, the article is used where we don't use "some" or "a few" in English:

A-t-il des amis ici?	Does he have friends here?

2. The article is omitted:

a. When an expression of quantity is used:

J'ai beaucoup d'argent.	I have a lot of money.
Combien de livres avez-vous?	How many books do you have?

Exceptions: *bien* much, many, and *la plupart* most, the majority:

bien des hommes	many men
le plupart des hommes	most men

b. When the noun is preceded by an adjective:

J'ai acheté de belles cravates.	I bought some nice ties.

c. When the sentence is negative:

Il n'a pas d'amis.	He has no friends.
Mon ami n'a pas d'argent.	My friend hasn't any money.

28. NEGATION

A sentence is made negative by placing *ne* before the verb and *pas* after it:

Je sais.	I know.
Je ne sais pas.	I don't know.
Je ne l'ai pas vu.	I haven't seen it.

Other negative expressions:

ne . . . guère	hardly
ne . . . point	not (at all)
ne . . . rien	nothing
ne . . . nul, nulle	no one, no
ne . . . jamais	never
ne . . . personne	nobody
ne . . . plus	no longer
ne . . . ni . . . ni	neither . . nor
ne . . . que	only
ne . . . aucun, aucune	no one

29. WORD ORDER IN QUESTIONS

1. Questions with pronoun subjects:

There are two ways of asking a question with a pronoun subject:

a. Place the pronoun after the verb:

Parlez-vous français?	Do you speak French?

b. Place *est-ce que* ("is it that") before the sentence [1]:

Est-ce que je parle trop vite?	Am I talking too fast?
Est-ce que vous parlez français?	Do you speak French?

2. Questions with noun subjects:

When a question begins with a noun, the pronoun is repeated after the verb:

Votre frère parle-t-il français?	Does your brother speak French?
Votre soeur a-t-elle quitté la maison?	Has your sister left the house?

3. Questions introduced by interrogative words:

In questions which begin with an interrogative word (*quand, comment, où, pourquoi*), the order is usually interrogative word—noun subject—verb—personal pronoun:

Pourquoi votre ami a-t-il quitté Paris?	Why did your friend leave Paris?

30. ADVERBS

1. Most adverbs are formed from the adjectives by adding *-ment* to the feminine form:

froid	cold	*froidement*	coldly
certain	certain	*certaine- ment*	certainly
naturel	natural	*naturelle- ment*	naturally
facile	easy	*facilement*	easily

2. There are many irregular adverbs which must be learned separately:

[1] In the first person singular this is the usual way of asking a question.

vite   quickly   *mal*   badly

3. Adverbs are compared like adjectives (see page 287):

POSITIVE		COMPARATIVE		SUPERLATIVE	
loin	far	*plus loin*	farther	*le plus loin*	the farthest

4. Some common adverbs of place:

ici	here
là	there
à côté	at the side
de côté	aside
devant	before, in front of
derrière	behind
dessus	on top
dessous	underneath
dedans	inside
dehors	outside
partout	everywhere
nulle part	nowhere
loin	far
près	near
où	where
y	there
ailleurs	elsewhere
là-haut	up there
là-bas	over there

5. Some common adverbs of time:

aujourd'hui	today
demain	tomorrow
hier	yesterday
avant-hier	the day before yesterday
après-demain	the day after tomorrow
maintenant	now
alors	then

avant	before
autrefois	once, formerly
jadis	once, formerly
tôt	early
bientôt	soon
tard	late
souvent	often
ne . . . jamais	never
toujours	always, ever
longtemps	long, for a long time
tantôt	soon, presently
tantôt . . . tantôt	now . . . now, sometimes . . . sometimes
encore	still, yet
ne . . . plus	no longer, no more

6. Adverbs of manner:

bien	well
mal	ill, badly
ainsi	thus, so
de même	similarly
autrement	otherwise
ensemble	together
fort	much, very
volontiers	willingly
surtout	above all, especially
exprès	on purpose, expressly

7. Adverbs of quantity or degree:

beaucoup	much, many
assez	enough
ne . . . guère	not much, scarcely
peu	little
plus	more
ne . . . plus	no more
moins	less
encore	more
bien	much, many

trop	too, too much, too many
tellement	so much, so many

31. THE INFINITIVE

The commonest endings of the infinitive are:

I -*er parler* to speak (The First Conjugation)
II -*ir finir*   to finish (The Second Conjugation)
III -*re vendre* to sell   (The Third Conjugation)

32. THE PAST PARTICIPLE

1. Forms:

INFINITIVE	PAST PARTICIPLE
I *parler*	*parl-é*
II *finir*	*fin-i*
III *perdre*	*perd-u*

2. Agreement:
   a. When a verb is conjugated with *avoir,* the past participle agrees in gender and number with the preceding direct object:

La pièce que j'ai vue hier était mauvaise.	The play I saw yesterday was bad.
Avez-vous vu le livre qu'il a acheté?	Have you seen the book he bought?
Avez-vous donné la plume à Charles?	Did you give the pen to Charles?
Non, je l'ai donnée à Claire.	No, I gave it to Claire.

   b. In the case of reflexive verbs the past participle agrees with the reflexive direct object:

Ils se sont levés.	They got up.
Elle s'est lavée.	She washed herself.

    c. In the case of intransitive verbs conjugated with *être*, the past participle agrees with the subject:

Marie est arrivée hier.	Mary arrived yesterday.
Jean et Pierre se sont levés.	John and Peter got up.
Ils sont arrivés.	They arrived.
Nous sommes rentrés trés tard.	We came back very late.

33. THE INDICATIVE

SIMPLE TENSES

1. The present tense is formed by the verb stem plus the endings *-e, -es, -e, -ons, -ez, -ent*. It has several English translations:

je parle	I speak, I am speaking I do speak
ils mangent	They eat, they are eating, they do eat

2. The imperfect tense is formed by dropping the *-ant* of the present participle and adding *-ais, -ais, -ait, -ions, -iez, -aient*. It expresses a continued or habitual action in the past. It also indicates an action that was happening when something else happened:

Je me levais à sept heures.	I used to get up at seven o'clock.
Il dormait quand Jean est entré.	He was sleeping when John entered.
Il parlait souvent de cela.	He often spoke about that.

Il faisait nuit quand il est sorti. — It was night when he went out.

3. The future tense is formed by adding to the infinitive or future stem the endings, *-ai, -as, -a, -ons, -ez, -ont.* It indicates a future action:

Il arrivera demain. — He'll arrive tomorrow.
Je le vendrai demain. — I'll sell it tomorrow.

4. The past definite tense is formed by adding to the root the endings *-ai, -as, -a, -âmes, -âtes, -èrent* for *-er* verbs; the endings *-is, -is, -it, -îmes, -îtes, -irent* for *-ir* verbs; and for all other verbs either these last or *-us, -us, -ut, -ûmes, -ûtes, -urent.* It expresses an action begun and ended in the past, and it is not generally used in the first person. This tense is used in formal narrative; in conversation and informal writing, the past indefinite tense (see below) is used:

Le roi fut rué. — The king was killed.
Les soldats entrèrent dans la ville. — The soldiers entered the city.

5. The past indefinite tense or "conversational past" is formed by adding the past participle to the present indicative of *avoir* or, in a few cases, *être.* It is used to indicate a past action which has been completed.

Il ne m'a rien dit. — He didn't tell me anything.
J'ai fini mon travail. — I finished my work. I have finished my work.
L'avez-vous vu? — Have you seen him? Did you see him?

Ils sont arrivés.	They arrived.

6. The past perfect tense is formed by adding the past participle to the imperfect of *avoir* or, in a few cases, *être*. It translates the English past perfect:

Il l'avait fait.	He had done it.
Lorsque je revins, il était parti.	When I came back, he had gone.

7. The past anterior tense is formed by adding the past participle to the past definite of *avoir* or, in a few cases, *être*. It is used for an event that happened just before another event. It is rarely found except after *quand* and *lorsque* "when," *après que* "after," *dès que* "as soon as." It is used only in literary style.

Après qu'il eut dîné il sortit.	As soon as he had eaten, he went out.
Quand il eut fini il se leva.	When he had finished, he got up.

8. The future perfect tense is formed by adding the past participle to the future of *avoir* or, in a few cases, *être*. It translates the English future perfect:

Il aura bientôt fini.	He will soon have finished.

Sometimes it indicates probability:

Il le lui aura sans doute dit.	No doubt he must have told him.
Il aura été malade.	He probably was sick.
Je me serai trompé.	I must have been mistaken.

9. The most common intransitive verbs which are conjugated with the verb *être* in the compound tenses are the following:

aller, arriver, descendre, entrer, monter, mourir,

naître, partir, rester, retourner, sortir, tomber, venir, revenir.

Examples:

Je suis venu.	I have come.
Il est arrivé.	He has arrived.
Nous sommes partis.	We have left.

10. Reflexive verbs are conjugated with the auxiliary *être* in the past indefinite:

Je me suis lavé les mains.	I have washed my hands.
Je me suis levé à sept heures ce matin.	I got up at seven o'clock this morning.

CONDITIONAL

1. The conditional is formed by adding to the infinitive the endings *-ais, -ais, -ait, -ions, -iez, -aient*. It translates English "would" or "should":

Je le prendrais si j'étais à votre place.	I would take it if I were you.
Je ne ferais jamais une chose pareille.	I would never do such a thing.

2. The conditional perfect if formed by adding the past participle to the conditional of *avoir* or, in a few cases, *être*. It translates the English "if I had" or "if I would have," etc.:

Si j'avais su, je n'y serais jamais allé.	If I had (would have) known, I should never have gone there.
Si j'avais eu assez d'argent je l'aurais acheté.	If I had (would have had) the money, I would have bought it.

34. THE IMPERATIVE

1. The imperative of most verbs is generally
   formed from the present indicative tense. (In
   the verbs of the first conjugation, however,
   the second person singular loses the final *s*):

donner	to give	*finir*	to finish
donne (fam.)	give	*finis* (fam.)	finish
donnez	give	*finissez*	finish
donnons	let us give	*finissons*	let us finish

vendre	to sell
vends (fam.)	sell
vendez	sell
vendons	let us sell

2. Imperatives of *être* and *avoir:*

être	to be	*avoir*	to have
sois (fam.)	be	*aie* (fam.)	have
soyez	be	*ayez*	have
soyons	let us be	*ayons*	let us have

35. VERBS FOLLOWED BY THE INFINITIVE

1. Some verbs are followed by the inifinitive
   without a preceding preposition:

Je vais parler à Jean.	I am going to talk to John.
J'aime parler français.	I like to speak French.
Je ne sais pas danser.	I don't know how to dance.

2. Some verbs are followed by *à* plus the infinitive:

J'apprends à parler français.	I am learning to speak French.
Je l'aiderai à le faire.	I'll help him do it.

3. Some verbs are followed by *de* plus the infinitive:

Il leur a demandè de fermer la porte.	He asked them to shut the door.

36. THE SUBJUNCTIVE

The indicative makes a simple statement; the subjunctive indicates a certain attitude toward the statement—uncertainty, desire, emotion, etc. The subjunctive is used in subordinate clauses when the statement is unreal, doubtful, indefinite, subject to some condition, or is affected by will, emotion, etc.

FORMS

1. Present Subjunctive:

   Drop the *-ent* of the third person plural present indicative and add *-e, -es, -e, -ions, -iez, -ient.* See the forms of the regular subjunctive in the Regular Verb Charts.

   The irregular verbs *avoir* and *être:*

que j'aie	*que je sois*
que tu aies	*que tu sois*
qu'il ait	*qu'il soit*
que nous ayons	*que nous soyons*
que vous ayez	*que vous soyez*
qu'ils aient	*qu'ils soient*

2. Imperfect Subjunctive:

   Drop the ending of the first person singular of the past definite and add *-sse, -sses, -t,*

-ssions, -ssiez, -ssent, putting a circumflex over the last vowel of the third person singular:

(that) I gave, might give	(that) I finished, might finish
que je donnasse	*que je finisse*
que tu donnasses	*que tu finisses*
qu'il donnât	*qu'il finît*
que nous donnassions	*que nous finissions*
que vous donnassiez	*que nous finnissiez*
qu'ils donnassent	*qu'ils finissent*

(that) I sold, might sell

que je vendisse
que tu vendisses
qu'il vendît
que nous vendissions
que vous vendissiez
qu'ils vendissent

3. Perfect Subjunctive:

   Add the past participle to the present subjunctive of *avoir* (or, in a few cases, *être):*

   avoir: *que j'aie donné, que tu aies donné, etc.*
   être: *que je sois allé, que tu sois allé, etc.*

4. Pluperfect Subjunctive:

   Add the past participle to the imperfect subjunctive of *avoir* (or, in a few cases, *être):*

   avoir: *j'eusse donné, etc.*
   être: *je fusse allé, etc.*

USES

1. After verbs of command, request, permission, etc.:

Je tiens à ce que vous y alliez.	I insist on your going there.

2. After expressions of approval and disapproval, necessity, etc.:

Il n'est que juste que vous le lui disiez.	It's only fair that you tell him that.
Il faut que vous fassiez cela.	You have to do that.

3. After verbs of emotion (desire, regret, fear, joy, etc.):

Je voudrais bien que vous veniez avec nous.	I'd like you to come with us.
Je regrette que vous ne puissiez pas venir.	I'm sorry you can't come.

4. After expressions of doubt, uncertainty, denial:

Je doute que j'y aille.	I doubt that I'll go there.
Il est possible qu'il ne puisse pas venir.	It's possible that he may not be able to come.

5. In relative clauses with an indefinite antecedent:

Il me faut quelqu'un qui fasse cela.	I need someone to do that.

6. In adverbial clauses after certain conjunctions denoting purpose, time, concession, etc.:

Je viendrai à moins   I'll come unless it
   qu'il ne pleuve.   rains.
Asseyez-vous en   Sit down until it's
   attendant que ce   ready.
   soit prêt.

7. In utterances expressing a wish or command:

Qu'ils s'en aillent!   Let them go away!
Dieu vous bénisse!   God bless you!
Vive la France!   Long live France!

VERB CHARTS

I. FORMS OF THE REGULAR VERBS

A. CLASSES I, II, III

Infinitive	Pres. & Past Participles	Present Indicative	Present Subjunctive†	Conversational Past	Past Subjunctive	Imperfect Indicative
-er ending parler	parlant parlé	parl + e es e ons ez ent	parl + e es e ions iez ent	j'ai + parlé tu as il a nou avons vous avez ils ont	que j'aie + parlé que tu aies qu'il ait que nous ayons que vous ayez qu'ils aient	parl + ais ais ait ions iez aient
-ir ending finir	finissant fini	fin + is is it issons issez issent	finiss + e es e ions iez ent	j'ai + fini tu as il a nous avons vous avez ils ont	que j'aie + fini que tu aies qu'il ait que nous ayons que vous ayez qu'ils aient	finiss + ais ais ait ions iez aient
-re ending vendre	vendant vendu	vend + s s — ons ez ent	vend + e es e ions iez ent	j'ai + vendu tu as il a nous avons vous avez ils ont	que j'aie + vendu que tu aies qu'il ait que nous ayons que vous ayez qu'ils aient	vend + ais ais ait ions iez aient

† Like the past subjunctive, the present subjunctive verb is always preceded by *que* or *qu'* + the appropriate pronoun, as in "Il faut que je parte" and "Je veux que quitte la maison."

322

parler

Past Perfect	Future	Future Perfect	Conditional	Conditional Perfect	Imperative
j'avais + parlé	parler + ai	j'aurai + parlé	parler + ais	j'aurais + parlé	parle
tu avais	as	tu auras	ais	tu aurais	
il avait	a	il aura	ait	il aurait	
nous avions	ons	nous aurons	ions	nous aurions	parlons
vous aviez	ez	vous aurez	iez	vous auriez	parlez
ils avaient	ont	ils auront	aient	ils auraient	

finir

Past Perfect	Future	Future Perfect	Conditional	Conditional Perfect	Imperative
j'avais + fini	finir + ai	j'aurai + fini	finir + ais	j'aurais + fini	finis
tu avais	as	tu auras	ais	tu aurais	
il avait	a	il aura	ait	il aurait	
nous avions	ons	nous aurons	ions	nous aurions	finissons
vous aviez	ez	vous aurez	iez	vous auriez	finissez
ils avaient	ont	ils auront	aient	il auraient	

vendre

Past Perfect	Future	Future Perfect	Conditional	Conditional Perfect	Imperative
j'avais + vendu	vendr + ai	j'aurai + vendu	vendr + ais	j'aurais + vendu	vends
tu avais	as	tu auras	ais	tu aurais	
il avait	a	il aura	ait	il aurait	
nous avions	ons	nous aurons	ions	nous aurions	vendons
vous aviez	ez	vous aurez	iez	vous auriez	vendez
ils avaient	ont	ils auront	aient	ils auraient	

B. VERBS ENDING IN -CER AND -GER

Infinitive	Pres. & Past Participles	Present Indicative	Present Subjunctive	Conversational Past		Past Subjunctive		Imperfect Indicative
(1) **placer**	*plaçant* placé	place places place *plaçons* placez placent	place places place placions placiez placent	j'ai tu as il a nous avons vous avez ils ont	+ placé	que j'aie que tu aies qu'il ait que nous ayons que vous ayez qu'ils aient	+ placé	*plaçais plaçais plaçait* placions placiez *plaçaient*
(2) **manger**	*mangeant* mangé	mange manges mange mangeons mangez mangent	mange manges mange mangions mangiez mangent	j'ai tu as il a nous avons vous avez ils ont	+ mangé	que j'aie que tu aies qu'il ait que nous ayons que vous ayez qu'ils aient	+ mangé	*mangeais mangeais mangeait* mangions mangiez *mangeaient*

(1) Similarly conjugated: *commencer, lancer, etc.*
(2) Similarly conjugated: *plonger, ranger, arranger, etc.*

324

Past Perfect	Future	Future Perfect	Conditional	Conditional Perfect	Imperative
j'avais + placé	placer + ai	j'aurai + placé	placer + ais	j'aurais + placé	place
tu avais	as	tu auras	ais	tu aurais	
il avait	a	il aura	ait	il aurait	plaçons
nous avions	ons	nous aurons	ions	nous aurions	placez
vous aviez	ez	vous aurez	iez	vous auriez	
ils avaient	ont	ils auront	aient	ils auraient	
j'avais + mangé	manger + ai	j'aurai + mangé	manger + ais	j'aurais + mangé	mange
tu avais	as	tu auras	ais	tu aurais	
il avait	a	il aura	ait	il aurait	mangeons
nous avions	ons	nous aurons	ions	nous aurions	mangez
vous aviez	ez	vous aurez	iez	vous auriez	
ils avaient	ont	ils auront	aient	il auraient	

C. VERBS ENDING IN -ER WITH CHANGES IN THE STEM

Infinitive	Pres. & Past Participles	Present Indicative	Present Subjunctive	Conversational Past	Past Subjunctive	Imperfect Indicative
(1) **acheter**	achetant acheté	achète achètes achète achetons achetez achètent	achète achètes achète achetions achetiez achètent	j'ai + acheté tu as il a nous avons vous avez ils ont	que j'aie + acheté que tu aies qu'il ait que nous ayons que vous ayez qu'ils aient	achet + ais ais ait ions iez aient
(2) **appeler**	appelant appelé	appelle appelles appelle appelons appelez appellent	appelle appelles appelle appelions appeliez appellent	j'ai + appelé tu as il a nous avons vous avez ils ont	que j'aie + appelé que tu aies qu'il ait que nous ayons que vous ayez qu'ils aient	appel + ais ais ait ions iez aient
(3) **payer**†	payant payé	paie/paye paies/payes paie/paye payons payez paient/payent	paie/paye paies/payes paie/paye payions payiez paient/payent	j'ai + payé tu as il a nous avons vous avez il ont	que j'aie + payé que tu aies qu'il ait que nous ayons que vous ayez qu'ils aient	pay + ais ais ait ions iez aient
(4) **préférer**	préférant préféré	préfère préfères préfère préférons préférez préfèrent	préfère préfères préfère préférions préfériez préfèrent	j'ai + préféré tu as il a nous avons vous avez il ont	que j'aie + préféré que tu aies qu'il ait que nous ayons que vous ayez qu'ils aient	préfér + ais ais ait ions iez aient

(1) Verbs like *acheter:* mener, amener, emmener, se promener, lever, se lever, élever

(2) Verbs like *appeler:* se rappeler, jeter

(3) Verbs like *payer:* essayer, employer, ennuyer, essuyer, nettoyer (See note below.)

Past Perfect	Future	Future Perfect	Conditional	Conditional Perfect	Imperative
j'avais + acheté	*acheter* + ai	j'aurai + acheté	*acheter* + ais	j'aurais + acheté	
tu avais	as	tu auras	ais	tu aurais	*achète*
il avait	a	il aura	ait	il aurait	
nous avions	ons	nous aurons	ions	nous aurions	*achetons*
vous aviez	ez	vous aurez	iez	vous auriez	*achetez*
ils avaient	ont	ils auront	aient	ils auraient	
j'avais + appelé	*appeller* + ai	j'aurai + appelé	*appeller* + ais	j'aurais + appelé	
tu avais	as	tu auras	ais	tu aurais	*appelle*
il avait	a	il aura	ait	il aurait	
nous avions	ons	nous aurons	ions	nous aurions	appelons
vous aviez	ez	vous aurez	iez	vous auriez	appelez
ils avaient	ont	ils auront	aient	ils auraient	
j'avais + payé	*paier* or payer + ai	j'aurai + payé	*paier* or payer + ais	j'aurais + payé	
tu avais	as	tu auras	ais	tu aurais	*paie/paye*
il avait	a	il aura	ait	il aurait	
nous avions	ons	nous aurons	ions	nous aurions	payons
vous aviez	ez	vous aurez	iez	vous auriez	payez
ils avaient	ont	ils auront	aient	ils auraient	
j'avais + préféré	*préférer* + ai	j'aurai + préféré	*préférer* + ais	j'aurais + préféré	
tu avais	as	tu auras	ais	tu aurais	*préfère*
il avait	a	il aura	ait	il aurait	
nous avions	ons	nous aurons	ions	nous aurions	préférons
vous aviez	ez	vous aurez	iez	vous auriez	préférez
ils avaient	ont	ils auront	aient	ils auraient	

(4) Verbs like *préférer*: espérer, répéter, célébrer, considérer, suggérer, protéger

† Verbs ending in *-ayer* may use *i* or *y* in the present (except for *nous* and *vous* forms), the future, and the conditional, as in *payer, essayer*. Verbs ending in *-oyer, -uyer* change *y* to *i* as in *essuyer, ennuyer, employer, nettoyer*).

D. VERBS ENDING IN -OIR

Infinitive	Pres. & Past Participles	Present Indicative	Present Subjunctive	Conversational Past		Past Subjunctive		Imperfect Indicative	
(1) recevoir	recevant	reçois	reçoive	j'ai	+ reçu	que j'aie	+ reçu	recev +	ais
	reçu	reçois	reçoives	tu as		que tu aies			ais
		reçoit	reçoive	il a		qu'il ait			ait
		recevons	recevions	nou avons		que nous ayons			ions
		recevez	receviez	vous avez		que vous ayez			iez
		reçoivent	reçoivent	ils ont		qu'ils aient			aient

(1) Verbs like recevoir: devoir, (dois, doive, dû)

328

Past Perfect		Future	Future Perfect		Conditional	Conditional Perfect		Imperative
j'avais	+ reçu	recevr + ai	j'aurai	+ reçu	recevr + ais	j'aurais	+ reçu	
tu avais		as	tu auras		ais	tu aurais		reçois
il avait		a	il aura		ait	il aurait		
nous avions		ons	nous aurons		ions	nous aurions		recevons
vous aviez		ez	vous aurez		iez	vous auriez		recevez
ils avaient		ont	ils auront		aient	ils auraient		

E. VERBS ENDING IN -NDRE

Infinitive	Pres. & Past Participles	Present Indicative	Present Subjunctive	Conversational Past	Past Subjunctive	Imperfect Indicative
(2) **craindre**	craignant	crains	craigne	j'ai	que j'aie	craign + ais
	craint	crains	craignes	tu as	que tu aies	ais
		craint	craigne	il a + craint	qu'il ait + craint	ait
		craignons	craignions	nou avons	que nous ayons	ions
		craignez	craigniez	vous avez	que vous ayez	iez
		craignent	craignent	ils ont	qu'ils aient	aient
(3) **eteindre**	éteignant	éteins	éteigne	j'ai	que j'aie	éteign + ais
	éteint	éteins	éteignes	tu as	que tu aies	ais
		éteint	éteigne	il a + éteint	qu'il ait + éteint	ait
		éteignons	éteignions	nou avons	que nous ayons	ions
		éteignez	éteigniez	vous avez	que vous ayez	iez
		éteignent	éteignent	ils ont	qu'ils aient	aient

(2) Verbs like *craindre*: *plaindre*, to pity. The reflexive form, *se plaindre*, means "to complain," and in the compound tenses is conjugated with *être*.

(3) Verbs like *éteindre*: *peindre*, to paint; *teindre*, to dye.

Past Perfect	Future	Future Perfect	Conditional	Conditional Perfect	Imperative
j'avais + *craint*	craindr + ai	j'aurai + *craint*	craindr + ais	j'aurais + *craint*	*crains*
tu avais	as	tu auras	ais	tu aurais	
il avait	a	il aura	ait	il aurait	*craignons*
nous avions	ons	nous aurons	ions	nous aurions	*craignez*
vous aviez	ez	vous aurez	iez	vous auriez	
ils avaient	ont	ils auront	aient	ils auraient	
j'avais + *éteint*	éteindr + ai	j'aurai + *éteint*	éteindr + ais	j'aurais + *éteint*	*éteins*
tu avais	as	tu auras	ais	tu aurais	
il avait	a	il aura	ait	il aurait	*éteignons*
nous avions	ons	nous aurons	ions	nous aurions	*éteignez*
vous aviez	ez	vous aurez	iez	vous auriez	
ils avaient	ont	ils auront	aient	ils auraient	

F. COMPOUND TENSES OF VERBS CONJUGATED WITH *ÊTRE*

Conversational past	Past subjunctive	Past perfect	Future perfect	Conditional perfect
je suis allé(e)	que je sois allé(e)	j'étais allé(e)	je serai allé(e)	je serais allé(e)
tu es allé(e)	que tu sois allé(e)	tu étais allé(e)	tu seras allé(e)	tu serais allé(e)
il est allé	qu'il soit allé	il était allé	il sera allé	il serait allé
elle est allée	qu'elle soit allée	elle était allée	elle sera allée	elle serait allée
nous sommes allé(e)s	que nous soyons allé(e)s	nous étions allé(e)s	nous serons allé(e)s	nous serions allé(e)s
vous êtes allé(e)(s)	que vous soyez allé(e)(s)	vous étiez allé(e)(s)	vous serez allé(e)(s)	vous seriez allé(e)(s)
ils sont allés	qu'ils soient allés	ils étaient allés	ils seront allés	ils seraient allés
elles sont allées	qu'elles soient allées	elles étaient allées	elles seront allées	elles seraient allées

G. COMPOUND TENSES OF REFLEXIVE VERBS (ALL REFLEXIVE VERBS ARE CONJUGATED WITH *ÊTRE*).

Conversational past	Past subjunctive	Past perfect	Future perfect	Conditional perfect
je me suis levé(e)	que je me sois levé(e)	je m'étais levé(e)	je me serai levé(e)	je me serais levé(e)
tu t'es levé(e)	que tu te sois levé(e)	tu t'étais levé(e)	tu te seras levé(e)	tu te serais levé(e)
il s'est levé	qu'il se soit levé	il s'était levé	il se sera levé	il se serait levé
elle s'est levée	qu'elle se soit levée	elle s'était levée	elle se sera levée	elle se serait levée
nous nous sommes levé(e)s	que nous nous soyons levé(e)s	nous nous étions levé(e)s	nous nous serons levé(e)s	nous nous serions levé(e)s
vous vous êtes levé(e)(s)	que vous vous soyez levé(e)(s)	vous vous étiez levé(e)(s)	vous vous serez levé(e)(s)	vous vous seriez levé(e)(s)
ils se sont levés	qu'ils se soient levés	ils s'étaient levés	ils se seront levés	ils se seraient levés
elles se sont levées	qu'elles se soient levées	elles s'étaient levées	elles se seront levées	elles se seraient levées

H. INFREQUENTLY USED AND "LITERARY" TENSES (CLASSES I, II, III)

(1) Past Definite†			(2) Past Anterior			(3) Imperfect Subjunctive		
parlai	finis	perdis	eus parlé	eus fini	eus perdu	parlasse	finisse	perdisse
parlas	finis	perdis	eus parlé	eus fini	eus perdu	parlasses	finisses	perdisses
parla	finit	perdit	eut parlé	eut fini	eut perdu	parlât	finît	perdît
parlâmes	finîmes	perdîmes	eûmes parlé	eûmes fini	eûmes perdu	parlassions	finissions	perdissions
parlâtes	finîtes	perdîtes	eûtes parlé	eûtes fini	eûtes perdu	parlassiez	finissiez	perdissiez
parlèrent	finirent	perdirent	eurent parlé	eurent fini	eurent perdu	parlassent	finissent	perdissent

(1) Used in formal narrative only. In informal conversation and writing, use the conversational past (*J'ai parlé*, etc.)

(2) Used, in literary style only, after *quand, lorsque, après que, dès que* for an event that happened just before another event. Example: *Après qu'il eut dîné il sortit*. As soon as he had eaten, he went out.

(3) "that I spoke," "that I might speak," etc. This tense is infrequently found in ordinary conversation, but is used fairly often in literary works.

† All other regular verbs use either the *-er, -ir,* or *-re* endings, depending upon the conjugation to which they belong. The past definite forms of irregular verbs must be memorized.

(4) Past Perfect Subjunctive

que j'eusse parlé	que j'eusse fini	que j'eusse perdu
que tu eusses parlé	que tu eusses fini	que tu eusses perdu
qu'il eût parlé	qu'il eût fini	qu'il eût perdu
que nous eussions parlé	que nous eussion fini	que nous eussions perdu
que vous eussiez parlé	que vous eussiez fini	que vous eussiez perdu
qu'ils eussent parlé	qu'ils eussent fini	qu'ils eussent perdu

(4) "that I had spoken," "that I might have spoken," etc. A predominantly literary tense.

II. FREQUENTLY USED IRREGULAR VERBS

(1) The correct auxiliary verb is indicated in parentheses below each verb.
(2) For compound tenses, use the appropriate form of the auxiliary verb + past participle.

Infinitive	Pres. & Past Participles	Present Indicative	Present Subjunctive	Imperfect Indicative	Future	Conditional	Imperative
acquérir to acquire (*avoir*)	acquériant acquis	acquiers acquiers acquiert acquérons acquérez acquièrent	acquière acquières acquière acquérions acquériez acquièrent	acquér + ais ais ait ions iez aient	acquerr + ai as a ons ez ont	acquerr + ais ais ait ions iez aient	acquiers acquérons acquérez
aller to go (*être*)	allant allé(e)(s)	vais vas va allons allez vont	aille ailles aille allions alliez aillent	all + ais ais ait ions iez aient	ir + ai as a ons ez ont	ir + ais ais ait ions iez aient	va allons allez
(s')asseoir† to sit (down) (*être*)	asseyant assie(e)(s)	assieds assieds assied asseyons asseyez asseyent	asseye asseyes asseye asseyions asseyiez asseyent	assey + ais ais ait ions iez aient	asseyer + ai as a *or* assiér + a *or* assoir + ez ont	asseyer + ais ais ait *or* assiér + ait *or* assoir + ions iez aient	assieds-toi asseyons-nous asseyez-vous

† There is a variant form of the conjugation of *s'asseoir* based on the present participle *assoyant* and first person singular *assois*, but this is rather archaic and is rarely used. There are also two variant forms for the future stem: *assiér*- and *assoir*-. *Assiér*- is frequently used.

334

		Present	Subjunctive	Imperfect		Future		Conditional		Imperative
avoir to have (*avoir*)	ayant eu	ai as a avons avez ont	aie aies ait ayons ayez aient	av	+ ais ais ait ions iez aient	aur	+ ai as a ons ez ont	aur	+ ais ais ait ions iez aient	aie ayons ayez
battre to beat (*avoir*)	battant battu	bats bats bat battons battez battent	batte battes batte battions battiez battent	batt	+ ais ais ait ions iez aient	battr	+ ai as a ons ez ont	battr	+ ais ais ait ions iez aient	bats battons battez
boire to drink (*avoir*)	buvant bu	bois bois boit buvons buvez boivent	boive boives boive buvions buviez boivent	buv	+ ais ais ait ions iez aient	boir	+ ai as a ons ez ont	boir	+ ais ais ait ions iez aient	bois buvons buvez
conclure to conclude (*avoir*)	concluant conclu	conclus conclus conclut concluons concluez concluent	conclue conclues conclue concluions concluiez concluent	conclu	+ ais ais ait ions iez aient	conclur	+ ai as a ons ez ont	conclur	+ ais ais ait ions iez aient	conclus concluons concluez

Infinitive	Pres. & Past Participles	Present Indicative	Present Subjunctive	Imperfect Indicative	Future	Conditional	Imperative
conduire to drive to lead (*avoir*)	conduisant conduit	conduis conduis conduit conduisons conduisez conduisent	conduise conduises conduise conduisions conduisiez conduisent	conduis + ais ais ait ions iez aient	conduir + ai as a ons ez ont	conduir + ais ais ait ions iez aient	conduis conduisons conduisez
connaître to know (*avoir*)	connaissant connu	connais connais connaît connaissons connaissez connaissent	connaisse connaisses connaisse connaissions connaissiez connaissent	connaiss + ais ais ait ions iez aient	connaîtr + ai as a ons ez ont	connaîtr + ais ais ait ions iez aient	connais connaissons connaissez
courir to run (*avoir*)	courant couru	cours cours court courons courez courent	coure coures coure courions couriez courent	cour + ais ais ait ions iez aient	courr + ai as a ons ez ont	courr + ais ais ait ions iez aient	cours courons courez

336

Infinitive	Participles	Present	Subjunctive	Imperfect		Future		Conditional		Imperative
croire to believe *(avoir)*	croyant cru	crois crois croit croyons croyez croient	croie croies croie croyions croyiez croient	croy +	ais ais ait ions iez aient	croir +	ai as a ons ez ont	croir +	ais ais ait ions iez aient	crois croyons croyez
cueillir to gather to pick *(avoir)*	cueillant cueilli	cueille cueilles cueille cueillons cueillez cueillent	cueille cueilles cueille cueillions cueilliez cueillent	cueill +	ais ais ait ions iez aient	cueiller +	ai as a ons ez ont	cueiller +	ais ais ait ions iez aient	cueille cueillons cueillez
devoir to owe ought *(avoir)*	devant dû	dois dois doit devons devez doivent	doive doives doive devions deviez doivent	dev +	ais ais ait ions iez aient	devr +	ai as a ons ez ont	devr +	ais ais ait ions iez aient	*not used*
dire to say to tell *(avoir)*	disant dit	dis dis dit disons dites disent	dise dises dise disions disiez disent	dis +	ais ais ait ions iez aient	dir +	ai as a ons ez ont	dir +	ais ais ait ions iez aient	dis disons dites

Infinitive	Pres. & Past Participles	Present Indicative	Present Subjunctive	Imperfect Indicative	Future	Conditional	Imperative
dormir to sleep (*avoir*)	dormant dormi	dors dors dort dormons dormez dorment	dorme dormes dorme dormions dormiez dorment	dorm + ais ais ait ions iez aient	dormir + ai as a ons ez ont	dormir + ais ais ait ions iez aient	dors dormons dormez
écrire to write (*avoir*)	écrivant écrit	écris écris écrit écrivons écrivez écrivent	écrive écrives écrive écrivions écriviez écrivent	écriv + ais ais ait ions iez aient	écrir + ai as a ons ez ont	écrir + ais ais ait ions iez aient	écris écrivons écrivez
envoyer to send (*avoir*)	envoyant envoyé	envoie envoies envoie envoyons envoyez envoient	envoie envoies envoie envoyions envoyiez envoient	envoy + ais ais ait ions iez aient	enverr + ai as a ons ez ont	enverr + ais ais ait ions iez aient	envoie envoyons envoyez
être to be (*avoir*)	étant été	suis es est sommes êtes	sois sois soit soyons soyez	ét + ais ais ait ions iez	ser + ai as a ons ez	ser + ais ais ait ions iez aient	sois soyons soyez

faillir† to fail (avoir)	faillant, failli	not used	not used	not used	faillir + ai, as, a, ons, ez, ont	faillir + ais, ais, ait, ions, iez, aient	not used
faire to do, to make (avoir)	faisant, fait	fais, fais, fait, faisons, faites, font	fasse, fasses, fasse, fassions, fassiez, fassent	fais + ais, ais, ait, ions, iez, aient	fer + ai, as, a, ons, ez, ont	fer + ais, ais, ait, ions, iez, aient	fais, faisons, faites
falloir to be necessary, must (used only with il) (avoir)	no pres. part., fallu	il faut	il faille	il fallait	il faudra	il faudrait	not used

*† Used in expressions such as *Il a failli tomber*, He nearly fell (lit., he failed to fall).

339

Infinitive	Pres. & Past Participles	Present Indicative	Present Subjunctive	Imperfect Indicative	Future	Conditional	Imperative
fuir to flee *(avoir)*	fuyant fui	fuis fuis fuit fuyons fuyez fuient	fuie fuies fuie fuyions fuyiez fuient	fuy + ais ais ait ions iez aient	fuir + ai as a ons ez ont	fuir + ais ais ait ions iez aient	fuis fuyons fuyez
haïr to hate *(avoir)*	haïssant haï	hais hais hait haïssons haïssons haïssent	haïsse haïsses haïsse haïssions haïssiez haïssent	haïss + ais ais ait ions iez aient	haïr + ai as a ions ez ont	haïr + ais ais ait ions iez aient	haïs haïssons haïssez
lire to read *(avoir)*	lisant lu	lis lis lit lisons lisez lisent	lise lises lise lisions lisiez lisent	lis + ais ais ait ions iez aient	lir + ai as a ons ez ont	lir + ais ais ait ions iez aient	lis lisons lisez

				Imperfect	Future	Conditional	Imperative
mettre to put to place (*avoir*)	mettant mis	mets mets met mettons mettez mettent	mette mettes mette mettions mettiez mettent	mett + ais ais ait ions iez aient	mettr + ai as a ons ez ont	mettr + ais ais ait ions iez aient	mets mettons mettez
mourir to die (*être*)	mourant mort(e)(s)	meurs meurs meurt mourons mourez meurent	meure meures meure mourions mouriez meurent	mour + ais ais ait ions iez aient	mourr + ai as a ons ez ont	mourr + ais ais ait ions iez aient	meurs mourons mourez
mouvoir† to move (*avoir*)	mouvant mû	meus meus meut mouvons mouvez meuvent	meuve meuves meuve mouvions mouviez meuvent	mouv + ais ais ait ions iez aient	mouvr + ai as a ons ez ont	mouvr + ais ais ait ions iez aient	meus mouvons mouvez
naître to be born (*être*)	naissant né(e)(s)	nais nais naît naissons naissez naissent	naisse naisses naisse naissions naissiez naissent	naiss + ais ais ait ions iez aient	naîtr + ai as a ons ez ont	naîtr + ais ais ait ions iez aient	nais naissons naissez

† *Mouvoir* is seldom used except in compounds like *émouvoir*, to move (emotionally).

Infinitive	Pres. & Past Participles	Present Indicative	Present Subjunctive	Imperfect Indicative	Future	Conditional	Imperative
ouvrir to open (*avoir*)	ouvrant ouvert	ouvre ouvres ouvre ouvrons ouvrez ouvrent	ouvre ouvres ouvre ouvrions ouvriez ouvrent	ouvr + ais ais ait ions iez aient	ouvrir + ai as a ons ez ont	ouvrir + ais ais ait ions iez aient	ouvre ouvrons ouvrez
partir to leave to depart (*être*)	partant parti(e)(s)	pars pars part partons partez partent	parte partes parte partions partiez partent	part + ais ais ait ions iez aient	partir + ai as a ons ez ont	partir + ais ais ait ions iez aient	pars partons partez
plaire to please (to be pleas- ing to) (*avoir*)	plaisant plu	plais plais plaît plaisons plaisez plaisent	plaise plaises plaise plaisions plaisiez plaisent	plais + ais ais ait ions iez aient	plair + ai as a ons ez ont	plair + ais ais ait ions iez aient	plais plaisons plaisez

342

	pleuvant plu	il pleut	il pleuve	il pleuvait	il pleuvra	il pleuvrait	*not used*
pleuvoir to rain (used only with *il*) (*avoir*)	pleuvant plu	il pleut	il pleuve	il pleuvait	il pleuvra	il pleuvrait	*not used*
pouvoir† to be able, can (*avoir*)	pouvant pu	peux (puis)† peux peut pouvons pouvez peuvent	puisse puisses puisse puissions puissiez puissent	pouv + ais ais ait ions iez aient	pourr + ai as a ons ez ont	pourr + ais ais ait ions iez aient	*not used*
prendre to take (*avoir*)	prenant pris	prends prends prend prenons prenez prennent	prenne prennes prenne prenions preniez prennent	pren + ais ais ait ions iez aient	prendr + ai as a ons ez ont	prendr + ais ais ait ions iez aient	prends prenons prenez
résoudre to resolve (*avoir*)	résolvant résolu	résous résous résout résolvons résolvez résolvent	résolve résolves résolve résolvions résolviez résolvent	résolv + ais ais ait ions iez aient	résoudr + ai as a ons ez ont	résoudr + ais ais ait ions iez aient	résous résolvons résolvez

†The interrogative of *pouvoir* in the first person singular is always *Puis-je?*

343

Infinitive	Pres. & Past Participles	Present Indicative	Present Subjunctive	Imperfect Indicative	Future	Conditional	Imperative
rire to laugh (*avoir*)	riant ri	ris ris rit rions riez rient	rie ries rie riions riiez rient	ri + ais ais ait ions iez aient	rir + ai as a ons ez ont	rir + ais ais ait ions iez aient	ris rions riez
savoir to know (*avoir*)	sachant su	sais sais sait savons savez savent	sache saches sache sachions sachiez sachent	sav + ais ais ait ions iez aient	saur + ai as a ons ez ont	saur + ais ais ait ions iez aient	sache sachons sachez
suffire to be enough, to suffice (*avoir*)	suffisant suffi	suffis suffis suffit suffisons suffisez suffisent	suffise suffises suffise suffisions suffisiez suffisent	suffis + ais ais ait ions iez aient	suffir + ai as a ons ez ont	suffir + ais ais ait ions iez aient	suffis suffisons suffisez
suivre to follow (*avoir*)	suivant suivi	suis suis suit suivons suivez suivent	suive suives suive suivions suiviez suivent	suiv + ais ais ait ions iez aient	suivr + ai as a ons ez ont	suivr + ais ais ait ions iez aient	suis suivons suivez

French Verb Conjugations

se taire — to be quiet, to say nothing (être)

Participle: tu(e)(s)

Person	Present	Subjunctive	Future	Conditional	Imperative
je	tais	taise	—	—	
tu	tais	taises	—	—	tais-toi
il	tait	taise	—	—	
nous	taisons	taisions	—	—	taisons-nous
vous	taisez	taisiez	—	—	taisez-vous
ils	taisent	taisent	—	—	

tenir — to hold, to keep (avoir)

Participles: tenant / tenu

Person	Present	Subjunctive	Imperfect	Future	Conditional	Imperative
je	tiens	tienne	ten + ais	tiendr + ai	tiendr + ais	
tu	tiens	tiennes	ten + ais	tiendr + as	tiendr + ais	tiens
il	tient	tienne	ten + ait	tiendr + a	tiendr + ait	
nous	tenons	tenions	ten + ions	tiendr + ons	tiendr + ions	tenons
vous	tenez	teniez	ten + iez	tiendr + ez	tiendr + iez	tenez
ils	tiennent	tiennent	ten + aient	tiendr + ont	tiendr + aient	

vaincre — to conquer (avoir)

Participles: vainquant / vaincu

Person	Present	Subjunctive	Imperfect	Future	Conditional	Imperative
je	vaincs	vainque	vainqu + ais	vainer + ai	vaincr + ais	
tu	vaincs	vainques	vainqu + ais	vainer + as	vaincr + ais	vaincs
il	vainc	vainque	vainqu + ait	vainer + a	vaincr + ait	
nous	vainquons	vainquions	vainqu + ions	vainer + ons	vaincr + ions	vainquons
vous	vainquez	vainquiez	vainqu + iez	vainer + ez	vaincr + iez	vainquez
ils	vainquent	vainquent	vainqu + aient	vainer + ont	vaincr + aient	

valoir — to be worth (avoir)

Participles: valant / valu

Person	Present	Subjunctive	Imperfect	Future	Conditional	Imperative
je	vaux	vaille	val + ais	vaudr + ai	vaudr + ais	
tu	vaux	vailles	val + ais	vaudr + as	vaudr + ais	vaux †
il	vaut	vaille	val + ait	vaudr + a	vaudr + ait	
nous	valons	valions	val + ions	vaudr + ons	vaudr + ions	valons
vous	valez	valiez	val + iez	vaudr + ez	vaudr + iez	valez
ils	valent	vaillent	val + aient	vaudr + ont	vaudr + aient	

† The imperative of *valoir* is not often used.

345

		Present	Imperfect	Future	Conditional	Subjunctive	Imperative
venir to come (*être*)	venant venu(e)(s)	viens viens vient venons venez viennent	ven + ais ais ait ions iez aient	viendr + ai as a ons ez ont	viendr + ais ais ait ions iez aient	vienne viennes vienne venions veniez viennent	viens venons venez
vivre to live (*avoir*)	vivant vécu	vis vis vit vivons vivez vivent	viv + ais ais ait ions iez aient	vivr + ai as a ons ez ont	vivr + ais ais ait ions iez aient	vive vives vive vivions viviez vivent	vis vivons vivez
voir to see (*avoir*)	voyant vu	vois vois voit voyons voyez voient	voy + ais ais ait ions iez aient	verr + ai as a ons ez ont	verr + ais ais ait ions iez aient	voie voies voie voyions voyiez voient	vois voyons voyez
vouloir to wish to want (*avoir*)	voulant voulu	veux veux veut voulons voulez veulent	voul + ais ais ait ions iez aient	voudr + ai as a ons ez ont	voudr + ais ais ait ions iez aient	veuille veuilles veuille voulions vouliez veuillent	veuillez†

†This is the only form of the imperative of *vouloir* generally used.

ANSWERS
LESSON 41

Drills and Exercises

II. A. Je viens de l'acheter.
         Tu viens de l'acheter.
         Il vient de l'acheter.
         Elle vient de l'acheter.

         Nous venons de l'acheter.
         Vous venez de l'acheter.
         Ils viennent de l'acheter.
         Elles viennent de l'acheter.

     B. Je tiens à le voir.
         Tu tiens à le voir.
         Il tient à le voir.
         Elle tient à le voir.

         Nous tenons à le voir.
         Vous tenez à le voir.
         Ils tiennent à le voir.
         Elles tiennent à le voir.

     C. J'ai envie de lui parler.
         Tu as envie de lui parler.
         Il a envie de lui parler.
         Elle a envie de lui parler.

         Nous avons envie de lui parler.
         Vous avez envie de lui parler.
         Ils ont envie de lui parler.
         Elles ont envie de lui parler.

III. A. Me voici.   *Here I am.*
         Te voici.   *Here you are.*
         Le voici.   *Here he is.*
         La voici.   *Here she is.*

Nous voici.	*Here we are.*
Vous voici.	*Here you are.*
Les voici.	*Here they are.*
	(m. & f.)

B.
Me voilà.	*There I am.*
Te voilà.	*There you are.*
Le voilà.	*There he is.*
La voilà.	*There she is.*
Nous voilà.	*There we are.*
Vous voilà.	*There you are.*
Les voilà.	*There they are.*

IV. 1. Je vais retrouver (rencontrer) Charles.
  2. Il ne va pas voir Jeanne.
  3. Allons-nous trouver une table libre?
  4. Je veux téléphoner.
  5. Voulez-vous parler français?
  6. Elle veut fixer un rendez-vous.
  7. Il faut s'asseoir à l'intérieur.
  8. Il faut payer l'addition.
  9. Elle peut faire un petit tour (*or* une petite promenade).
  10. Nous pouvons fêter votre arrivée.
  11. Je sais lire un journal français.
  12. Savez-vous écrire une lettre en français?
  13. Je commence à défaire les bagages.
  14. Commencez-vous à comprendre?
  15. Elle tient à le voir.
  16. Je refuse de rester ici.
  17. Il a demandé à Robert de rester.
  18. Je suis content d'être à Paris.
  19. C'est le moment de rencontrer Michel.
  20. J'ai le droit d'accompagner Michel.
  21. Avons-nous le droit d'entrer?

Quiz

1. Je viens d'arriver.
   I have just come.

2. Tout de suite, messieurs.
   Right away, gentlemen.

3. Tiens, voici déjà le garçon qui nous apporte les boissons.
   Look, here is the waiter with our drinks already.

4. Et on ne demande jamais aux clients de partir?
   And they never ask the customers to leave?

5. A la terrasse, bien entendu.
   On the terrace, naturally (or of course).

6. Il fait chaud.
   It's hot.

7. J'ai envie de marcher.
   I feel like walking.

8. Je vais régler l'addition et laisser un pourboire.
   I am going to settle the bill and leave a tip.

9. Oui, et c'était une excellente traversée.
   Yes, and it was an excellent crossing.

10. Le voici.
    Here he is.

LESSON 42

Drills and Exercises

II. Elle est Anglaise./Il est Anglais.
   Elle est Chinoise./Il est Chinois.
   Elle est Américaine./Il est Américain.
   Elle est Italienne./Il est Italien.
   Elle est Espagnole./Il est Espagnol.

III. 1. En choisissant cela, il s'est trompé.
He made a mistake in choosing that.

2. En choisissant cela, elle a bien fait.
She did well by choosing that.

3. En choisissant cela, elle ne s'est pas trompée.
In choosing that, she made no mistake.

4. En choisissant cela, elle avait raison.
She did right to choose that.

5. En choisissant cela, nous avons payé trop cher.
Because of choosing that, we paid too much money.

IV. 1. Pourriez-vous nous dire . . . ?

2. Pourriez-vous nous montrer . . . ?

3. Pourriez-vous nous indiquer un magasin?

4. Auriez-vous un quotidien?

5. Si je ne me trompe, voici un journal littéraire. (Note the absence of *pas.*)

6. Voici quelque chose d'intéressant.

7. Voici quelque chose d'ennuyeux.

8. Voici quelque chose d'important.

9. Il nous faut des disques et des bandes (magnétiques).

10. Puis-je voir Jeanne?

11. Puis-je parler à Charles?

12. Choisissons entre ce numéro-ci et ce numéro-là.

13. Regardez cet article-ci. Ne regardez pas cet article-là.

14. Je n'aime pas ces journaux-ci. Je préfère ces journaux-là.

15. Je n'aime pas ces revues-ci. Je préfère ces revues-là.

16. Montrez-moi ce magnétophone-là.

17. Prenez ces bandes (magnétiques)-là.

18. Prenez ces disques-ci.

19. Voici ce que vous cherchez.

20. Voici ce que je veux dire.

21. Ce que je veux? Une carte routière!

22. Ce qu'il cherche? Une bande (magnétique)!

23. Ce qu'elle lit? Notre *Michelin!*

24. J'ai tout ce que vous cherchez.

25. Je comprends tout ce qu'elle dit.

26. Il aime ce qui est important.

27. Nous lisons ce qui est nécessaire.

28. Voyez-vous ce qui se passe?

29. En lisant, on apprend à lire.

30. En écrivant, on apprend à écrire.

Quiz

1. Je ne connais pas les journaux.
   I am not familiar with the newspapers.

2. Pourriez-vous nous aider?
   Could you help me?

3. Ces journaux paraissent une fois par semaine.
   These newspapers appear (or come out) once a week.

4. Tant d'images!
   So many pictures!

5. Je commence par *Le Monde.*
   I'll begin with Le Monde.

6. Nous avons des revues de tous les genres.
   We have all kinds of magazines.

7. C'est ça, madame.
   That's right, ma'am.

8. Avez-vous un plan de la ville?
   Do you have a map of the city?

LESSON 43

Drills and Exercises

II. Quelle belle maison!
   What a beautiful house!

   Quel livre intéressant!
   What an interesting book!

   Quel bon garçon!
   What a good boy!

   Quelle robe exquise!
   What a lovely dress!

   Quelles jolies images!
   What pretty pictures!

   Quels beaux arbres!
   What beautiful trees!

III. 1. Quand je le verrai, je le saluerai.
   When I (will) see him, I'll say hello (lit.: I will greet him).

   2. Quand il viendra, dites-lui de manger.
   When he comes (will come), tell him to eat.

   3. Quand il sortira, fermez la porte.
   When he goes out (will go out), close the door.

4. Quand vous quitterez la salle, on commencera la discussion.
   When you leave (will leave) the room, we will begin the discussion.

5. Quand il achètera la voiture, il fera un voyage.
   When he buys (will buy) the car, he will take a trip.

IV. 1. Je voudrais chercher un numéro.
    2. Voudriez-vous parler à Charles?
    3. Quelle téléphoniste!
    4. Je ne vois rien.
    5. Il ne trouve rien.
    6. Vous ne voulez rien?
    7. Elle n'a rien vu.
    8. Nous n'avons rien trouvé.
    9. Ils n'ont rien voulu.
   10. Qu'est-ce que vous avez trouvé? Rien.
   11. Qu'est-ce que vous voulez? Rien.
   12. Qu'est-ce que vous dites? Rien.
   13. Veuillez parler plus fort (*or* Parlez plus fort, s'il vous plaît).

V. Achetez un jeton.
   Cherchez le numéro dans le Bottin.
   Décrochez le récepteur.
   Mettez le jeton dans la fente.
   Attendez le signal.
   Demandez le numéro au service de renseignements.
   Composez votre numéro.
   Enfoncez le bouton A.
   Parlez avec votre correspondant.
   Raccrochez si vous avez un faux numéro.
   Commencez de nouveau.

VI. Mme: Allo! C'est ici Passy 58–17?

M.: Oui, madame.

Mme: Je voudrais parler avec (*or* à) Monsieur Dupont, s'il vous plaît.

M.: C'est de la part de qui?

Mme: Ici Madame Lenclos.

M.: Ne quittez pas, s'il vous plaît. Je le regrette, madame, mais sa ligne est occupée. Voulez-vous attendre? Ça pourrait être long.

Mme: Non, merci. Je préfère laisser un mot.

M.: Comme vous voulez, madame.

Mme: Veuillez lui dire que je le rappellerai demain.

M.: Je ferai la commission.

Mme: Merci beaucoup. Au revoir, mademoiselle.

M.: Au revoir, madame.

Quiz

1. C'est pour quelle ville?
   What city is it for?

2. Cela ne fait rien, monsieur.
   That's nothing (or it doesn't matter), sir.

3. Le Bottin est à droite.
   The Bottin [telephone directory] is on the right.

4. Dès que j'aurai la communication.
   As soon as I (will) have the connection.

5. Veuillez entrer.
   Please go in.

6. Je vous dérange encore une fois.
   I am disturbing you once again.

7. C'est dans Paris même.
   It's in Paris itself.

8. Il vous faudra un jeton.
   You'll need a token.

9. J'y suis, jusqu'ici.
   I understand, so far (lit.: *I am here, up to here*).

10. Je saurai me débrouiller.
    I'll know how to manage.

LESSON 44

Drills and Exercises

II. Parle/Parlez/Parlons
Finis/Finissez/Finissons
Sois/Soyez/Soyons
Apprends/Apprenez/Apprenons
Mange/Mangez/Mangeons
Choisis/Choisissez/Choisissons
Mets/Mettez/Mettons

III. 1. Quelle est l'adresse?
2. Nous devons prendre un autobus.
3. Elle doit prendre le métro.
4. Cela doit être l'arrêt d'autobus.
5. J'ai dû prendre un billet.
6. Ils ont dû prendre un carnet de deuxièmes.
7. Elle devra faire la queue.
8. Ils devront payer.
9. Il devrait payer, mais il ne veut pas payer.
10. Il aurait dû partir.
11. Elles auraient dû venir.
12. Allons regarder la Tour Eiffel.
13. Allons passer l'après-midi avec Marie.
14. Comment fait-on pour arriver à l'Opéra?
15. Comment fait-on pour trouver un taxi?

16. Il n'y a qu'un portillon automatique.

17. Il n'y a que deux correspondances à faire.

18. Il a dit qu'elle prendrait un taxi.

19. Il a dit qu'ils auraient l'argent.

20. Ils sont plus riches que les autres.

21. Les billets sont plus chers en première.

22. On parle anglais ici.

23. On peut voir la Tour Eiffel d'ici.

24. On fait la queue ici.

25. Elle veut que vous alliez.

26. Je suis content qu'elle soit heureuse.

27. Nous doutons qu'il puisse faire cela.

28. J'irai à moins qu'il ne pleuve.

Quiz

1. Pour rentrer, prenons un taxi.
   To get back, let's take a taxi.

2. Allons prendre nos billets.
   Let's go get our tickets (lit.: *Let's go to take our tickets*).

3. L'escalier se trouve au bout du couloir.
   The staircase is at the end of the corridor.

4. Nous devrons faire la queue.
   We will have to stand in line.

5. Il y a encore de la place.
   There is still room.

6. Vous payez selon la longueur du parcours.
   You pay according to the length of the trip.

7. Oui, ça vaudrait mieux.
   Yes, that would be better.

8. Celui-là doit être occupé.
   That one must be taken (lit.: *occupied*).

9. C'est quelle adresse, s'il vous plaît?
   What address is it, please?

10. Tu avais raison.
    You were right.

LESSON 45

Drills and Exercises

II. A. Je me couche à neuf heures.
     I go to bed at nine.

   Tu te couches à neuf heures.
   You go to bed at nine.

   Il se couche à neuf heures.
   He goes to bed at nine.

   Elle se couche à neuf heures.
   She goes to bed at nine.

   Nous nous couchons à neuf heures.
   We go to bed at nine.

   Vous vous couchez à neuf heures.
   You go to bed at nine.

   Ils se couchent à neuf heures.
   They (masc.) *go to bed at nine.*

   Elles se couchent à neuf heures.
   They (fem.) *go to bed at nine.*

   B. Je me suis trompé(e).
      I made a mistake (or *I was mistaken*).

   Tu t'es trompé(e).
   You made a mistake.

Il s'est trompé.
He made a mistake.

Elle s'est trompée.
She made a mistake.

Nous nous sommes trompé(e)s.
We made a mistake.

Vous vous êtes trompé(e)s.
You made a mistake.

Ils se sont trompés.
They (masc.) *made a mistake.*

Elles se sont trompées.
They (fem.) *made a mistake.*

III. A. Nous nous sommes lavé(e)s.
  We washed.

  B. Nous nous sommes levé(e)s.
  We got up.

  C. Nous nous sommes trompé(e)s.
  We were mistaken (or *We made a mistake*).

  D. Nous nous sommes dépêché(e)s.
  We hurried.

  E. Nous nous sommes arrêté(e).
  We stopped.

IV. 1. Demandez le chemin au concierge (*or* à la
  concierge).
  2. Ne demandez pas le chemin à ce monsieur.
  3. Je ne saurais pas aller à pied.
  4. De quel coté voulez-vous aller? Du côté de
  Paris.
  5. Du côté du Louvre.
  6. Si on allait voir la Sainte-Chapelle?

7. Si on allait faire une promenade?

8. Nous nous sommes égarés.

9. Nous nous sommes dirigés vers le Quartier Latin.

10. Marchons-nous dans le bon sens?

11. Vous marchez dans le mauvais sens.

12. Tournez à droite.

13. Je dois tourner à gauche.

14. Vous auriez dû continuer tout droit.

15. Elle doit rebrousser chemin.

16. La Sorbonne est à deux pas d'ici? Oui, elle est tout près d'ici.

Quiz

1. Si on faisait une promenade à pied?
   How about taking a walk?

2. C'est facile.
   It's easy.

3. Regardez ce plan de Paris.
   Look at this map of Paris.

4. Il faut continuer tout droit.
   You have to go (to continue) straight ahead.

5. Vous allez dans le mauvais sens.
   You are walking in the wrong direction.

6. Nous avons tourné à gauche.
   We turned left.

7. Ah oui, une fois que nous avons trouvé le bon chemin.
   Oh, yes, once we found the right path.

8. C'est nous qui nous sommes trompés.
   It is we who made the mistake.

9. Quel dommage!
   What a pity!

10. N'oublie pas que nous avons vu Notre-Dame.
    Don't forget that we saw Notre Dame.

LESSON 46

Drills and Exercises

II. 1. Donnez-moi celui-ci.
   2. Je préfère ceux-là.
   3. Regardez celles-ci.
   4. Prenez ceux-ci.

III. 1. Celui dont je vous ai parlé a été vendu.
      The one I spoke to you about (lit., *about which I spoke to you*) *has been sold.*

   2. Celui dont je vous ai parlé coûte trop cher.
      The one that I spoke to you about costs too much.

   3. Celui dont je vous ai parlé ne me plaît pas.
      I don't like the one (or the person) I spoke to you about.

   4. Celui dont je vous ai parlé est excellent.
      The one I spoke to you about is excellent.

   5. Celui dont je vous ai parlé est le frère de Michel.
      The person (or *the one*) *about whom I spoke to you is Michael's brother.*

   6. Celui dont je vous ai parlé est venu me voir.
      The one (or *the person*) *whom I spoke to you about came to see me.*

IV. 1. Il le lui donne.
   He is giving it to him.

 2. Il nous les montre.
   He is showing them to us.

 3. Ne me le donnez pas.
   Don't give it to me.

 4. Il m'en montre.
   He shows some to me.

 5. Je l'y mets.
   I am putting it there.

V. 1. Ne la leur montrez pas.
   Don't show it to them.

 2. Ne les lui vendez pas.
   Don't sell them to him.

 3. Ne m'en donnez pas.
   Don't give any to me.

 4. Ne nous la racontez pas.
   Don't tell it to us.

 5. Ne me le prête pas.
   Don't lend it to me.

VI. 1. Je préfère celui-là en soie.
 2. J'aime celle-ci en rayon.
 3. Il aime ceux-là en laine.
 4. Elle aime celles-là en lin.
 5. Nous préférons celles-ci en coton.
 6. Elle préfère ceux-ci en nylon.
 7. Quelle est votre pointure?
 8. Quelle est votre taille?
 9. Je voudrais celui-ci en rose.

10. Je voudrais celle-là en bleu marine.

11. Je voudrais ceux-ci en blanc.

12. Je voudrais ceux-là en rouge.

13. Je voudrais celles-ci en jaune.

14. Il voudrait celles-là en gris.

15. La robe aux manches longues.

16. Celui-ci vous va à merveille.

17. Celle-là te va parfaitement.

18. Voici quelque chose de beau.

19. Il n'y a rien d'autre ici.

20. Il va vous les envoyer.

21. Il va les lui envelopper.

22. Donnez-les-moi.

23. Ne le leur racontez pas.

24. Pourriez-vous me dire où se trouve l'autobus?

25. Sauriez-vous le nom de ce monsieur-là?

26. Je voudrais le voir.

27. Auriez-vous la bonté de m'indiquer l'heure?

Quiz

1. Je voudrais des gants pour tous les jours.
   I would like some gloves for every day.

2. Ceux-là sont assez jolis.
   Those are quite pretty.

3. Les pointures pour les gants sont les mêmes.
   Glove sizes are the same.

4. Je cherche une robe de soie.
   I am looking for a silk dress.

5. C'est une occasion.
   It's a bargain.

6. Je la trouve large aux épaules.
   I find it wide in the shoulders.

7. Qu'est-ce que vous désirez, madame?
   What do you wish, madam?

8. Je cherche des mouchoirs.
   I am looking for some handkerchiefs.

9. Ils se vendent à cent francs la douzaine.
   The sell for 100 francs a dozen.

10. Voici votre monnaie.
    Here is your change.

LESSON 47

Drills and Exercises

I. 1. Elle parle au garçon qu'elle a rencontré à la banque.
   She is speaking to the boy she met at the bank.

2. Elle parle de l'arbre qui est plein de fleurs.
   She is speaking about the tree that is full of flowers.

3. Elle parle aux enfants qui se rendent à l'épicerie.
   She is speaking to the children who are going to the grocery store.

4. Elle parle constamment du petit truc qu'elle a vu au magasin.
   She speaks constantly of the little gadget she saw in the store.

5. Elle parle souvent de la jolie petite fille du professeur.
   She speaks often about the pretty little daughter of the professor.

II. A. Tu es plus jolie que jamais.

Tu es plus intéressante que jamais.

Tu es plus belle que jamais.

Tu es plus aimable que jamais.

Tu es plus charmante que jamais.

Tu es plus bavarde que jamais.

B. Vous pouvez le voir plus tard.

Vous pouvez le faire plus tard.

Vous pouvez le demander plus tard.

Vous pouvez le dire plus tard.

Vous pouvez le chercher plus tard.

Vous pouvez le manger plus tard.

Vous pouvez le boire plus tard.

Vous pouvez le lire plus tard.

C. Nous pourrions vous le montrer.

Nous pourrions vous le donner.

Nous pourrions vous le demander.

Nous pourrions vous le dire.

Nous pourrions vous l'expliquer.

Nous pourrions vous le recommander.

III. 1. Je me fais laver les cheveux.

2. Je me fais teindre les cheveux.

3. Je me fais raser.

4. Je me fais faire une mise en plis.

5. Je me fais faire les ongles.

IV. 1. Je me suis fait raser.
I had myself shaved (or *I got myself shaved*).

2. Je me suis fait laver les vêtements.
I had my clothes washed.

3. Elle s'est fait faire les ongles.
She has had her nails done.

4. Elle s'est fait couper les cheveux.
   She had her hair cut.

V. 1. Qu'est-ce qu'il y a pour votre service, madame?

2. En quoi puis-je vous être utile, monsieur?

3. Monsieur (Madame) désire?

4. Je veux me faire faire une mise en plis.

5. Elle veut se faire faire un shampooing.

6. Il veut se faire couper les cheveux.

7. Elle veut se faire faire les ongles.

8. Elle veut se faire éclaircir les cheveux.

9. Ne les coupez pas trop courts sur la nuque.

10. Quel luxe que d'être chez le coiffeur!

11. Quel luxe que d'aller à Paris!

12. Voudriez-vous une mise en plis?

13. Je voudrais une coupe de cheveux.

14. Elle voudrait un shampooing.

15. Faites-le comme d'habitude.

16. Faites-le comme toujours.

17. Faites-le comme vous voulez.

18. Elle en aura pour longtemps.

19. Est-ce que j'en aurai pour longtemps?

20. La terrasse du café est toujours ouverte au public.

21. Voulez-vous aller avec lui à la bibliothèque pour parler aux étudiants?

22. Le critique du *Monde* m'a parlé des films d'aujourd'hui.

23. Viens avec moi à l'école de l'agriculture.

24. Chez nous on trouvera beaucoup de livres.

Quiz

1. Ils poussent plus vite que jamais.
   They are growing faster than ever.

2. Je vous les coupe comme d'habitude.
   I'll cut it (hair—les cheveux) as usual.

3. Vous en aurez pour longtemps.
   You will have a long wait.

4. Ma femme est á côté.
   My wife is next door.

5. Quel luxe que de se faire raser de temps en temps.
   What a luxury to have oneself shaved from time to time.

6. On vous reverra la semaine prochaine.
   We'll see you (again) next week.

7. Voilà quelque chose en plus pour vous.
   Here is something extra for you.

8. Te voilà, chérie!
   There you are, dear!

9. Il y a quelque chose de différent.
   There is something different.

10. Pas de manucure cette fois-ci?
    No manicure this time?

LESSON 48

Drills and Exercises

I. 1. Elle n'a que deux soeurs.
   She has only two sisters.

   2. Ils n'ont que quatre pièces.
   They only have four plays.

   Note: *la pièce* also means "the room."

   3. Elle ne veut que ton bonheur.
   She wants only your happiness.

   4. Nous n'avons qu'un peu d'argent.
   We only have a little money.

II. 1. vous avez de bonnes idées.
   You have (some) good ideas.

   Note: In this sentence, the word "some" could be either stated or merely implied.

   2. J'ai lu de bons livres.
   I've read some good books.

   3. Nous avons vu de bons films.
   We've seen some good films.

   4. J'ai mangé de bonnes frites.
   I ate some good French fries.

   5. Elle a écrit de bonnes lettres.
   She's written some good letters.

III. 1. Ne lui pardonne pas.

   2. Ne les regardons pas.

   3. Ne nous écoutez pas.

   4. Ne l'excusez pas.

   5. Ne te lève pas.

IV. A. Nous sommes entrés.

Nous sommes partis.

Nous sommes arrivés.

Nous sommes venus.

Nous sommes restés.

Nous sommes tombés.

B. Elle est sortie.

Elle est partie.

Elle est devenue riche.

Elle est restée.

Elle est née.

Elle est montée.

V. 1. Elle est descendue.
   She went down.

2. Ils sont venus.
   They have come.

3. Elles sont parties.
   They have left.

4. Nous sommes resté(e)s.
   We stayed.

5. Vous êtes entré(e)s.
   You came in.

VI. 1. Nous ne voulons que des places au centre.

2. Il n'y a que des places de côté.

3. Nous avons de bonnes pièces à Paris.

4. Nous avons de bonnes œuvres symphoniques.

5. Nous avons d'autres places.

6. Ne me montrez pas le programme.

7. Présentez-nous à Michel.

8. Donnez-lui l'argent. Ne lui donnez pas l'argent.

9. Aujourd'hui il part à neuf heures.
   Hier il est parti à neuf heures aussi.

10. Aujourd'hui vous restez sans dire un mot.
    Hier aussi vous êtes resté sans dire un mot.

11. Elle se plaît à voir les comédiens.

12. Nous nous plaisons à aller au théâtre.

13. Ils se plaisent à regarder la télé (*or* la télévision).

14. J'aurai le temps de le faire.

15. Aurez-vous l'occasion de le faire?

16. Ce qui m'intéresse c'est le décor.

17. Ce qui m'intéresse c'est l'action.

18. Quant à lui, il aime les dessins animés.

19. Je regrette qu'elle soit venue.

20. Donnez-moi du sucre.

21. Il a de l'argent.

22. Nous voudrions des pommes.

23. Allez au marché, parce que nous n'avons pas de lait.

24. Il a acheté de très bonnes chaussures.

Quiz

1. Quatre places, pas trop de côté.
   Four seats, not too far to the side.

2. J'ai encore de bonnes places.
   I still have some good seats.

3. Quel plaisir de vous revoir!
   What a pleasure to see you again!

4. La couleur vous va à merveille.
   The color becomes you wonderfully.

5. Permettez-moi, Charles.
   Permit me, Charles.

6. Par ici, s'il vous plaît.
   This way, please.

7. Que de monde!
   What a crowd!

8. A vrai dire, il me plâit.
   To tell the truth, I like him.

9. C'est la deuxième chaîne.
   It's the second channel.

10. Dépêchons-nous, alors!
    Let's hurry, then!

LESSON 49

Drills and Exercises

II. 1. Il y a quatre peintures au mur.

   2. Il y a vingt personnes dans la salle.

   3. Il y a des garçons devant l'école.

   4. Il y a de la bonne viande chez le boucher.

   5. Il y du sucre dans le placard.

III. 1. N'y va pas.
      Don't go there.

   2. N'y allez pas.
      Don't go there.

   3. Il n'y va pas.
      He isn't going there.

4. Il n'y est pas allé.
   He didn't go there.

5. Nous n'y sommes pas allés.
   We haven't gone there.

6. Elles n'y sont pas allées.
   They didn't go there.

IV. 1. L'homme dont je t'avais parlé est arrivé.
   The man about whom I spoke to you has come.

2. La femme dont j'avais fait la connaissance hier s'appelle Mme Dupont.
   The name of the woman (whom) I met yesterday is Mme Dupont.

3. Les hommes dont j'avais entendu parler sont partis pour Paris.
   The men (whom) I've heard about have left for Paris.

4. Les femmes dont vous connaissez les fils ont aussi des filles.
   The women whose sons you know also have daughters.

5. Le livre dont vous avez besonin n'est pas à la bibliothèque.
   The book (that) you need is not at the library.

V. 1. Elle vous fera visiter le Louvre.

2. Nous lui ferons voir les peintures.

3. Je leur ferai regarder les statues.

4. Voilà l'Opéra! Il y a aussi un bel Opéra à Milan.

5. Voilà la Place de la Concorde. Il y a aussi une belle place à Rome.

6. Voilá le Louvre! Il y a aussi un beau musée à New-York.

7. Voici les objets d'art dont il vous a parlé.

8. Voici les sculptures dont ils lui ont parlé.

9. Voici les peintures dont elle leur a parlé.

10. Voici les chefs-d'œuvre dont nous vous avons parlé.

11. Voilà les peintres dont nous entendons toujours parler.

12. Voilà les Impressionnistes dont j'entends toujours parler.

13. Ma femme se connaît en musique.

14. Je me connais en livres.

VI. 1. Je voudrais aller au Louvre.

2. Allons-y tout de suite (*or* Allons-y immédiatement).

3. Où se trouvent les peintures (*or* Où sont les peintures)?

4. Je voudrais voir aussi les statues (*or* Je voudrais voir également les statues).

5. Regardez! Voilá les chefs-d'œuvre (*or* Regardez! Voilà les œuvres maîtresses).

Quiz

1. Un franc chacun, s'il vous plaît.
   One franc each, please.

2. Nous aurions dû venir dimanche.
   We should have come Sunday.

3. Mon mari se connaît en peinture.
   My husband knows about painting.

4. On peut admirer les chefs-d'œuvre.
   One can admire the masterpieces.

5. Suivez-moi, s'il vous plaît.
   Follow me, please.

6. Qu'elle [la peinture] est bien exposée!
   How well displayed it [the painting] is!

7. Je ne les vois nulle part.
   *I see them nowhere (or I don't see them any-
   where).*

8. Allons-y tout de suite.
   Let's go there right away.

9. Je préfère le cubisme.
   I prefer cubism.

10. Ne les cherchons pas maintenant.
    Let's not look for them now.

LESSON 50

Drills and Exercises

II. La maison que tu as vendue est belle.

La maison qu'il a vendue est belle.

La maison qu'elle a vendue est belle.

La maison que nous avons vendue est belle.

La maison que vous avez vendue est belle.

La maison qu'ils ont vendue est belle.

La maison qu'elles ont vendue est belle.

III. 1. Le marchand qui vend la cafetière est sym-
       pathique.

2. La dame qui achète les meubles est ma
   femme.

3. Le marchand que vous voyez est sympathique.

4. La dame que nous aimons est ici.

5. Les habits que je porte sont vieux.

6. Les bagues que vous avez sont belles.

7. C'est l'allée la plus longue du marché.

8. C'est la toile la plus riche de la galerie.

9. C'est l'homme le plus intéressant de Paris.

10. C'est le meilleur dessin de la collection.

11. C'est le plus vieux tableau de la collection.

12. Il y aura des meubles au marché.

13. Il y aura des peintures à la galerie.

14. Il faudra marchander.

15. Il faudra porter de vieux habits.

16. Elle a l'air élégant.

17. Est-ce que j'ai l'air riche?

18. Ils n'ont pas l'air sympathique.

19. Je me demande s'il a un canapé.

20. On se demande s'ils ont des peintures.

21. Nous nous demandons si vous avez des objets d'art.

22. Je voudrais le voir de près.

23. Je voudrais le voir de loin.

24. Elle voudrait le voir d'ici.

25. Vous le trouverez au bout de l'allée.

26. Vous le trouverez en face de la galerie.

27. Est-ce que je le trouverai au coin de la rue?

28. Montrez-moi un fauteuil bleu ciel.

29. Violà un canapé vert foncé.

30. Je voudrais une tapisserie rouge clair.

31. Préférez-vous la tapisserie de droite?

32. Je préfère la toile du milieu.

33. Elle préfère la tapisserie de gauche.

Quiz

1. Nous avons si souvent entendu parler du
   Marché aux Puces.
   We have heard so often of the Flea Market.

2. Si on y allait tous les trois?
   How about all three of us going there?

3. Il y aura quelque chose que nous pourrions
   acheter.
   There will be something that we could buy.

4. Il ne faut pas avoir l'air trop riche.
   One mustn't look too rich (lit.: *to have a too
   rich air*).

5. Il faut marchander.
   One must bargain.

6. Regardez en face.
   Look across the way.

7. Ne soyez pas trop impulsif.
   Don't be too impulsive.

8. Celui qui a gagné un diplôme . . .
   The one who has graduated (lit.: *has earned a
   diploma*) . . .

9. Il nous reste encore quelques-unes [les toiles].
   We still have a few [canvases] *left.*

10. Elle [la toile] doit être très chère.
    It [the canvas] *must be very expensive.*

LESSON 51

Drills and Exercises

II.   1. Qu'est-ce que se passe?

    2. Qu'est-ce qui ne marche pas?

    3. Qu'est-ce qui vous ennuie?

    4. Qu'est-ce qui est arrivé?

    5. Qu'est-ce qui l'inquiète?

III.   1. J'en ai acheté.
      I bought some.

    2. J'en voudrais.
      I'd like some.

    3. Nous en avons assez.
      We have enough (of it, of them).

    4. Il m'en a donné quatre.
      He gave me four (of them).

    5. Prêtez-m'en.
      Lend me some.

IV.   1. Des photos? Il en a fait plusieurs.

    2. J'en voudrais quatre.

    3. Ne me donnez pas de pellicules; j'en ai assez.

    4. Avez-vous assez de pellicules pour l'appareil?

    5. Oui, mais il n'y a pas assez de lumière.

    6. Qu'est-ce qui est sur la table?

    7. Qu'est-ce qui va arriver?

    8. Qu'est-ce qui vous ennuie?

    9. Pour apprendre, il faut comprendre.

    10. Je n'ai pas assez d'argent pour acheter ces pellicules.

    11. Faut-il prendre un avion pour y aller?

Quiz

1. Tu as assez d'inversibles?
   Do you have enough slide film?

2. Je voudrais des films en noir et blanc.
   I'd like some films in black and white (or *some black and white films*).

3. Il nous en faudra au moins deux.
   We'll need at least two.

4. Je voudrais me souvenir des couleurs.
   I'd like to remember the colors.

5. Les voici.
   Here they are.

6. Je l'ai acheté aux Etats-Unis.
   I bought it in the United States.

7. Veuillez aussi donner un coup d'œil à cet appareil?
   Would you please also glance (or *take a look*) *at this camera?*

8. Y a-t-il autre chose?
   Is there anything else?

9. Je vois jusqu'à l'Arc de Triomphe.
   I see up to the Arch of Triumph.

10. Je ferais mieux d'employer le pose-mètre.
    I'd better (lit. *I would be better to*) *use the light meter.*

LESSON 52

Drills and Exercises

II. A. Croit-il que tu sois stupide?

Croit-il qu'il soit stupide?

Croit-il qu'elle soit stupide?

Croit-il que nous soyons stupides?

Croit-il que vous soyez stupide(s)?

Croit-il qu'ils soient stupides?

Croit-il qu'elles soient stupides?

B. Il ne pense pas que tu aies de l'argent.

Il ne pense pas qu'il ait de l'argent.

Il ne pense pas qu'elle ait de l'argent.

Il ne pense pas que nous ayons de l'argent.

Il ne pense pas que vous ayez de l'argent.

Il ne pense pas qu'ils aient de l'argent.

Il ne pense pas qu'elles aient de l'argent.

III. 1. Ils sont allés en Italie l'année dernière.

2. Il y a une belle cathédrale à Chartres.

3. En France, on parle français.

4. Nous avons reçu une lettre du Canada français.

5. Elle est revenue de Paris hier.

6. Ce vin vient du Portugal.

7. Ils voyagent toujours en voiture.

8. Je suis rentré à pied.

9. Je ne pense pas qu'elle soit très jolie.

10. Croyez-vous qu'il soit venu hier?

11. Je ne crois pas qu'ils puissent faire ceci.

Quiz

1. Je voudrais voyager en dehors de Paris.
   I would like to travel outside of Paris.

2. Vous pouvez aller n'importe où.
   You can go anywhere (lit.: *You can go no matter where*).

3. Vous pouvez y aller en chemin de fer.
   You can go there by railroad.

4. J'ai besoin d'une carte routière.
   I need a road map.

5. Vous gagnerez ainsi beaucoup de temps.
   You will save a lot of time that way.

6. Qu'est-ce que vous avez décidé?
   What have you decided?
      (lit.: *What is it that you have decided?*)

7. On peut voir les jeux d'eau seulement les dimanches.
   You can see the fountains only on Sundays.

8. Voudriez-vous bien nous retenir des chambres d'hôtel?
   Would you please reserve hotel rooms for us?

9. Si vous y tenez, vous pourriez le faire.
   If you insist you can do it.

10. Il y a de très bons vins en Provence.
    There are some very good wines in Provence.

LESSON 53

Drills and Exercises

II. A. Il mange trois fois par jour.
   He eats three times a day.

   B. Ils se voient deux fois par jour.
   They see each other twice a day.

   C. Elles sortent une fois par jour.
   They go out once a day.

   D. Il me téléphone plusieurs fois par jour.
   He telephones me several times a day.

   E. Nous les changeons une fois par jour.
   We change them once a day.

III. A. Il nous faut trois livres.

   B. Il lui faut un ami.

   C. Il leur faut de l'argent.

   D. Il vous faut des conseils.

   E. Il lui faut du sommeil.

IV. 1. Quelle est sa question?

   2. Quel est votre problème?

   3. Quelles étaient ses raisons?

   4. Quelle robe préférez-vous?

   5. Quelle voiture a-t-il achetée?

   6. Quel voyage feront-ils?

   7. Je la vois une fois par an.

   8. Les enfants vont à l'école cinq jours par semaine.

   9. Combien de fois par jour mangez-vous?

   10. Il me faut une voiture pour mon travail.

   11. Il lui fallait de l'argent.

12. Vous faut-il une nouvelle voiture?

13. Elle pensait travailler hier soir.

14. Que pensez-vous faire samedi?

15. Je pense aller au cinéma.

Quiz

1. C'est pour vous deux.
   It's for the two of you.

2. Qu'est-ce qui est inclus dans le tarif?
   What's included in the rate?

3. Quant à l'essence, c'est trop cher.
   As for gasoline, it's too expensive.

4. Nous payerons quand nous rendrons la voiture.
   We will pay when we (will) return the car.

5. Mais si on la laisse ailleurs?
   But if we leave it somewhere else?

6. Cela revient moins cher.
   It's less expensive.

7. Vous pouvez l'acheter comptant.
   You can buy it for cash.

8. Ce sont des voitures d'occasion.
   These are secondhand (or used) cars.

9. Voudriez-vous faire un essai?
   Would you like to try it out?

10. Il faudra que nous y réfléchissions un peu.
    We will have to think it over a little.

LESSON 54

Drills and Exercises

I. 1. Elle y restera.
    She will stay there.

2. J'y passerai mes vacances.
    I will spend my vacation there.

3. Il lui parle.
    He is speaking to him.

4. J'y ai trouvé mes chaussettes.
    I found my shoes there.

5. Il y est entré.
    He went in there.

6. Elle lui lit le roman.
    She is reading the novel to him (or *her*).

7. Il leur a posé une question.
    He asked them a question.

8. Il y a passé trois semaines.
    He spent three weeks there.

II. 1. Je n'y suis pas.

2. Je n'y reste pas.

3. Il n'y obéit pas.

4. Elle n'y répond pas.

5. Nous n'y pensons pas.

6. N'y allez pas.

7. N'y va pas.

8. N'y allons pas.

9. N'y répondons pas.

10. N'y entrez pas.

III. 1. Elle va partir ce soir.
    She is going to leave this evening.

  2. Ils vont sortir plus tard.
    They are leaving later.

  3. Elles vont arriver à sept heures.
    They will arrive at seven.

  4. Nous allons faire une promenade.
    We are going to take a walk.

  5. Elle va voir sa sœur demain.
    She is seeing her sister tomorrow.

IV. 1. J'y vais dans trois semaines.

  2. Nous y sommes restés pendant un mois.

  3. Son voyage? Elle y pense tous les jours.

  4. Nous allons partir demain.

  5. Va-t-elle venir plus tard?

  6. Je vais remplacer le pneu crevé.

  7. C'est une longue histoire.

  8. Quelle belle voiture!

  9. Il n'est pas très heureux aujourd'hui.

Quiz

  1. Je ne sais pas, au juste.
    I don't know, exactly.

  2. Il y a un drôle de bruit.
    There is a funny noise.

  3. Je croyais en avoir encore quelques litres.
    I thought I still had a few litres.

  4. Nous allons faire un voyage à travers la France.
    We are going to take a trip across France.

  5. Il y a un pneu de rechange dans le coffre.
    There's a spare tire in the trunk.

6. Je vais vérifier les bougies s'il le faut.
   I'll check the sparkplugs if necessary.

7. Elle [la voiture] est neuve.
   It [the car] is new.

8. Pas du tout, monsieur.
   Not at all, sir.

9. J'aurai besoin de la voiture.
   I'll need the car.

10. Nous faisons de notre mieux.
    We do our best.

LESSON 55

Drills and Exercises

II. A. 1. J'ai entendu dire qu'elle est arrivée.
         I heard that she has arrived.

    2. J'ai entendu dire que vous étiez malade.
       I've heard that you were sick.

    3. J'ai entendu dire qu'ils sont très pauvres.
       *I've heard (people say) that they are very
       poor.*

    4. J'ai entendu dire que tu étais parti hier.
       I heard that you had left yesterday.

    5. J'ai entendu dire qu'il ne veut pas venir.
       I heard (tell) that he doesn't want to come.

B. 1. Il ne veut pas que vous ayez de la peine.
      He doesn't want you to take any trouble.

2. Il ne veut pas qu'elle sache la vérité.
   He doesn't want her to know the truth.

3. Il ne veut pas que nous parlions trop fort.
   He doesn't want us to speak too loudly.

4. Il ne veut pas que je fasse ce voyage.
   He doesn't want me to take this trip.

5. Il ne veut pas qu'ils aillent à Paris.
   He doesn't want them to go to Paris.

6. Il ne veut pas que je finisse ce travail.
   He doesn't want me to finish this work.

7. Il ne veut pas qu'elles apprennent cette nouvelle.
   He doesn't want them to learn this news.

III. 1. Avez-vous entendu parler de ce livre?

   2. J'ai entendu dire qu'elle partira demain.

   3. Je vois venir l'ouvreuse.

   4. Il ne veut pas que je sois triste.

   5. Voulez-vous que je vienne à trois heures?

   6. Je veux que vous partiez tout de suite!

   7. Les livres que j'ai lus étaient excellents.

   8. Je les ai lus l'année dernière.

   9. Elle est arrivée en retard.

  10. Nous nous sommes recontrés, mais nous ne
      nous somes pas écrit.

  11. Mangeons ensemble.

  12. Je commençais à lire quand il est entré.

  13. Nous commençons à nous fatiguer.

  14. Elle mangeait lentement.

Quiz

1. Regarde cette queue devant le poste de douane.
   Look at that line in front of the customs station.

2. C'est la douane entre la France et l'Espagne.
   It's the customs station between France and Spain.

3. Je ne crois pas qu'ils soient stricts.
   I don't believe that they're strict.

4. Nous voici enfin à la frontière.
   Here we are at last at the border.

5. Ce ne sera qu'une courte visite.
   This will only be a short visit.

6. Pas que je sache.
   Not that I know of.

7. Tout ce que nous avons est pour nous.
   Everything that we have is for us.

8. Tout est en règle.
   Everything is in order.

9. Te souviens-tu de notre dernier voyage?
   Do you remember our last trip?

10. On les a fouillées.
    They searched them.

LESSON 56

Drills and Exercises

II. 1. Reposez-vous avand de commencer.
Rest before you begin.

2. Il faut réfléchir avant de commencer.
It's necessary to reflect before beginning.

3. Vous devez manger avant de commencer.
You must eat before you begin.

4. Il pourrait vous parler avant de commencer.
He'll be able to speak to you before he begins.

5. Avant de commencer, je viendrai vous voir.
Before I begin, I'll come to see you.

6. Avant de commencer, elle a téléphoné à son amie.
Before beginning, she telephoned her friend.

7. Pensez bien avant de commencer ce travail.
Think well before you begin this work.

8. Réfléchissez bien avant de commencer ce que vous allez faire.
Reflect carefully before beginning what you are going to do.

Note: *Avant de commencer* means literally, "before beginning," but it is often freely translated, as in some of the preceding sentences.

III. 1. Il parle constamment.

2. Il parle prudemment.

3. Il parle poliment.

4. Il parle intelligemment.

5. Il parle suffisamment.

IV. 1. Elle a dit au revoir avant de partir.

2. Avant de dire "non," faites un effort.

3. Je me lave les mains avant de manger.

4. Après les avoir lus, j'ai rendu les livres à Marie.

5. Après être rentrée, elle s'est couchée.

6. Après nous être lavé les mains, nous nous asseyons à manger.

7. Si elle a assez d'argent, elle achètera ce manteau.

8. Je vous écrirais plus souvent si j'en avais le temps.

9. S'il avait neigé, je serais resté chez moi.

10. Heureusement, nous avons assez d'argent.

11. Elle est évidemment très intelligente.

12. Vous avez absolument raison.

13. J'aurais dû lui parler.

14. Ils seraient partis.

Quiz

1. Vous n'avez qu'à le contresigner.
   You need only to countersign it.

2. Il faudra que vous me montriez une pièce d'identité.
   You will have to show me some identification.

3. Donnez-le-moi [l'argent] en gros billets.
   Give it [the money] to me in large bills.

4. Je voudrais expédier une caisse.
   I'd like to ship a case.

5. Et la deuxième question?
   And the second question (or matter)?

6. C'est exact.
   That's right.

7. Il s'occupe de tout.
   He takes care of everything.

8. Il s'agit du paiement.
   It's a question of the payment.

9. Je n'ai pas suffisamment d'argent (*or* assez d'argent).
   I don't have enough money.

10. Quels seront les impôts à payer?
    What taxes will have to be paid?

LESSON 57

Drills and Exercises

II. A. Il veut la voir.
      He wants to see her.

   B. Il voulait la voir.
      He wanted to see her.

   C. Il voudra la voir.
      He will want to see her.

   D. Il voudrait la voir.
      He would like to see her.

   E. Il a voulu la voir.
      He has wanted to see her.

   F. Il avait voulu la voir.
      He had wanted to see her.

   G. Il aurait voulu la voir.
      He would have wanted to see her.

Note: *La* as a direct object means either "her" or "it" (when referring to a feminine noun). Thus, these sentences could also be translated, "He wants to see it," "He wanted to see it," etc.

III. 1. Je vous reverrai dans trois semaines.
   2. Pouvez-vous finir le travail en une heure?
   3. J'ai quelque chose à vous dire.
   4. Avez-vous un télégramme à envoyer?
   5. Nous avons à écrire plusieurs lettres.
   6. Je ne peux pas vous parler maintenant.
   7. Elle va le faire plus tard.
   8. Je voudrais le voir bientôt.

Quiz

1. Je voudrais envoyer ces lettres.
   I would like to send these letters.

2. Par avion?
   By airmail?

3. Il lui parviendra en une heure.
   It will reach him within an hour.

4. Y a-t-il du courrier pour moi?
   Is there some mail for me?

5. Comment fait-on pour envoyer un télégramme?
   How does one go about sending a telegram?

6. Combien est-ce?
   How much is it?

7. J'ai aussi un colis à expédier.
   I have also a package to send.

8. Ce colis pèse au dessus d'un kilo.
   This package weighs more than a kilo.

9. C'est le bureau le plus proche.
   It's the nearest office.

10. Je voulais aussi le faire assurer.
    I wanted also to have it insured.

LESSON 58

Drills and Exercises

II. A. Je ne préfère pas ce livre-ci.
       I don't prefer this book.

   B. Ils ne préfèrent pas les autres chemises.
      They don't prefer the other shirts.

   C. Nous ne répétons pas la leçon.
      We aren't repeating the lesson.

   D. La mère no protège pas ses enfants.
      The mother doesn't protect her children.

   E. Elle ne mène pas une vie heureuse.
      She doesn't lead a happy life.

   F. Il ne ramène pas les enfants de l'école.
      He isn't taking the children from school.

   G. Nous n'achetons pas les robes les plus chères.
      We aren't buying the most expensive dresses.

III. 1. Je lui demanderai de venir.

   2. Ils ont commencé à marcher rapidement.

   3. Ne partez pas sans me parler.

   4. Elle ramène son enfant de l'école à midi.

   5. Quel tissu préférez-vous?

   6. Le col est trop empesé.

   7. Le bas du pantalon est trop serré.

   8. Le bifteck est bien cuit.

Quiz

1. Vous avez plusieurs choses à faire laver.
    You have several things to have washed.

2. J'ai une assez longue liste.
    I have a rather long list.

3. Je me rappelle qu'il ne les aime pas empesées
    [les chemises].
    *I remember that he doesn't like them starched
    [the shirts].*

4. Ce bouton vient de sauter.
    This button has just come off.

5. Vous allez tout laver à la main.
    You are going to wash everything by hand.

6. Combien de temps faudra-t-il?
    How much time will it take?

7. Vous l'aurez dans la journée.
    You will have it within the day (the same day).

8. Il faut mesurer la largeur de pantalon.
    One must measure the width of the trousers.

9. A propos, je voudrais deux fentes latérales.
    By the way, I would like two side slashes.

10. Est-ce que vous trouvez la jaquette à votre gré?
    Do you find the jacket to your liking?

LESSON 59

Drills and Exercises

II. 1. J'attends depuis deux jours.
       I've been waiting for two days.

2. Elle est malade depuis un mois.
   She's been sick for a month.

3. Je veux vous parler depuis trois semaines.
   I've been wanting to speak to you for three weeks.

4. Il conduit depuis quatre ans.
   He's been driving for four years.

5. Je demeure dans cet hôtel depuis une quinzaine de jours.
   I've been living in that hotel for two weeks.

III. 1. Elle travaille depuis quatre heures.

2. Il m'attend depuis midi.

3. Je demeure ici depuis cinq ans.

4. Il se peut qu'elle ne sache pas la réponse.

5. Il se peut qu'il ait faim.

6. Il se peut qu'ils soient arrivés trop tard.

7. Avez-vous mal à la tête?

8. Elle a les cheveux blonds.

9. Il se peut qu'il ait mal à la gorge.

10. Ils sont arrivés il y a une heure (*or* Il y a une heure qu'ils sont arrivés).

11. Elle a étudié il y a deux heures (*or* Il y a deux heures qu'elle a étudié).

12. Nous attendons depuis un jour.

13. Je lui ai parlé il y a une semaine (*or* Il y a une semaine que je lui ai parlé).

Quiz

1. Qu'est-ce qui ne va pas?
   What's wrong? or *What's the trouble?*

2. Il se peut que le nerf soit à vif.
   It's possible that the nerve is exposed.

3. Rejetez la tête en arrière.
   Put your head back.

4. Je ne vais pas bien, Jeanne.
   I'm not well, Jane.

5. Votre mari doit garder le lit.
   Your husband must stay in bed.

6. Il doit faire des repas légers.
   He must take light meals.

7. Quels sont vos honoraires?
   What is your fee? •

8. Vous pouvez manger de tout.
   You can eat everything.

9. Je voudrais revoir votre mari dans l'après-midi.
   I'd like to see your husband again in the afternoon.

10. Je vous la [l'ordonnance] prépare tout de suite.
    I'll prepare it [the prescription] for you right away (or *immediately*).

LESSON 60

Drills and Exercises

II. 1. Il faut que j'aille à la banque maintenant.
   2. Il faut que nous fassions notre travail maintenant.
   3. Il faut qu'elle prenne l'avion.
   4. Le dimanche ils vont à l'église.
   5. Elle est allée à l'église dimanche.
   6. Il est professeur.

7. C'est un bon professeur.
8. Ce n'est pas facile.
9. Il n'est pas facile à dire.
10. Il est possible qu'elle ne puisse pas venir.
11. Ce stylo? C'est à moi (*or* C'est le mien).

Quiz

1. Y a-t-il une temple près de l'hôtel?
   Is there a (Protestant) church near the hotel?

2. On célèbre tous les cultes, y compris le culte protestant.
   All religions are practiced, including the Protestant religion.

3. C'est tout en français, bien entendu.
   It's all in French, naturally.

4. Les offices ont lieu le vendredi soir.
   Services take place (or are held) on Friday.

5. Si vous voulez assister à un service, allez-y.
   If you wish to attend a service, go there.

6. Je parlais au sujet de temples.
   I spoke about (Protestant) churches.

7. Je vais donner un coup de fil à Michel.
   I'm going to ring (make a phone call to) Michael.

8. Si cela vous convient, on irait ensemble.
   If that's all right with you, we'd go together.

9. Il se marie à 9h. 30 du matin.
   He is getting married at 9:30 in the morning.

10. Pensez-vous que nous puissions assister à ce mariage civil?
    Do you think we might attend this civil marriage?